Interactive Computing Series

Microsoft® FrontPage® 2002

Introductory Edition

Kenneth C. Laudon • Kenneth Rosenblatt

David Langley

Boston   Burr Ridge, IL   Dubuque, IA   Madison, WI   New York   San Francisco   St. Louis
Bangkok   Bogotá   Caracas   Kuala Lumpur   Lisbon   London   Madrid   Mexico City
Milan   Montreal   New Delhi   Santiago   Seoul   Singapore   Sydney   Taipei   Toronto

McGraw-Hill Higher Education
*A Division of The **McGraw-Hill** Companies*

MICROSOFT FRONTPAGE 2002 INTRODUCTORY EDITION
Published by McGraw-Hill/Irwin, an imprint of The McGraw-Hill Companies, Inc., 1221 Avenue of the Americas, New York, NY 10020. Copyright 2002, by The McGraw-Hill Companies, Inc. All rights reserved. No part of this publication may be reproduced or distributed in any form or by any means, or stored in a database or retrieval system, without the prior written consent of The McGraw-Hill Companies, Inc., including, but not limited to, in any network or other electronic storage or transmission, or broadcast for distance learning.

This book is printed on acid-free paper.

2 3 4 5 6 7 8 9 0 QPD/QPD 0 9 8 7 6 5 4 3

ISBN 0-07-247178-6

Publisher: *George Werthman*
Developmental editor I: *Diana Del Castillo*
Senior marketing manager: *Jeff Parr*
Senior project manager: *Pat Frederickson*
Senior production supervisor: *Michael R. McCormick*
Senior designer: *Pam Verros*
Supplement producer: *Mark Mattson*
Cover photograph: *Bill Brooks/© Masterfile*
Interior design: *Asylum Studios*
Cover designer: *JoAnne Schopler*
Compositor: *Azimuth Interactive, Inc.*
Typeface: *10/12 Times*
Printer: *Quebecor Printing Book Group/Dubuque*

Library of Congress Control Number: 2001098504

www.mhhe.com

Information Technology at McGraw-Hill/Irwin

At McGraw-Hill Higher Education, we publish instructional materials targeted at the higher education market. In an effort to expand the tools of higher learning, we publish texts, lab manuals, study guides, testing materials, software, and multimedia products.

At McGraw-Hill/Irwin (a division of McGraw-Hill Higher Education), we realize that technology has created and will continue to create new mediums for professors and students to use in managing resources and communicating information with one another. We strive to provide the most flexible and complete teaching and learning tools available as well as offer solutions to the changing world of teaching and learning.

MCGRAW-HILL/IRWIN IS DEDICATED TO PROVIDING THE TOOLS FOR TODAY'S INSTRUCTORS AND STUDENTS TO SUCCESSFULLY NAVIGATE THE WORLD OF INFORMATION TECHNOLOGY.

- **Seminar series**—Technology Connection seminar series offered across the country every year demonstrates the latest technology products and encourages collaboration among teaching professionals.

- **Osborne/McGraw-Hill**—This division of The McGraw-Hill Companies is known for its best-selling Internet titles: *Harley Hahn's Internet & Web Yellow Pages*, and the *Internet Complete Reference*. Osborne offers an additional resource for certification and has strategic publishing relationships with corporations such as Corel Corporation and America Online. For more information visit Osborne at www.osborne.com.

- **Digital solutions**—McGraw-Hill/Irwin is committed to publishing digital solutions. Taking your course online does not have to be a solitary venture, nor does it have to be a difficult one. We offer several solutions that will allow you to enjoy all the benefits of having course material online. For more information visit www.mhhe.com/solutions/index.mhtml.

- **Packaging options**—For more about our discount options, contact your local McGraw-Hill/Irwin Sales representative at 1-800-338-3987 or visit our Web site at www.mhhe.com/it.

Interactive Computing Series

GOALS/PHILOSOPHY

The ***Interactive Computing Series*** provides you with an illustrated interactive environment for learning software skills using Microsoft Office. The text uses both "hands-on" instruction, supplementary text, and independent exercises to enrich the learning experience.

APPROACH

The ***Interactive Computing Series*** is the visual interactive way to develop and apply software skills. This skills-based approach coupled with its highly visual, two-page spread design allows the student to focus on a single skill without having to turn the page. A Lesson Goal at the beginning of each lesson prepares the student to apply the skills with a real-world focus. The Quiz and Interactivity sections at the end of each lesson measure the student's understanding of the concepts and skills learned in the two-page spreads and reinforce the skills with additional exercises.

ABOUT THE BOOK

The ***Interactive Computing Series*** offers *two levels* of instruction. Each level builds upon the previous level.

Brief lab manual—covers the basics of the application, contains two to four chapters.

Introductory lab manual—includes the material in the Brief textbook plus two to four additional chapters. The Introductory lab manuals prepare students for the *Microsoft Office User Specialist Proficiency Exam (MOUS Certification)*.

Each lesson is divided into a number of Skills. Each **Skill** is first explained at the top of the page in the Concept. Each **Concept** is a concise description of why the Skill is useful and where it is commonly used. Each **Step (Do It!)** contains the instructions on how to complete the Skill. The appearance of the **MOUS Skill** icon on a Skill page indicates that the Skill contains instruction in at least one of the required MOUS objectives for the relevant exam. Though the icons appear in the Brief manuals as well as the Introductory manuals, only the Introductory manuals may be used in preparation for MOUS Certification.

using the book

Figure 1

> **WD 3.32**   THREE
>
> ### skill — Finding and Replacing Text
>
> **concept** — The Find command enables you to search a document for individual occurrences of any word, phrase, or other unit of text. The Replace command enables you to replace one or all occurrences of a word that you have found. Together, the Find and Replace commands form powerful editing tools for making many document-wide changes in just seconds.
>
> **do it!**
>
> Use Find and Replace to spell a word consistently throughout a document.
>
> 1. Open student file, wddoit12.doc, and save it as Report12.doc.
> 2. If necessary, place the insertion point at the beginning of the document. Word will search the document from the insertion point forward.
> 3. Click Edit, and then click Replace. The Find and Replace dialog box appears with the Replace tab in front and the insertion point in the Find What text box.
> 4. In the Find What box, type the two words per cent. Click in the Replace With box, and type the one word percent (see Figure 3-37).
> 5. Click [Replace All] to search the document for all instances of per cent and to replace them with percent. A message box appears to display the results. In this case, one replacement was made (see Figure 3-38). In short documents the Find and Replace procedure takes so little time that you usually cannot cancel it before it ends. However, in longer documents you can cancel a search in progress by pressing [Esc].
> 6. Click [OK] to close the message box. Click [Close] to close the Find and Replace dialog box.
> 7. Save and close the document, Report12.doc, with your change.
>
> **more** — Clicking the Replace All button in the Find and Replace dialog box replaces every instance of the text you have placed in the Find What box. To examine and replace a word or phrase manually instead of automatically, start by clicking the Find Next button. If you desire to replace that instance, click the Replace button. Continue checking the document like this, clicking the Find Next button and then, if desired, the Replace button. Keep clicking the pairs of buttons until you have run through the entire document. Unless you absolutely must do otherwise, use the method for shorter documents only.
>
> The first button under the Replace With box usually displays the word More. Click this button when you want to display the Search Options area of the dialog box. With the area displayed, the More button converts to a Less button. Clicking on the Less button will hide the Search Options area. The Search drop-down list under Search Options determines the direction of the search relative to the insertion point. You can search upward or downward through the document or keep the Word default setting of All to check the whole document, including headers, footers, and footnotes. The Format drop-down list enables you to search criteria for fonts, paragraphs, tabs, and similar items. The Special drop-down list enables you to search for paragraph marks, tab characters, column breaks and related special characters. The No Formatting button removes all formatting criteria from searches. For information on the Search Option activated by the check boxes, consult Table 3-3.
>
> The Find tab of the Find and Replace dialog box matches the Replace tab except it lacks the replace function and only searches documents for items that you specify.

Skill: Each lesson is divided into a number of specific skills

Concept: A concise description of why the skill is useful and when it is commonly used

Do It!: Step-by-step directions show you how to use the skill in a real-world scenario

Hot Tips: Icons introduce helpful hints or troubleshooting tips

More: Provides in-depth information about the skill and related features

In the book, each skill is described in a two-page graphical spread (Figure 1). The left side of the two-page spread describes the skill, the concept, and the steps needed to perform the skill. The right side of the spread uses screen shots to show you how the screen should look at key stages.

Figure 1 (continued)

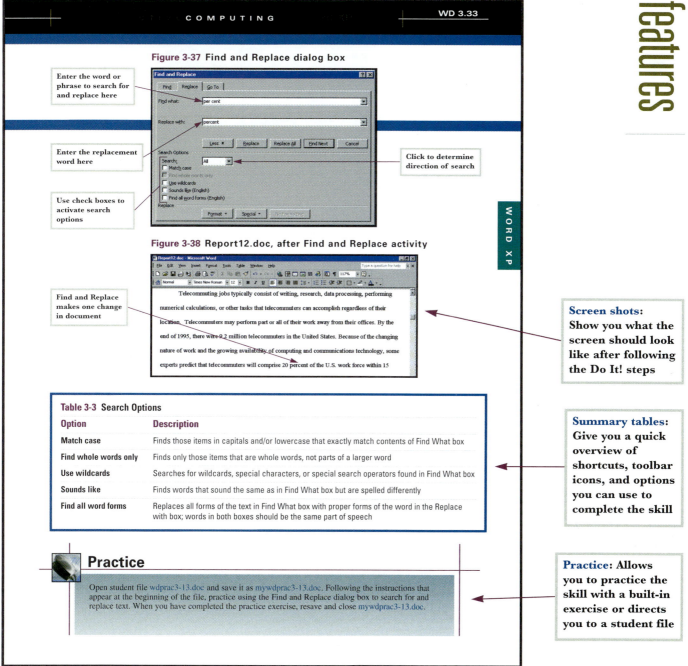

END-OF-LESSON FEATURES

In the book, the learning in each lesson is reinforced at the end by a Quiz and a skills review called Interactivity, which provides step-by-step exercises and real-world problems for the students to solve independently.

teaching resources

The following is a list of supplemental material available with the Interactive Computing Series:

Skills Assessment

SimNet eXPert (Simulated Network Assessment Product)—SimNet provides a way for you to test students' software skills in a simulated environment. SimNet is available for Microsoft Office 97, Microsoft Office 2000, and Microsoft Office XP. SimNet provides flexibility for you in your course by offering:

- Pre-testing options
- Post-testing options
- Course placement testing
- Diagnostic capabilities to reinforce skills
- Proficiency testing to measure skills
- Web or LAN delivery of tests
- Computer based training materials (New for Office XP)
- MOUS preparation exams
- Learning verification reports
- Spanish Version

Instructor's Resource Kits

The Instructor's Resource Kit provides professors with all of the ancillary material needed to teach a course. McGraw-Hill/Irwin is dedicated to providing instructors with the most effective instruction resources available. Many of these resources are available at our Information Technology Supersite www.mhhe.com/it. Our Instructor's Kits are available on CD-ROM and contain the following:

>**Diploma by Brownstone**—is the most flexible, powerful, and easy-to-use computerized testing system available in higher education. The diploma system allows professors to create an Exam as a printed version, as a LAN-based Online version, and as an Internet version. Diploma includes grade book features, which automate the entire testing process.
>
>**Instructor's Manual**—Includes:
>–Solutions to all lessons and end-of-unit material
>–Teaching Tips
>–Teaching Strategies
>–Additional exercises
>
>**PowerPoint Slides**—NEW to the *Interactive Computing Series*, all of the figures from the application textbooks are available in PowerPoint slides for presentation purposes.
>
>**Student Data Files**—To use the *Interactive Computing Series*, students must have Student Data Files to complete practice and test sessions. The instructor and students using this text in classes are granted the right to post the student files on any network or stand-alone computer, or to distribute the files on individual diskettes. The student files may be downloaded from our IT Supersite at www.mhhe.com/it.
>
>**Series Web Site**—Available at www.mhhe.com/cit/apps/laudon.

Digital Solutions

Pageout—is our Course Web site Development Center. Pageout offers a Syllabus page, Web site address, Online Learning Center Content, online exercises and quizzes, gradebook, discussion board, an area for students to build their own Web pages, and all the features of Pageout Lite. For more information please visit the Pageout Web site at www.mhla.net/pageout.

Digital Solutions (continued)

OLC/Series Web Sites—Online Learning Centers (OLCs)/Series Sites are accessible through our Supersite at www.mhhe.com/it. Our Online Learning Centers/Series Sites provide pedagogical features and supplements for our titles online. Students can point and click their way to key terms, learning objectives, chapter overviews, PowerPoint slides, exercises, and Web links.

The McGraw-Hill Learning Architecture (MHLA)—is a complete course delivery system. MHLA gives professors ownership in the way digital content is presented to the class through online quizzing, student collaboration, course administration, and content management. For a walk-through of MHLA visit the MHLA Web site at www.mhla.net.

Packaging Options—For more about our discount options, contact your local McGraw-Hill/Irwin Sales representative at 1-800-338-3987 or visit our Web site at www.mhhe.com/it.

Visit www.mhhe.com/it

THE ONLY SITE WITH ALL YOUR CIT AND MIS NEEDS.

acknowledgments

The *Interactive Computing Series* is a cooperative effort of many individuals, each contributing to an overall team effort. The Interactive Computing team is composed of instructional designers, writers, multimedia designers, graphic artists, and programmers. Our goal is to provide you and your instructor with the most powerful and enjoyable learning environment using both traditional text and new interactive multimedia techniques. Interactive Computing is tested rigorously in both CD-ROM and text formats prior to publication.

Our special thanks to George Werthman, our Publisher; Sarah Wood, our Developmental Editor; and Jeffrey Parr, Marketing Director for Computer Information Systems. They have provided exceptional market awareness and understanding, along with enthusiasm and support for the project, and have inspired us all to work closely together. In addition, Steven Schuetz provided valuable technical review of our interactive versions, and Charles Pelto contributed superb quality assurance.

The Azimuth team members who contributed to the textbooks and CD-ROM multimedia program are:

Ken Rosenblatt (Editorial Director, Writer)
Russell Polo (Technical Director)
Robin Pickering (Developmental Editor, Writer)
David Langley (Writer)
Chris Hahnenberger (Multimedia Designer)

APPROVED COURSEWARE

What does this logo mean?

It means this courseware has been approved by the Microsoft® Office User Specialist Program to be among the finest available for learning *Microsoft Word 2002, Microsoft Excel 2002, Microsoft Access 2002, and Microsoft PowerPoint 2002*. It also means that upon completion of this courseware, you may be prepared to become a Microsoft Office User Specialist. The Interactive Computing Series Microsoft Office XP books are available in two levels of coverage: Brief level and Intro level. The Interactive Computing Series Introductory books are approved courseware to prepare you for the MOUS level 1 exam.

What is a Microsoft Office User Specialist?

A Microsoft Office User Specialist is an individual who has certified his or her skills in one or more of the Microsoft Office desktop applications of Microsoft Word, Microsoft Excel, Microsoft PowerPoint®, Microsoft Outlook® or Microsoft Access, or in Microsoft Project. The Microsoft Office User Specialist Program typically offers certification exams at the "Core" and "Expert" skill levels.* The Microsoft Office User Specialist Program is the only Microsoft approved program in the world for certifying proficiency in Microsoft Office desktop applications and Microsoft Project. This certification can be a valuable asset in any job search or career advancement.

More Information:

To learn more about becoming a Microsoft Office User Specialist, visit www.mous.net.

To purchase a Microsoft Office User Specialist certification exam, visit www.DesktopIQ.com.

To learn about other Microsoft Office User Specialist approved courseware from McGraw-Hill/Irwin, visit http://www.mhhe.com/catalogs/irwin/cit/mous/index.mhtml.

---

* The availability of Microsoft Office User Specialist certification exams varies by application, application version and language. Visit www.mous.net for exam availability.

Microsoft, the Microsoft Office User Specialist Logo, PowerPoint and Outlook are either registered trademarks or trademarks of Microsoft Corporation in the United States and/or other countries.

Who benefits from Microsoft® Office User Specialist certification?

Employers
Microsoft Office User Specialist ("MOUS") certification helps satisfy employers' needs for qualitative assessments of employees' skills. Training, coupled with MOUS certification, offers organizations of every size the ability to enhance productivity and efficiency by enabling their employees to unlock many advanced and laborsaving features in Microsoft Office applications. MOUS certification can ultimately improve the bottom line.

Employees
MOUS certification demonstrates employees' productivity and competence in Microsoft Office applications, the most popular business applications in the world. Achieving MOUS certification verifies that employees have the confidence and ability to use Microsoft Office applications in meeting and exceeding their work challenges.

Instructors
MOUS certification validates instructors' knowledge and skill in using Microsoft Office applications. It serves as a valuable credential, demonstrating their potential to teach students these essential applications. The MOUS Authorized Instructor program is also available to those who wish to further demonstrate their instructional capabilities.

Students
MOUS certification distinguishes students from their peers. It demonstrates their efficiency in completing assignments and projects, leaving more time for other studies. Improved confidence toward meeting new challenges and obstacles is yet another benefit. Achieving MOUS certification gives students the marketable skills necessary to set them apart in the competitive job market.

To learn more about MOUS certification, visit www.mous.net

To purchase a MOUS certification exam, visit www.DesktopIQ.com

---

Microsoft and the Microsoft Office User Specialist Logo are either registered trademarks or trademarks of Microsoft Corporation in the United States and/or other countries.

contents

FrontPage® 2002
Introductory Edition

Preface   v

LESSON ONE

Introducing Microsoft FrontPage   FP 1.1

Introducing Microsoft FrontPage	FP 1.2
Starting FrontPage	FP 1.4
Exploring the FrontPage Screen	FP 1.6
Opening a Web Page	FP 1.8
Saving a Web Page	FP 1.10
Using the Page View	FP 1.12
Getting Help in FrontPage	FP 1.14
Exiting FrontPage	FP 1.16
Shortcuts	FP 1.18
Quiz	FP 1.19
Interactivity	FP 1.21

LESSON TWO

Creating Web Sites   FP 2.1

Creating a New Web Page Using a Template	FP 2.2
Creating a New Web Using a Template	FP 2.4
Using a Web Wizard	FP 2.6
Using the Import Web Wizard	FP 2.10
Adding Text to a Web Page	FP 2.12
Formatting Text on a Web Page	FP 2.14
Adding and Formatting Lists	FP 2.16
Spell Checking and Editing a Web Page	FP 2.18
Using the Find Command	FP 2.20
Previewing a Web Page in a Browser	FP 2.22
Shortcuts	FP 2.24
Quiz	FP 2.25
Interactivity	FP 2.27

Skill covers at least one MOUS Certification Core objective.

FrontPage® 2002 continued

LESSON THREE

Formatting and Adding Objects to Web Pages — FP 3.1

Creating Tables	FP 3.2
Formatting Tables	FP 3.4
Applying Themes to Webs	FP 3.6
Applying Custom Themes	FP 3.8
Applying Themes to Individual Pages	FP 3.10
Creating Text Hyperlinks	FP 3.12
Editing Hyperlinks	FP 3.14
Adding Images	FP 3.16
Formatting Images	FP 3.18
Image Mapping	FP 3.20
Creating a Hover Button	FP 3.22
Creating a Marquee	FP 3.24
Inserting Text Boxes	FP 3.26
Adding Check Boxes and Option Buttons	FP 3.28
Creating a Drop-Down List Box	FP 3.30
Creating a Push Button	FP 3.32
Shortcuts	FP 3.34
Quiz	FP 3.35
Interactivity	FP 3.37

LESSON FOUR

Publishing and Maintaining Web Pages — FP 4.1

Creating a Web Hierarchy	FP 4.2
Adding a Navigation Bar	FP 4.4
Viewing and Printing the Web Structure	FP 4.6
Organizing Files in Folders View	FP 4.8
Verifying Hyperlinks	FP 4.10
Renaming and Changing URLs	FP 4.12
Changing Page Titles in Banners	FP 4.14
Opening an Office Document in a Web	FP 4.16
Using the Office Clipboard	FP 4.18
Creating and Printing Reports	FP 4.20
Publishing a Web	FP 4.22
Shortcuts	FP 4.24
Quiz	FP 4.25
Interactivity	FP 4.27

Skill covers at least one MOUS Certification Core objective.

FrontPage® 2002 continued

LESSON FIVE 5

Advanced Formatting — FP 5.1

Importing Text	FP 5.2
Importing Web Pages	FP 5.4
Importing Images	FP 5.6
Advanced Image Formatting	FP 5.8
Editing Graphics on Web Pages	FP 5.10
Placing Text over an Image	FP 5.14
Using the Format Painter	FP 5.16
Inserting a Hit Counter	FP 5.18
Inserting a Time Stamp 🖐	FP 5.20
Creating a Search Form	FP 5.22
Formatting Web Page Transitions	FP 5.24
Using Style Sheets	FP 5.26
Shortcuts	FP 5.28
Quiz	FP 5.29
Interactivity	FP 5.31

LESSON SIX 6

Modifying Tables — FP 6.1

Deleting Table Rows and Columns 🖐	FP 6.2
Drawing Tables and Columns	FP 6.4
Resizing Table Cells	FP 6.6
Merging Table Cells 🖐	FP 6.8
Converting Text into a Table	FP 6.10
Inserting Captions	FP 6.12
Shortcuts	FP 6.14
Quiz	FP 6.15
Interactivity	FP 6.17

🖐 Skill covers at least one MOUS Certification Core objective.

XV

FrontPage® 2002 continued

LESSON SEVEN 7

Advanced Web Management and Design — FP 7.1

Using Global Find and Replace	FP 7.2
Checking the Spelling of a Web	FP 7.4
Using Shared Borders	FP 7.6
Adding and Modifying Banners	FP 7.8
Using Dynamic HTML Effects	FP 7.10
Inserting an ActiveX Control	FP 7.12
Adding a Photo Gallery ⓢ	FP 7.14
Reaching a Target Audience	FP 7.18
Creating Frames Pages	FP 7.20
Saving Frames Pages	FP 7.22
Manipulating Frames Pages	FP 7.24
Creating No-Frames Pages	FP 7.26
Shortcuts	FP 7.28
Quiz	FP 7.29
Interactivity	FP 7.31

LESSON EIGHT 8

Creating and Managing Tasks — FP 8.1

Creating New Tasks ⓢ	FP 8.2
Adding a Task Linked to a Page ⓢ	FP 8.4
Starting and Completing Tasks ⓢ	FP 8.6
Sorting Tasks ⓢ	FP 8.8
Viewing Task History ⓢ	FP 8.10
Shortcuts	FP 8.12
Quiz	FP 8.13
Interactivity	FP 8.15

Glossary — FP 1

Index — FP 11

File Directory — FP 13

MOUS Objectives Map — FP 15

ⓢ Skill covers at least one MOUS Certification Core objective.

Introducing Microsoft FrontPage

skills

- ≶ Introducing Microsoft FrontPage
- ≶ Starting FrontPage
- ≶ Exploring the FrontPage Screen
- ≶ Opening a Web Page
- ≶ Saving a Web Page
- ≶ Using the Page View
- ≶ Getting Help in FrontPage
- ≶ Exiting FrontPage

The Internet is the worldwide collection of computers and computer networks that use Internet protocols to communicate with one another. (A protocol is a set of communication rules governing the exchange of data between files or on any type of network, including the Internet.) The World Wide Web is the largest subdivision of the Internet and, as such, is one of the parts that people use most often. The World Wide Web is made up of literally millions of Web sites, which are groups of related Web pages—that is, home pages and their related pages of text, graphics, and multimedia that people read and view.

Pages created for the World Wide Web often resemble ordinary computer documents, but are formatted in Hypertext Markup Language, or HTML. HTML is the standard language that trained programmers use to create Web sites. This language uses strings of text, or tags, to tell Web browsers how to display page elements such as text and graphics. This language also tells Web browsers how to respond to user actions such as entering data, clicking a button on a Web page, or clicking a hyperlink.

HTML contains hundreds of tags, or markers, that are somewhat cryptic and often quite complicated for ordinary computer users. That is where Microsoft's FrontPage 2002 application comes in handy. FrontPage is a Web site authoring application. Web authoring applications help you to quickly create, edit, and enhance Web pages. In general, you will find Web authoring programs such as FrontPage are much faster in generating Web pages than is raw HTML. FrontPage provides an organized environment and many helpful tools for entering text, inserting graphics, and integrating these and other elements such as page banners, navigation buttons, and hyperlinks.

In the next four lessons, you will learn the basic steps of Web page and site design. Lesson 1 explains the basic elements of FrontPage: how to start the software, open a Web page, save a Web page, and get help. Lesson 2 explains how to create new Web pages, use the Web Wizard, and edit a Web page. Lesson 3 explains how to customize Web pages by adding hyperlinks, tables, and custom themes. And Lesson 4 explains how to organize, maintain, and publish Web pages.

Lesson Goal:

In this lesson you will learn how to start and explore FrontPage, open and save a Web page, and use Page view to view the Web page. You also will learn how to get help in FrontPage and how to exit the application.

skill: Introducing Microsoft FrontPage

concept

As a Web authoring application, FrontPage takes the time and tedium out of designing, writing, and formatting Web pages. In the past, authoring attractive Web pages required extensive knowledge of HTML. While knowledge of HTML is useful to anyone who wants to create truly effective Web sites, especially sites with advanced designs and features, more user-friendly Web-authoring applications such as FrontPage make it possible to build Web pages without knowing HTML. The barriers to Web site construction are slowly but surely being erased, and FrontPage 2002 is an additional step in knocking down those barriers.

There are many FrontPage users, including small businesses, non-profit institutions, social and cultural clubs, athletic leagues, and similar organizations. Private individuals and larger businesses also use FrontPage. These users can design and develop their own Web sites using FrontPage because it puts the power of Web site design and development in a user-friendly, integrated way directly into the hands of such users.

Figure 1-1 provides an example of a Web page designed in FrontPage 2002 and highlights some of its most essential features:

- **Text**—Although the page that appears in Figure 1-1 is relatively free of text, it still contains a title and some text hyperlinks. Since Figure 1-1 represents a home page, this relative lack of text is quite common. As you go through this book, however, you will have many opportunities to add and format text on your Web pages.

- **Hyperlinks**—The words Home, Back, Info, and so on are colored, underlined areas of text, identifying them as hyperlinks. (Sometimes hyperlinks vary from this format.) When clicked, these hyperlinks would take you to other Web pages within the main site. The last hyperlink, E-Mail Us, would open an electronic mail program for messaging the owner or operator (Webmaster) of the Web site. Home pages almost always contain internal links, but often contain links to Web pages in other Web sites as well.

- **Frames**—are physical subdivisions of a Web page. In Figure 1-1 there are three frames. The top frame contains the main title of the Web site's home page. The left frame contains the hyperlinks of the home page, and the right frame contains a graphic. You can design frames that are scrollable and resizable and that also contain borders.

- **Graphics**—are images such as solid or dotted lines, page banners, Clip Art, photographs, cartoons, or other visual elements on a page. Some graphics even are dynamic—that is, they provide moving images and occasionally sound. Such images identify pages and their topics or functions, break large sections of text into related subsections, illustrate textual material, function as hyperlinks, display additional information, and so on.

INTERACTIVE COMPUTING FrontPage 2002   FP 1.3

Figure 1-1 Web Page in FrontPage 2002

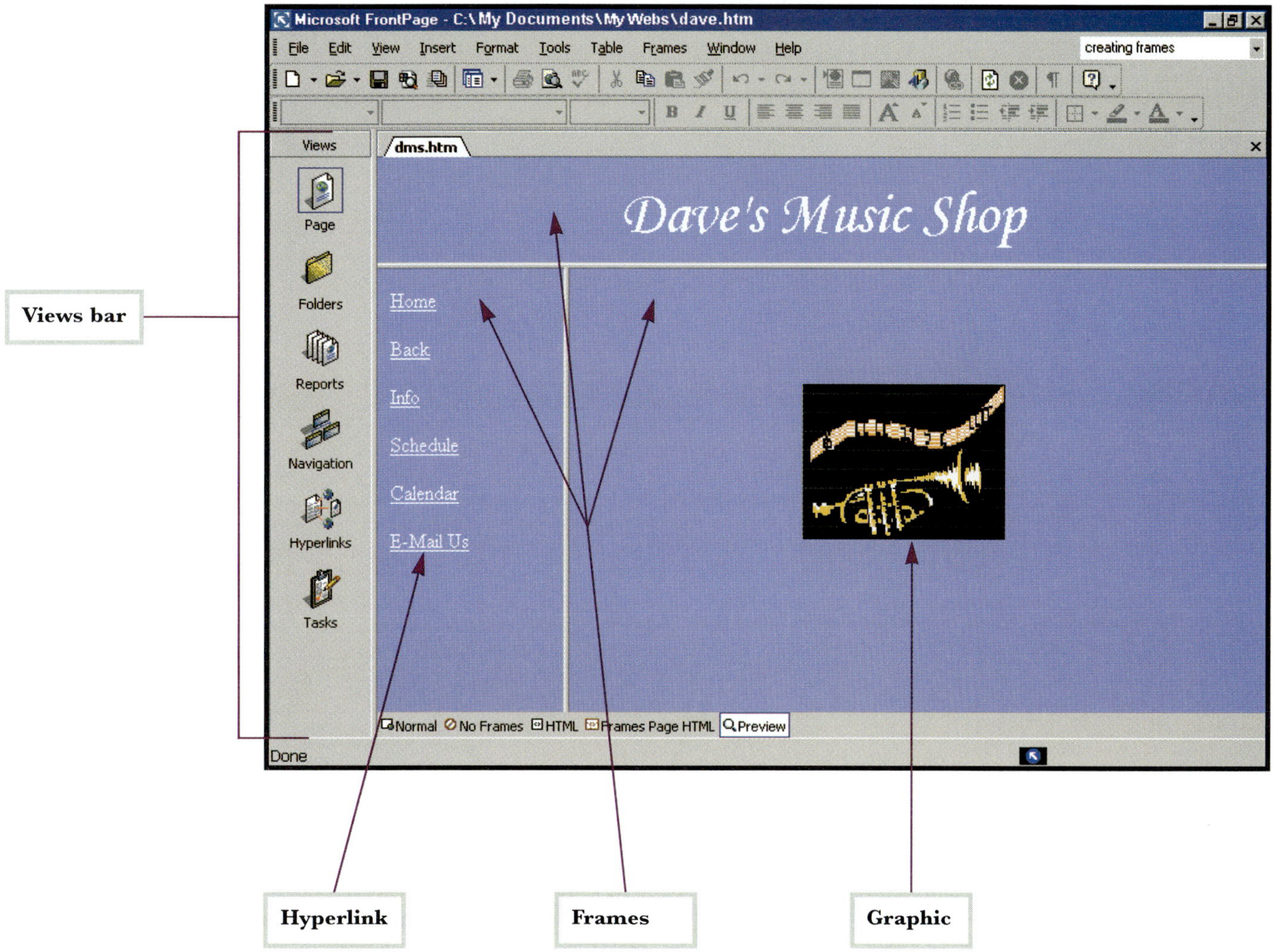

Views bar

Hyperlink   Frames   Graphic

skill: Starting FrontPage

concept

Before you can view or edit a Web page, you must open the FrontPage 2002 application. FrontPage opens with a new blank Web page file.

do it!

Start the FrontPage application.

1. Make sure the computer, monitor, and any other necessary peripheral devices are turned on. The Windows desktop should appear on your screen. Your screen may differ slightly from the one shown in the graphic.

2. Locate the Windows taskbar, usually found at the bottom of your screen. Use your mouse to guide the pointer over the Start button  present on the Windows taskbar and click it. The Start menu appears.

3. Point to Programs. A submenu is displayed, similar to the one shown in Figure 1-2. If you do not see Microsoft FrontPage listed separately on the Programs submenu, you may find it under even another submenu for Microsoft Office programs.

4. Click the Microsoft FrontPage command. FrontPage will open with a blank Web page.

more

Each computer varies in its setup, depending on its hardware and software configurations. Therefore, your startup procedure may be slightly different from the one described above. Notice that your mouse has two buttons. Whenever you are told to click a mouse button, click the left button, unless otherwise indicated.

Figure 1-2 Windows desktop

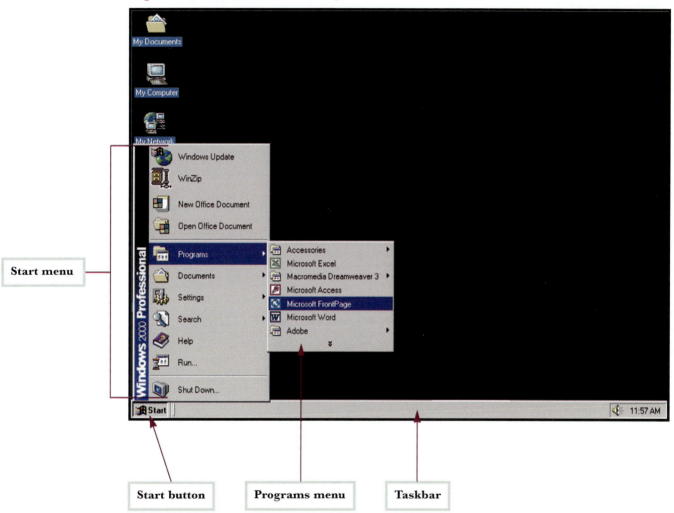

skill: Exploring the FrontPage Screen

concept

FrontPage opens to a blank Web page enclosed in a frame. View buttons are located on the left side of the FrontPage window on the Views bar. The Views bar facilitates Web site management. The buttons on the Views bar are labeled according to the functions they control. These buttons are designed for working with Webs. A Web is a group of related and interconnected Web pages intended to be explored as a Web site. A Web page is a document that can be viewed over the Internet with its own URL or Uniform Resource Locator. A URL is a unique address for locating a Web site or document. For example, the URL for the manufacturer of the FrontPage application is www.microsoft.com. A Web site is a group of Web pages that are linked together to form a cohesive, navigable Web. The FrontPage window is displayed in Figure 1-3.

The specific buttons on the Views bar are as follows:

- Page button: This button allows you to create and edit an individual Web page. Most formatting and the addition of graphics and other elements are done in this view.
- Folders button: This button enables you to view and organize the files and folders associated with a Web.
- Reports button: This button provides reports and updates on the status of files and hyperlinks, which enable you to keep your Web site up to date.
- Navigation button: This button displays the navigational structure of your Web site. You can also add navigation buttons to a Web page in this view.
- Hyperlinks button: This button displays every hyperlink to and from every page in a Web.
- Tasks button: This button lists the uncompleted tasks in a Web.

The other elements in the FrontPage window are as follows:

- Title bar: The bar running across the top of the FrontPage window which contains the FrontPage icon, the name of the application, location of the page, and the Window controls in the right-hand corner.
- Window Controls: The Minimize button reduces the window to a program button on the Windows taskbar. The Maximize button will appear if the FrontPage window is not enlarged to fit the entire screen. The Restore button, which reverts the window to its previous size and location, will appear if the window is maximized. Finally, the Close button will close the application. The Maximize button replaces the Restore button when the FrontPage window is not enlarged to fit the entire screen.
- Menu bar: The row of menu titles below the Title bar. When you click a menu title, a drop-down list of commands related to the title appears.
- Standard toolbar: The row of icons used to execute common commands.
- Formatting toolbar: The row of list boxes and icons used to perform common text formatting commands.

INTERACTIVE COMPUTING   FrontPage 2002   FP 1.7

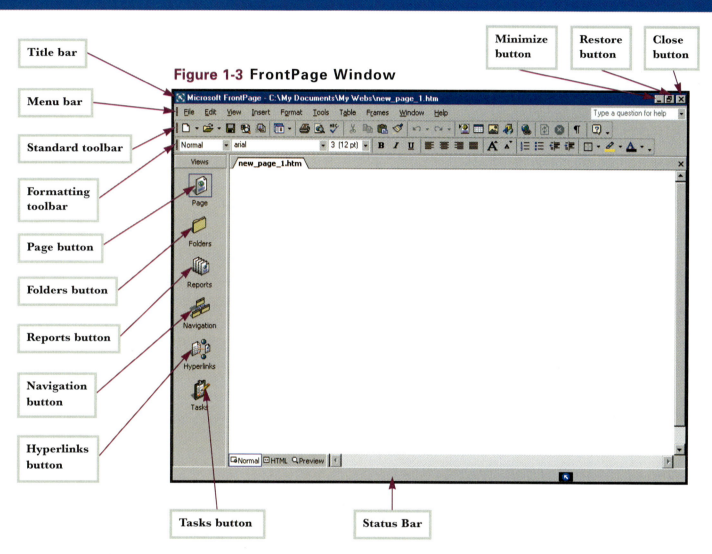

Figure 1-3 FrontPage Window

skill Opening a Web Page

concept

You will probably design your Web over a series of editing sessions. In order to work with a file, you must know how to reopen it after you saved it. You must know the name of the file and its location in order to open it.

do it!

Open an existing Web page.

1. Click File on the Menu bar. The File menu opens.
2. Click the Open command to display the Open File dialog box.
3. Click the arrow of the Look in drop-down list box, as shown in Figure 1-4, to locate your Student Files. They may be located on a floppy disk or in a folder on your hard disk. If they are located on a floppy disk, you must click 3 1/2 Floppy [A:] to access it. If they are on your desktop, you must click the folder, and double-click to open any subsequent sub-folders until you reach the desired files. Folders can be located using the buttons on the left-hand side of the Open File dialog box instead of the arrow button in the Look in list box.
4. After finding where your Student Files are stored, click the fpdoit1-4.htm student file.
5. Click Open.

more

You can open an existing Web page by clicking the Open Web command on the File menu. The Open Web dialog box operates similarly to the Open File dialog box. After you have created a Web or a file, you can bypass the Open File dialog box by clicking File on the Menu bar and selecting Recent Files, or Recent Webs. The corresponding submenus will display the latest Web pages or files you have accessed. These shortcuts are a new feature of FrontPage 2002. If you open a file directly from its folder in Windows Explorer, it will open in your default Web browser. A Web browser is an application that enables you to view Web pages on the Internet. However, in order to edit a Web page, you must open it from the FrontPage application.

Figure 1-4 Open File dialog box

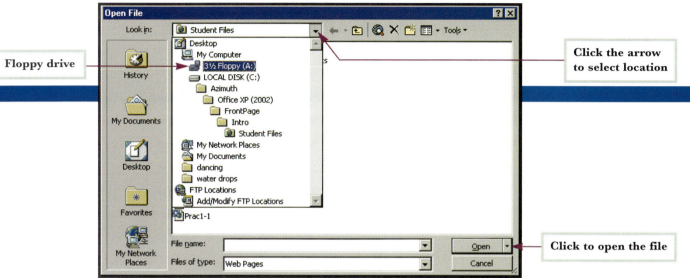

Figure 1-5 Web page opened in FrontPage

Practice

Locate and open the file fpprac1-4.htm from the location where you have stored the student files, then close the file.

LESSON ONE Introducing Microsoft FrontPage

skill
Saving a Web Page

concept

If you do not save your work frequently, you can lose lots of data and Web pages. Such losses can occur during power shortages or computer failure. Therefore, you should save Web pages to a hard drive, floppy disk, or network drive. If you save work frequently, any files that you open after a power loss will recover a recently saved version with most of your work still available for editing.

do it!

Save a Web page under a new name and in a new location.

1. Click File on the Menu bar, while the fpdoit1-4.htm student file is open.

2. Click the Save As command to open the Save As dialog box. On the left side of the dialog box, click the My Documents icon . The My Documents folder will appear in the Save in box near the top of the dialog box. Double-click the My Webs folder to place it in the Save in box. In recent versions of the Windows operating system, Microsoft has included the My Webs folder as the expected storage folder for Web pages and entire Webs. However, you can save such files in any customized folder that you desire, as explained in the More section below.

3. In the File name text box, delete the existing name, if any, and type skydive.htm as shown in Figure 1-6.

4. Click [Save] and close the file.

5. When you open the My Webs folder again, the Skydive Web page will be present with a logo similar to the aircraft.htm file, also shown in Figure 1-6.

more

The Save command and the Save As command perform different functions. The first time you save a document, the Save command on the File menu, or 💾 on the Standard toolbar will open the Save As dialog box. After you have named a file and stored it in a specific location, the Save command will simply overwrite the existing document. The Save As command will enable you to change the name and/or location of the existing document. It allows you to save and make changes to a document under a new name while maintaining the original file under the original file name. Both commands are accessed from the File menu. You can create a customized folder in any location by clicking the Create New Folder button 📁 in the Save As dialog box. By default, Webs are saved in folders titled My Webs. The more pages and Webs you create, the more My Webs folders there are. The next Web you create will be saved as My Webs1, then My Webs2, and so on.

Figure 1-6 Web Page saved with a different name

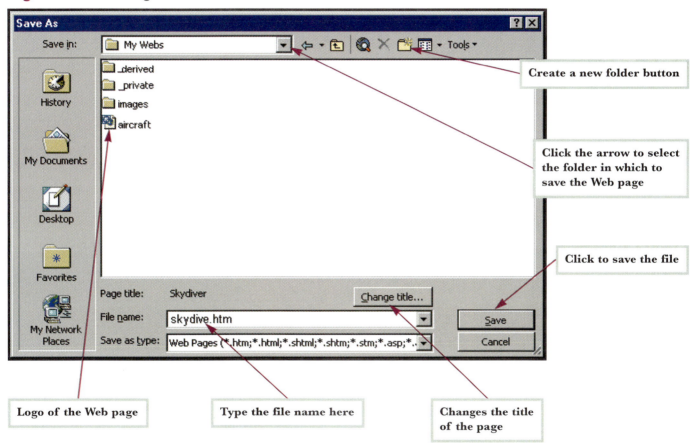

Practice

Save the file fpprac1-5.htm as myfile.htm in the My Webs folder.

skill: Using the Page View

concept

Most Web pages are designed in the Page view. Text, graphics, and other Web elements are added and reformatted in Page view. Page view is the only view explicitly used for creating, editing, and enhancing your Web pages. The other views are primarily used for managing your Web. Page view provides three formats for viewing Web pages: Normal, HTML, and Preview.

do it!

View a Web page in the three formats provided by Page view.

1. Open the Skydive Web page. By default the page will be displayed in the Normal view.
2. Three tabs are located on the lower left-hand side of the window. Click the HTML tab. This view displays your page in HTML format, as shown in Figure 1-7.
3. Click the Preview tab. The page will be displayed in the same way as it would appear in a browser window. You cannot format or edit your page from the Preview tab. You can only use this format to click on hyperlinks, and preview the visual effects. The Preview format is displayed in Figure 1-8. Since no effects have been added, it looks the same as the Normal format.

more

FrontPage is an HTML editor. It takes the work you create and edit in Normal view and converts it into Hypertext Markup Language or HTML format. If you know HTML, you can create a page using the HTML tab rather than the Normal tab. The results of your work can always be viewed in the Preview tab.

INTERACTIVE COMPUTING | FrontPage 2002 | FP 1.13

Figure 1-7 Web page in HTML format

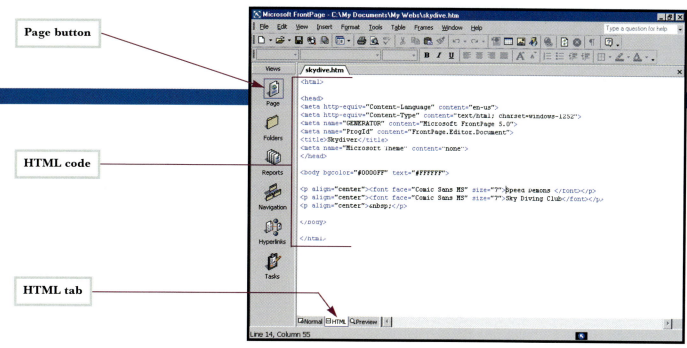

- Page button
- HTML code
- HTML tab

Figure 1-8 Web page in Preview format

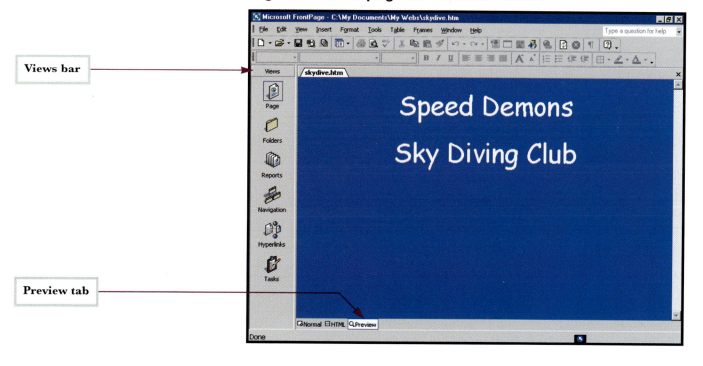

- Views bar
- Preview tab

Practice

Open the myfile.htm file you saved in the previous skill and use the Page view to view the page in the HTML and Preview formats.

Getting Help in FrontPage

concept

FrontPage has several help options. The Microsoft FrontPage Help window has three tabs: Index, Contents, and Answer Wizard. The Hide button, in the upper left-hand corner of the Microsoft FrontPage Help window, reduces the window to one section. The Hide button is then replaced by the Show button, which in turn, expands the Help window back to the two-paneled format.

do it!

Find help topics using the Index and Answer Wizard tabs of the Microsoft FrontPage window.

1. Click Help on the Menu bar.

2. Click the Microsoft FrontPage Help command. The Microsoft FrontPage Help dialog box appears. If the Office Assistant with a yellow balloon opens rather than the Help facility, type Show Help Index in the text box of the balloon. Press [Enter] or click the Search button. When the potentially relevant Help topics appear, click on the Use Help without the Office Assistant option, then move to Step 3.

3. Click the Index tab.

4. In the Type keywords text box, type Report. A list of Help topics is automatically displayed in the Or choose keywords section.

5. Double-click report in the Or choose keywords section. A list of topics relating to report will be displayed in the Choose a topic section, as shown in Figure 1-9.

6. Click the Web site reports topic. Read what it says about the Web site report.

7. Click the Answer Wizard tab. In the What would you like to do text box, type What is Navigation view.

8. Click Search. The Select topic to display list box provides an index of related topics. Click the Customize Navigation view and read what it says, as shown in Figure 1-10.

9. Close the Microsoft FrontPage Help window.

more

All three Help tabs direct you to the same information. If you are unsure of exactly what you are looking for, the Contents tab allows you to look at an expandable table of contents. General topics are listed next to book icons. Clicking the plus sign to the left of the book icon will display a list of more specific subtopics. The Index tab uses keywords to locate topics. It is useful if you know the name of the feature you wish to explore. The Answer Wizard enables you to request help on topics by asking a question in your own words. At the top left of the Help window are the navigation buttons. You can use these buttons to move back and forth between topics you have already viewed.

Another Help feature is the What's This? command. It is also accessed from the Help menu. When you click the What's This? command, the pointer turns into a. When you click a particular button or other screen element with this pointer, a ScreenTip appears describing its function in further detail.

Figure 1-9 Index tab

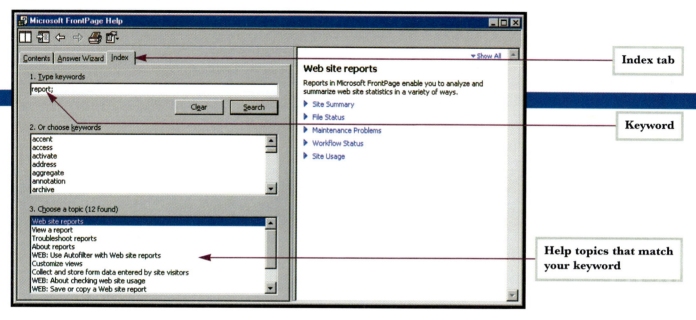

Figure 1-10 Answer Wizard tab

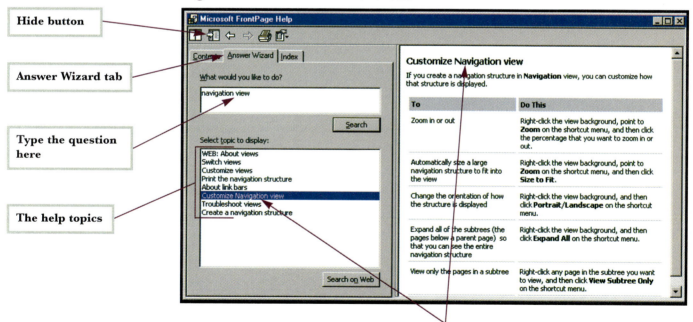

Practice

Use any of the Help features to look up information on Folders and on Hyperlinks.

skill Exiting FrontPage

concept

It is important to exit the FrontPage application properly. Exiting and closing the application properly will prevent data loss. You can exit the FrontPage either using the File menu or clicking ⊠. If you have forgotten to save your work, FrontPage prompts you to save the work before closing the application.

do it!

Exit the FrontPage program when you are finished working.

1. Click File on the Menu bar.
2. Select the Exit command and click it (Figure 1-11).
3. If you have made changes to the page without saving them, the Microsoft FrontPage dialog box (Figure 1-12) appears. Clicking [Yes] saves the changes and closes FrontPage. Clicking [No] closes the program without saving the changes, and clicking [Cancel] stops the program from closing.
4. If you have not made any changes, FrontPage simply closes.

more

The Close button ⊠ on the Title bar closes the application, while the Close button ⊠ in the upper right-hand corner of the active FrontPage window, closes the current Web page. The keyboard shortcut for exiting FrontPage is [Alt]+[F4], however to close the active file you can use [Ctrl]+[F4]. You can also close the program by accessing the Control menu. The Control menu is opened by clicking the FrontPage icon on the extreme left of the Title bar, or by right-clicking the Title bar.

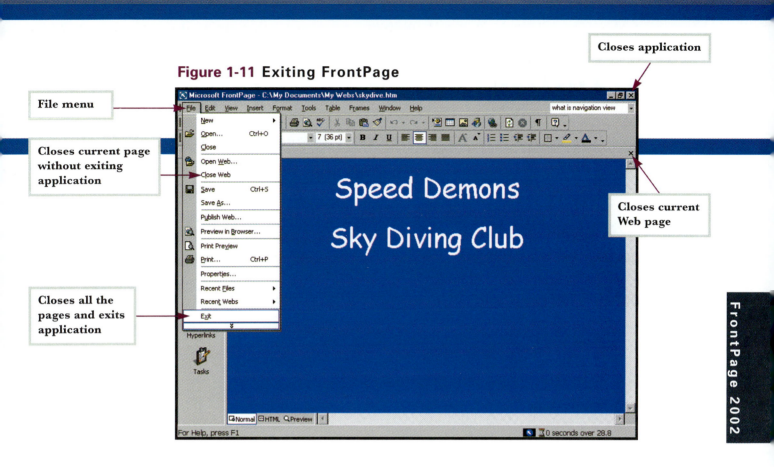

Figure 1-11 Exiting FrontPage

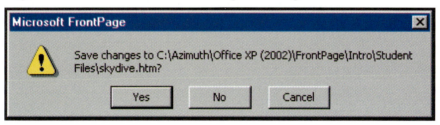

Figure 1-12 Microsoft FrontPage dialog box

Practice

Open the myfile.htm file you saved in a previous skill. Then close the file and exit FrontPage.

shortcuts

Function	Button/Mouse	Menu	Keyboard
Open file		Click File, then click Open	[Ctrl]+[O]
Save file		Click File, then click Save	[Ctrl]+[S]
Access Microsoft FrontPage Help		Click Help, then click Microsoft FrontPage Help	[F1]
Access What's This feature		Click Help, then click What's This?	[Shift]+[F1]

A. Identify Key Features

Name the items indicated by callouts in Figure 1-13.

Figure 1-13 Components of the FrontPage window

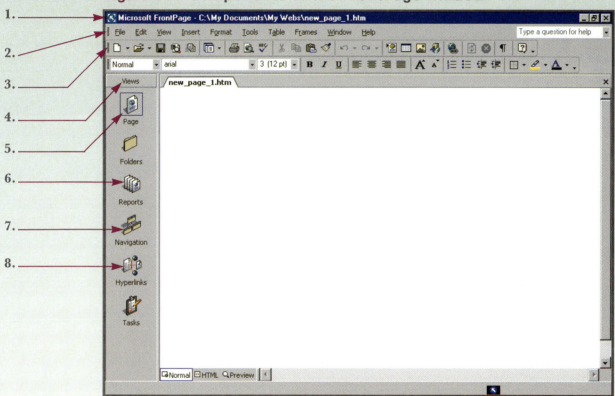

1. _____
2. _____
3. _____
4. _____
5. _____
6. _____
7. _____
8. _____

B. Select the Best Answer

9. Creating, editing, and most Web page formatting is done here
10. Web page address
11. This help feature looks up keywords
12. Overwrites an existing document
13. An assortment of Web pages that make up a Web site
14. The Start button is found here
15. Displays activities being performed and active elements at bottom of screen
16. Buttons at top right of window that allow you to alter the window size

a. Save
b. Windows taskbar
c. Page view
d. Window controls
e. Index
f. Status bar
g. Web
h. URL

quiz (continued)

C. Complete the Statement

17. The Contents tab is part of this feature:
  a. Views bar
  b. Menu bar
  c. The Help window
  d. Status bar

18. Click this command to open a Web site recently worked upon:
  a. File
  b. Recent Web
  c. Open File
  d. Old Web

19. This view gives you updates on your files and hyperlinks so that you can keep your Web up-to-date:
  a. Reports view
  b. Page view
  c. Hyperlinks view
  d. Update view

20. If you open a Web page directly from an icon in one of your desktop folders:
  a. It will not open at all
  b. All data will be lost
  c. It will open in FrontPage
  d. It will open in your default browser

21. This Help feature enables you to click items to display tool tips:
  a. Index
  b. Contents
  c. Answer Wizard
  d. What's This?

22. This contains graphical buttons that execute specific commands:
  a. Standard toolbar
  b. Menu bar
  c. Graphical toolbar
  d. Taskbar

23. The Control menu is accessed from the:
  a. File menu
  b. Taskbar
  c. Title bar
  d. Menu bar

24. The formatting language used to create Web pages:
  a. URL
  b. Web code
  c. FrontPage 2002 code
  d. HTML

25. To create a customizable folder in a storage location, click the:
  a. Custom Folder button on the File menu
  b. Create New Folder button in the Save As dialog box
  c. New Storage command on the Tools menu
  d. Any of the above

interactivity

Build Your Skills

1. Opening FrontPage 2002:

    a. Open the Start menu.

    b. Access the Programs menu.

    c. Click the Microsoft FrontPage command.

2. Open a Web page:

    a. Click File, then click Open.

    b. Navigate to the location where you have stored your Student Files.

    c. Locate the Web page fpskill1.htm, and open it.

3. Save a Web page:

    a. Click File, then click Save As.

    b. Locate the My Webs folder that is in the My Documents folder.

    c. Save the file as watertaxi.htm and close the file.

4. View a Web page in the Page view:

    a. Open the watertaxi.htm page.

    b. Click the Page view button on the Views bar, if it is not already selected.

    c. Click the HTML tab.

    d. Click the Preview tab.

5. Getting help in FrontPage:

    a. Click Help, then click Microsoft FrontPage Help.

    b. On the Contents tab, find the Creating Web Pages section under the heading, Designing Web Pages.

    c. On the Index tab, type in the keyword Graphic. See what Help topics appear in the lower-left window and which of those is selected and appears in the right window. Close the Microsoft FrontPage Help.

6. Exiting FrontPage:

    a. Click File, then click Exit.

    b. Do not save any changes that you made since you last saved watertaxi.htm.

interactivity (continued)

Problem Solving Exercises

1. Congratulations! You have been hired by a small publishing house, Diggs & Associates, as an office administrator. Your job profile involves creation and maintenance of a Web site. In order to maintain a competitive advantage, the publishers realized they would need a Web site to distribute information to agents, authors, and other potential business partners. Furthermore, they realized that certain business transactions could be conducted via the Internet. Your first job is to devise a rough draft of a Web site. Nothing concrete is necessary, just a few conceptual proposals including thematic examples and possible features. Some possible features to consider are a product ordering page and a guest book to record visitors to the site.

2. Make a list of the Web site components you advocate. Use your imagination; be creative and brainstorm with the Web site. All of your ideas may not be plausible but many can come to fruition. For example, images complete with animation can be added. Plug-ins and applets are other possibilities. These terms will be explained in future lessons if you are unfamiliar with them.

3. Devise a personally significant Web site. For example, if you are a soccer enthusiast, create a soccer Web site. Consider what type of information will be relevant and useful to visitors and what sites might complement yours. Search the Internet for related sites to link to yours.

4. Find one or more Web sites that you like and compile a list of the attributes that attracted you to them. Take detailed notes about what makes these sites attractive and engaging to visitors. Your notes should include everything from animation and graphics to theme, color, writing style, font size, and ont color. If possible, also take note of the flow of the pages. How are they linked? Try to draw a map or hierarchy of the Web site's pages.

Creating Web Sites

After you have defined a plan for your Web site, the next step is to create the necessary Web pages. You can create the design in several different ways. First, you can start with a blank page that automatically opens when you start the FrontPage application. Second, you can use a template or wizard to create a new page. A template is a preformatted Web page containing sample text and pictures that you can alter and format into unique pages. A wizard is a series of dialog boxes that guides you through the process of creating a Web page. Wizards and templates also can be used to create entire sites.

In this Lesson, you will open a template for creating a Guest Book. Such a book is a Web page for visitors to your Web site to write comments in a public guest log. After viewing the Guest Book template, you will close it and then open the Customer Support Web template. This template provides predesigned pages for an entire Web site devoted to identifying and serving customer needs, especially if the company performing those tasks is a software company.

The Web Wizard in the later Skills of this Lesson takes you through the process of choosing the overall elements of a Web site. You first add places for a mission statement and contact information on a home page. You then add places for Web changes, then articles and reviews, on a What's New page. You also create a feedback form Web page that asks your Web site's visitors to provide information such as their name, company affiliation, and contact data so you can send them the kinds of business-related information they seek.

skills

- Creating a New Web Page Using a Template
- Creating a New Web Using a Template
- Using a Web Wizard
- Using the Import Web Wizard
- Adding Text to a Web Page
- Formatting Text on a Web Page
- Adding and Formatting Lists
- Spell Checking and Editing a Web Page
- Using the Find Command
- Previewing a Web Page in a Browser

Additional Skills require you to add text to your Web pages, format that text, add and format lists of information, spell check and edit your Web pages, find a particular phrase on a page, and finally, preview a Web page in the default Web browser on your computer. All in all, this Lesson familiarizes you with the basic tools for building and viewing Web pages.

Lesson Goal:

In this lesson you will learn how to use wizards and templates. The Corporate Presence Wizard will build a rough Web, complete with a Home page, using the general organization and style of your choice. In addition, you will learn the fundamental tasks of adding and editing text, and check the spelling of the text in the Web page. You will also learn how to find and replace specific words and how to preview a published Web page.

skill: Creating a New Web Page Using a Template

concept

The fundamental building block of a Web site is a Web page. One of the easiest ways to get started on building a Web page is to use predefined templates that are provided by FrontPage. These templates can be easily modified to suit your specific needs.

do it!

Create a new Web page using a template.

1. Open the FrontPage application and click File on the Menu bar.
2. Point to New, and click Page or Web from the submenu that appears. This action displays a new Web page with the default file name new_page_1.htm in the left two-thirds of the program window and the New Page or Web task pane in the right one-third of the window.
3. In the New from Template section of the task pane, click the Page Templates hyperlink. This displays the Page Templates dialog box.
4. Click the Guest Book page, as shown in Figure 2-1. Click OK.
5. The new Web page appears in the FrontPage window complete with placeholder text, as shown in Figure 2-2. Placeholder text displays the text format and facilitates data entry.
6. Close the file. You do not need to save it.

more

A template is a basic structure or outline. FrontPage features many useful templates that you can choose from. Some templates are specifically designed to accommodate graphics, some come equipped with option buttons, and still others have predesigned return forms. Take advantage of these templates to create functional Web pages. Directly below and to the right of the FrontPage window are scroll bars equipped with scroll boxes and scroll arrows. Clicking the right or left scroll arrow on the horizontal scroll bar will move the view to the right or left. Clicking the up or down scroll arrow on the vertical scroll bar, will move the screen up or down one line at a time. You can move more quickly by clicking and dragging the scroll boxes up, down, left, or right. The size of the scroll box changes with the page size. The longer a page is top to bottom, the shorter the vertical scroll box. Conversely, as page width increases, horizontal scroll box size decreases.

Task panes are a new feature of Office XP applications for carrying out common program operations or selecting often-used options for common tasks. The FrontPage 2002 New Page or Web task pane enables you to open previously created files, open new blank pages or Webs, create new Webs or pages from existing Web pages, open Web templates, etc. The Clipboard task pane enables you to manage text and/or graphics that you have cut or copied to the Clipboard. The Search task pane can search for desired files, file names, and file properties, can perform advanced searches, and can control other aspects of search or find processes.

Step 3: Click to display the Page templates dialog box

Figure 2-1 Page Templates dialog box

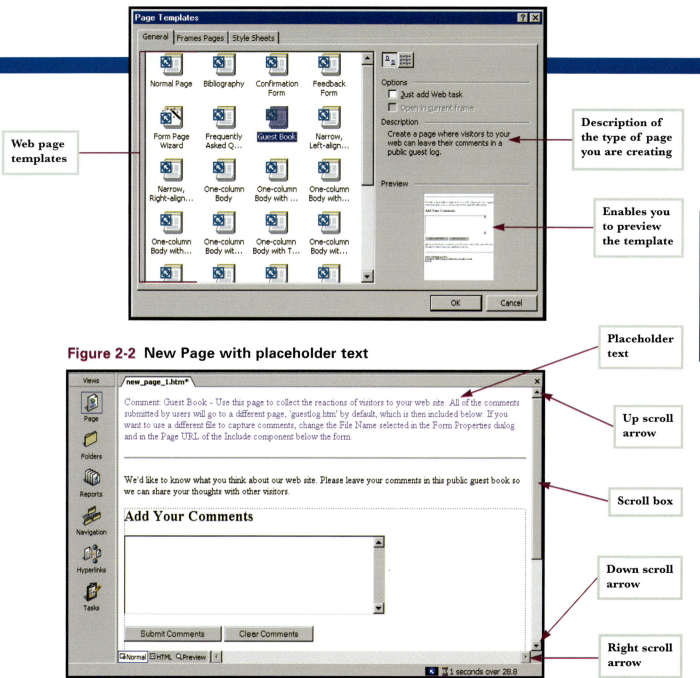

Figure 2-2 New Page with placeholder text

Practice

Open FrontPage and create a new Web page using the template of your choice. Save the Web page as try.htm. After saving the Web page, close the file.

skill Creating a New Web Using a Template

concept

A new multipage Web or a Web site can be started as easily as a new single Web page. If you have an idea of the theme and format you want, you can create a Web using a template. A Web template will create an entire Web site with a Home page and a general organizational structure and outline. You can replace placeholder text with your own data.

do it!

Create a Web using a template.

1. Click File on the Menu bar.
2. Point to New, and click Page or Web from the submenu that appears. This displays the New Page or Web Task Pane.
3. Click the Web Site Templates hyperlink. The Web Site Templates dialog box appears. Click Customer Support Web icon, as shown in Figure 2-3.
4. Click OK.
5. Your Web is created, complete with a Home page. Most Web servers require a default name for Home pages, usually, Index.htm. If you change it, FrontPage will automatically rename it if required by the server, when you publish the Web.
6. To view the structure of the Web, as shown in Figure 2-4, click the Navigation button on the Views bar. Scroll to the right to see the remaining area of the Web hierarchy.
7. You do not need to save this Web.

more

Every Web contains a Home page. A Home page is the first page that visitors see when they reach a site. Links are used to navigate between the various pages in a Web.

The New Web dialog box provides a description of each available template. The Customer Support Web furnishes a feedback mechanism to improve customer support services. The Project Web provides a team member directory and enables project team members to discuss ideas and concerns, post status reports, and schedule meetings. A Personal Web consists of a Home page, a Photo album page, an Interests page, and a page which links to the author's favorite sites.

Each of these Web templates serves different purposes. However, a template is not a restrictive structure. Web templates can be edited and reorganized. Themes can be applied during or after the creation process. Unnecessary pages can be deleted and additional pages can be inserted. For example, if a company wants to advertise using multiple photographs, the Web author can begin with the Personal Web template and add a Form page and a Guest book page. Start with a Web template that is suited to your requirements and edit it in any way you wish, to make it your own.

Figure 2-3 Web Site Templates dialog box

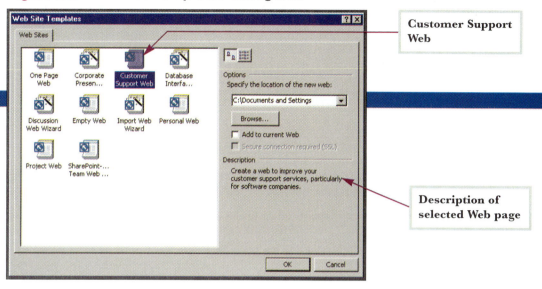

Figure 2-4 Structure of a Web

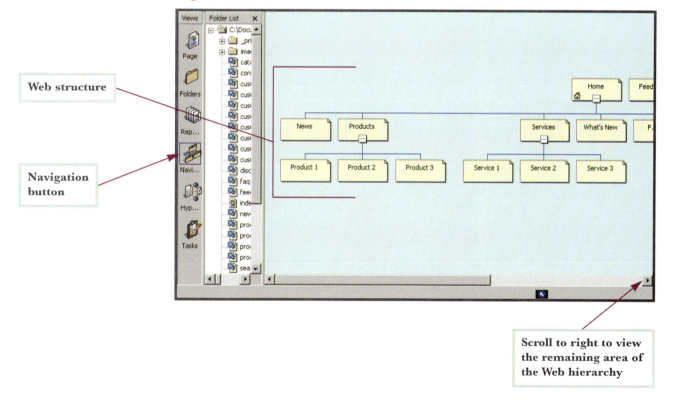

Practice

Create a Web using the Project Web template from the Web Site Templates dialog box. Go through the Navigation structure of this Web and then close the Web. You do not need to save this Web.

skill: Using a Web Wizard

concept

A *wizard* is an automated procedure that enables you to conveniently perform a complex operation. A series of dialog boxes prompts you to choose options that accomplish the task to your specifications. The easiest method for creating a Web is to choose a Web Wizard.

do it!

Use a wizard to create a new Web.

1. Click File, on the Menu bar.
2. Select New, and click Page or Web from the submenu that appears. The Page or Web Task Pane appears.
3. Click the Web Site Templates hyperlink. This displays the Web Site Templates dialog box.
4. Click Corporate Presence Wizard on the Web Sites tab.
5. Click [OK]. This displays the first dialog box of the Corporate Presence Web Wizard. The first dialog box is an introduction to the Wizard, shown below in Figure 2-5. Click [Next >].
6. The next dialog box allows you to choose the pages to include in your Web. Make sure that all of the check boxes are selected, except for the Products/Services check box. Click [Next >].
7. The next dialog box is a description of the Home page. Select the Mission Statement and Contact Information boxes, as shown in Figure 2-6. Click [Next >].
8. The next dialog box describes the What's New page. Select the Articles and Reviews, and Web Changes check boxes, as shown in Figure 2-7. Click [Next >].
9. The next dialog box sets up the Feedback Form. Retain the default settings and select the Mailing Address check box, as shown in Figure 2-8. Click [Next >]. 💿 Default settings are pre-selected settings (and, therefore, already checked off) by FrontPage.

(continued on FP 2.8)

Figure 2-5 Corporate Presence Web Wizard dialog box

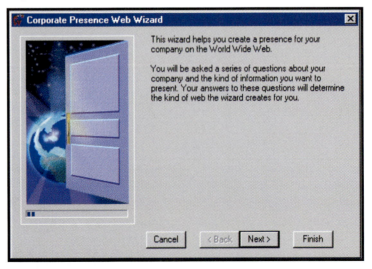

Figure 2-6 Description of the Home page

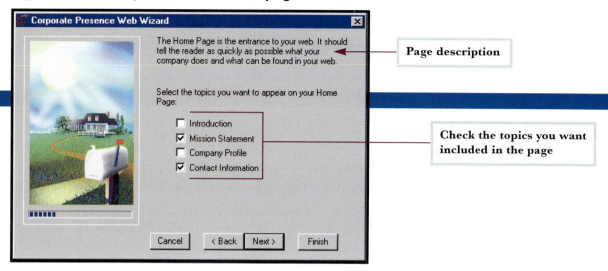

Figure 2-7 Description of What's New page

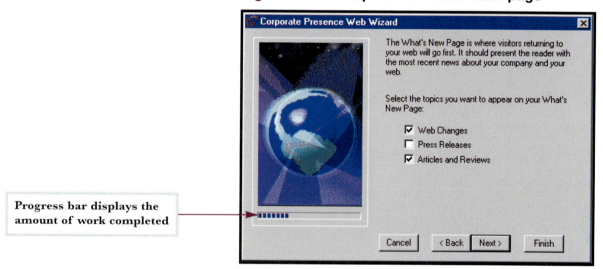

Figure 2-8 Description of the Feedback Form

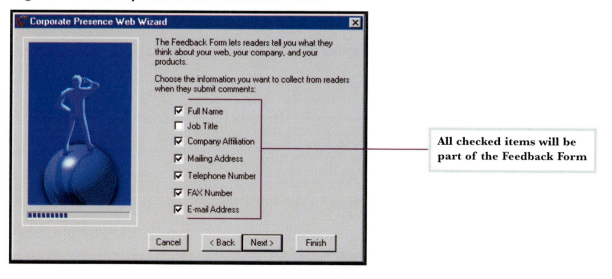

skill Using a Web Wizard (continued)

10. The next dialog box prompts you to specify whether you want the files to be compatible with database and spreadsheet programs. Accept the default settings and click Next>.

11. The next dialog box sets up the Table of Contents. Accept the default settings and click Next>.

12. The next dialog box adds objects to the top and bottom of each page. Leave the default settings checked. In addition, select the check boxes to place the company logo at the top of each page. The dialog box is shown in Figure 2-9. Click Next>.

13. The next dialog box prompts you to mark each unfinished page in your Web with the Under Construction icon. Accept the default settings, and click Next>.

14. Click in the company name text box to place the insertion point there. Delete the sample company name and type Speed Demons Sky Diving Club. Type in Skydiver as the one word version of that name. The address is 345 Rocky Rd., Falling Water, N.Y. 10566, as shown in Figure 2-10. Click Next>.

15. Type the telephone number and the fax number as (914) 555-9903. The Webmaster's e-mail address is Shanson@domain.skydiver.com. The e-mail address for general info is info@domain.speed_demon.com. Click Next>.

16. Click Next> without selecting a Web theme.

17. Click Finish. The Web opens in the Tasks view. The only tasks are for you to customize the pages. Click the Navigation view button to view the Web structure, as shown in Figure 2-11.

more

Web Wizards are most useful when creating a complicated Web, as they guide a user through the process of creating a complicated site. You can use wizards to create a Form Page, which is used to collect information from the user. You can also create Data Access Pages, which are Web pages created using Microsoft Access databases. There is even a Discussion Web Wizard, a Customer Support Web Wizard, and an Import Web Wizard.

You can type in the specified location of your Web folder in the Specify the Location of the New Web list box in the Web Site Templates dialog box. FrontPage will create a new folder with a specified name. For example, type the following text: C:\Windows\Desktop\Sydney's Web\. FrontPage will create a folder called Sydney's Web, on your desktop. If you do not type Windows before Desktop then the folder will be saved in your Desktop folder on the hard drive. If you do not specify the name of the folder or the location to save it, FrontPage will create a default folder called myweb, in Desktop folder. Each succeeding Web that you create will be labeled myweb1, myweb2, myweb3, etc.

The first letter, of the location in which you save the folder, specifies the drive where the folders are located. Generally, A: is the floppy disk drive, C: is the hard drive, and D: is the CD ROM drive. After specifying the drive, you specify the location, such as Desktop, or My Documents. This method can help you save a Web anywhere on your computer.

Figure 2-9 Objects to be added at top and bottom of page

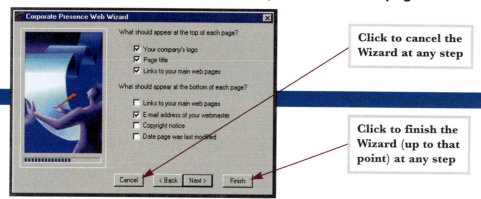

Figure 2-10 Details of the company to be added in the Web

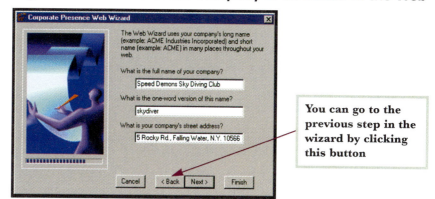

Figure 2-11 Web in Navigation view

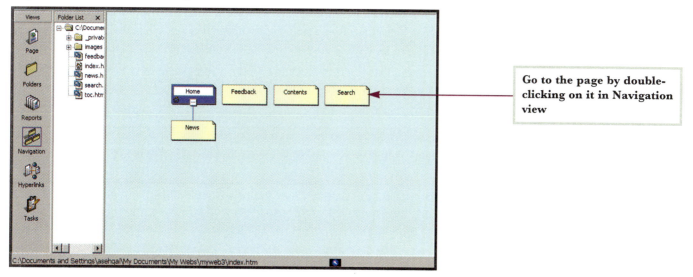

Practice

Create a Web called Discussion using the Discussion Web Wizard.

skill: Using the Import Web Wizard

concept

When you import a file to FrontPage you are creating a new Web using pre-existing files. A wizard, referred to as the Import Web Wizard makes the importing process easier. The Wizard creates a new Web that uses data imported from a previously created file. This Wizard enables you to add and delete data quickly without beginning a Web from scratch each time.

do it!

Use the Import Web Wizard to create a new Web by importing data from pre-existing files.

1. Click File on the Menu bar.
2. Select New, and click Page or Web from the submenu that appears. The New Page or Web Task Pane opens.
3. Click the Web Site Templates hyperlink. This displays the Web Site Templates dialog box.
4. Click Import Web Wizard. You can use the Import Web Wizard to transfer data from a published Web site to a new Web as well as to convert a folder to a Web.
5. In the Specify the Location of the New Web text box type C:\My Documents\Skydiver, as shown in Figure 2-12. This specifies that the Web will be saved in a folder called Skydiver in the My Documents folder on your machine. Click OK. The first Import Web Wizard dialog box opens.
6. Activate the From a source directory of files on a local computer or network option button. You will notice that this action deselects the only other option, From a World Wide Web site. Click Browse. The File Open dialog box will open.
7. In the File Open dialog box, find the location where you have stored the student file, and click the fpdoit2-4 folder, as shown in Figure 2-13. Click Open to close the dialog box and to return to the Import Web Wizard - Choose Source screen.
8. Click Next >. This displays the Import Web Wizard - Edit File List dialog box.
9. Click Next > again. This displays the Import Web Wizard - Finish dialog box. Click Finish.
10. Click the Navigation icon on the Views toolbar. Double-click the Index page in the Skydiver Web. It is the original Skydiver page you worked with earlier.
11. Save and close the file.

more

By default, FrontPage always opens a blank Web page. To open a previously saved Web page, double-click the page icon in the Folder List. You can also click the Navigation button on the Views bar and double-click the page you want to view, on the Navigation structure. At present, in the Navigation view, the Skydiver Web contains only one page. Double-clicking it will display the Speed Demons page in the Page view.

Figure 2-12 Web Site Templates dialog box

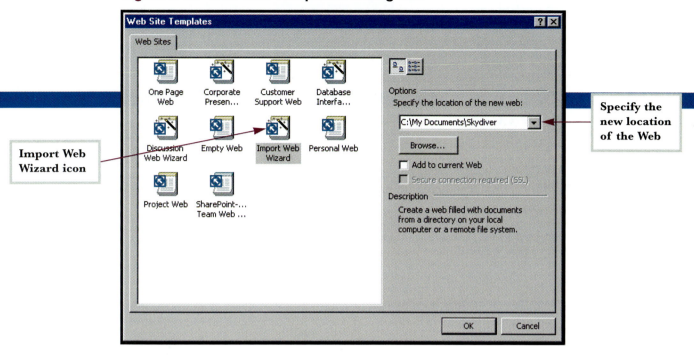

Figure 2-13 File Open dialog box

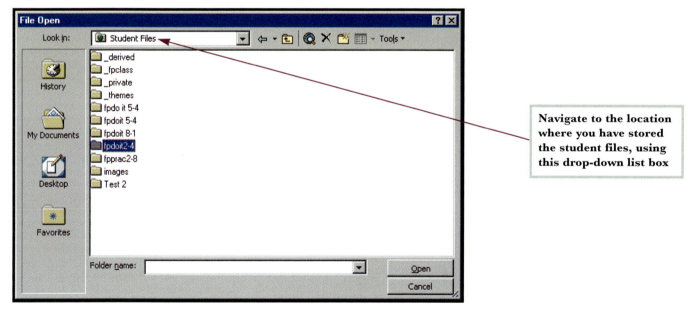

Practice

Create a new Web, called Caddy Shop. Import the file fpprac2-4.htm into the new Web.

skill | Adding Text to a Web Page

concept

Perhaps the most important job in creating a Web site is composing the text. Imparting information to visitors to your site is, after all, your primary goal. Adding text is the first step in the creation of a functional Web site.

do it!

Add text to a Web page. You will add text to the imported Home page in the Skydiver Web you have created.

1. Open the Index page in Page view from the Skydiver Web.

2. Place the mouse pointer at the end of the word Club, and click. A flashing insertion point, (a black bar, which marks where text will be added), should appear at the end of the word Club, as shown in Figure 2-14.

3. Press the [Enter] key four times.  The [Tab] key on the keyboard moves text several spaces, generally toward the right, depending on the format you apply. You can use the [Enter] key, [Tab] key, and [Space bar] key to affect where a page text appears.

4. Type A National Organization for those who live on the edge. Your page should look like Figure 2-15.

5. Click File and then click the Save command.

6. Close the Index page.

more

You can format or change the appearance of text, using the Formatting toolbar. Text formatting includes changing font, font style, size, color, and alignment. For example, if the text you just entered appears larger than that in Figure 2-15, you can decrease its size by selecting the phrase, then choosing a smaller font size—perhaps 4 (14 pt). Special effects, such as Marquee text, can also be added to enhance the way text appears.

Figure 2-14 Insertion point placed in text

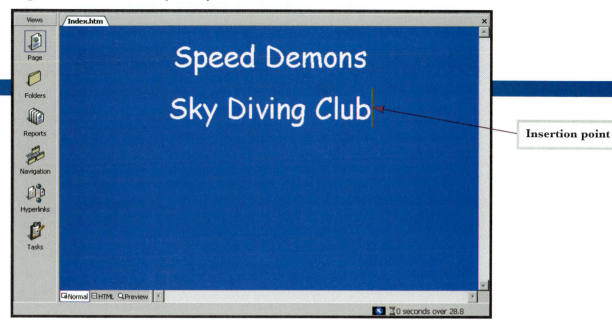

Figure 2-15 Page with new text added

Practice

Five lines below the last line of text on the Index page in the Caddy Shop Web, type Best Prices This Side of the Pond.

 Formatting Text on a Web Page

concept

FrontPage allows for many formatting options. These formatting options include changing the font or typeface, font style, font size, color, and alignment. Text can be aligned to the left, right, or center. It can also be underlined, italicized, or made bold. Many formatting commands can be accessed from the Formatting toolbar.

do it!

Change the font and font size of Web page text.

1. Open the Index page of the Skydiver Web.
2. Place the insertion point before the letter A in the second phrase. Click and drag the pointer to the end of the phrase, selecting it. The text should appear as shown in Figure 2-16.
3. Click the arrow in the Font Size drop-down list box on the Formatting toolbar (Figure 2-17).
4. Select the size 5 (18 pt) from the drop-down list. The selected sentence becomes bigger.
5. Click the Font drop-down list box. A list of fonts is displayed, as shown in Figure 2-17.
6. Click the Monotype Corsiva font. The text font changes to Monotype Corsiva.
7. Select the first two lines of the page.
8. Click the Underline button U on the Formatting toolbar. If you apply a format before typing, it will be applied to the entire page. On the other hand if you select the target text, the formatting will be applied only to the selected text.
9. Click once anywhere on the screen to deselect the selected text. Your page should now resemble Figure 2-18.
10. Save and close the file.

more

The word Font refers to typeface style. Some fonts are bold, some are ornate, and some are classic. You can even choose a comical or a serious font to set the tone for your page. Next to the Underline button are the Bold B and Italic I buttons, which can be used together or separately. The three style buttons are especially useful for headers, footers, and other text you want to emphasize. The three layout buttons, Align Left, Align Right, and Center control where text appears on the page. Sometimes you may need to use the alignment buttons in conjunction with the space bar to arrange text exactly as desired.

Figure 2-16 Selected page text

Figure 2-17 Formatting toolbar

Figure 2-18 Formatted text

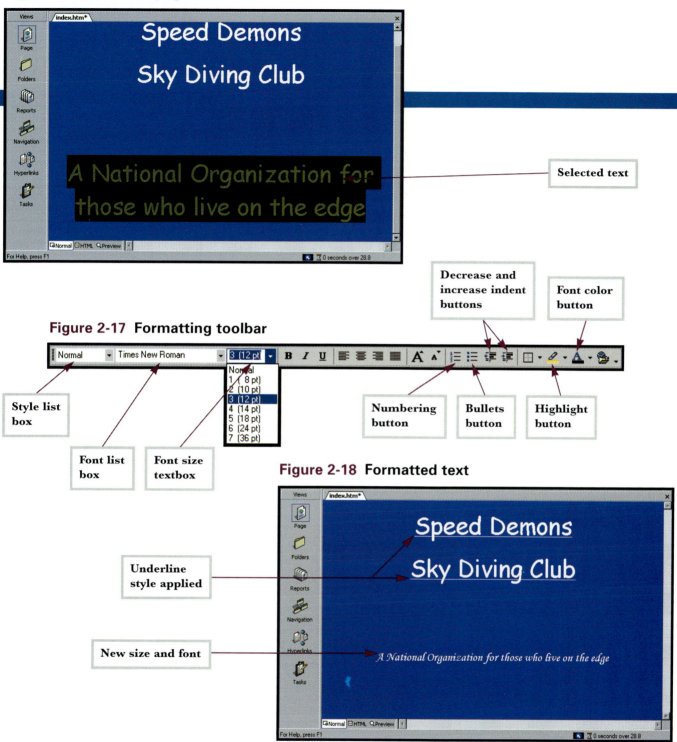

Practice

On the Index page of the Caddy Shop Web, format the text so that the address of the shop appears in the font Century Gothic and the text is underlined. Save and close the file.

skill: Adding and Formatting Lists

concept

FrontPage has many ways of organizing information on a Web Page. One simple and convenient way for organizing information on a Web page is to create a list. Lists consolidate information in a concise format. They can either be numbered or bulleted by using the corresponding buttons on the Formatting toolbar.

do it!

Add a new page with a list to a Web.

1. Open the Skydiver Web.
2. Open the Index page.
3. Click File on the Menu bar and point to New. Click Page or Web from the submenu. The New Page or Web Task Pane appears. Click the Blank Page hyperlink. A new page opens.
4. Type Organizational Goals in the first line of the page and then click the Center button on the Formatting bar.
5. Select the text and format it so that the font is Arial Black and the size is 5 (18 pt).
6. Place the insertion point after s in Goals and click once. Press the [Enter] key.
7. Click the Align Left button. Then click the Bullets button. Type Increase club membership. Press the [Enter] key again. Type Increase public awareness.
8. Follow the same procedure to expand the list by including the follow text: Catch media attention, Stress safety measures, and Make skydiving more affordable and enjoyable for all. The page is shown in Figure 2-19.
9. Right-click one of the bullets in the list. Click List Properties. The List Properties dialog box opens.
10. Click the bullets that are empty circles, as shown in Figure 2-20, and click OK.
    To change the properties of only one item in the list, right-click the item you want to change and click List Item Properties from the menu. The List Item Properties dialog box will open, presenting formatting options for that particular item.
11. Save the file in the Skydiver Web, accept the default name organizational_goals.html and close the file.

more

You can create a numbered list rather than a bulleted list using the Numbering button. Then you can right-click an item in a numbered list to access the pop-up menu. In the Numbers tab of the List Properties dialog box, you can label your list with capital or lowercase letters or Roman numerals.

Figure 2-19 Bulleted list

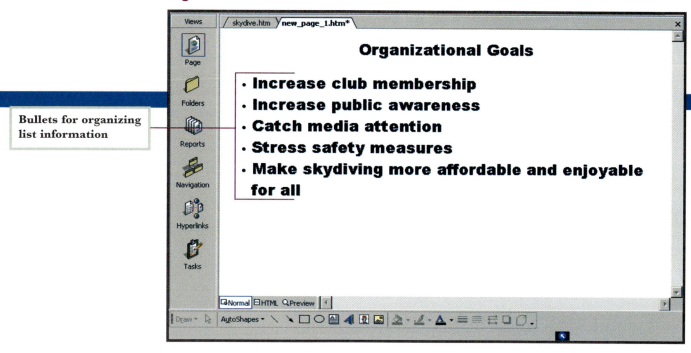

Bullets for organizing list information

Figure 2-20 List Properties dialog box

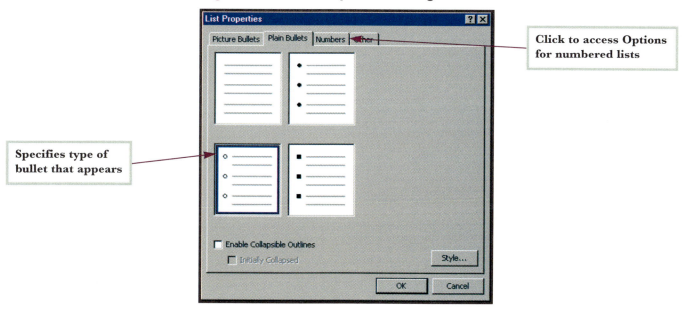

Click to access Options for numbered lists

Specifies type of bullet that appears

Practice

Create a new page in the Caddy Shop Web. At the top write Best selling items. Then create a numbered list, listing, in order, Tees, Balls, Clubs, Bags, Shoes, Shirts, Pants, Videos, and Books. Save the page as best_selling_items.htm and close the file.

skill
Spell Checking and Editing a Web Page

concept

Typing errors are inevitable. You can use the Spell Checker to locate mistakes while adding text to a Web page in the Normal tab. Red and green underlines, called Squigglies, will alert you to possible errors. Editing text is then a fairly simple task.

do it!

Check a Web page you have created for spelling errors and make the necessary corrections.

1. Open the page fpdoit2-8.htm from the location where you have stored the student files.
2. Click Tools on the Menu bar, then click Spelling.
3. The Spelling dialog box opens when a point is reached where a word is not in the FrontPage dictionary, as shown in Figure 2-21.
4. Click [Change] to replace the word with the suggested change.
5. Click [Cancel] to close the Spelling dialog box.
6. Place the mouse pointer after the letter k in the misspelled word, and click to place the insertion point. The misspelled word is shown in Figure 2-22. When a word is underlined in red, it indicates that it is not in the dictionary. You can do on-the-spot editing without accessing the Spell Checker.
7. Press the [Backspace] key on the keyboard to delete the letter k.
8. Type rm, so the word Determine is spelled correctly.
9. Save the file as Writing Tips.htm in your My Documents folder and close the file.

more

Clicking [Add] will add a word to the spell-checking dictionary. This is particularly useful if the checker frequently stops on your name, or for unusual words that are not in the dictionary. You can also select and right-click a word to access a pop-up menu. The pop-up menu will contain a list of possible replacements and the Add and Ignore commands.

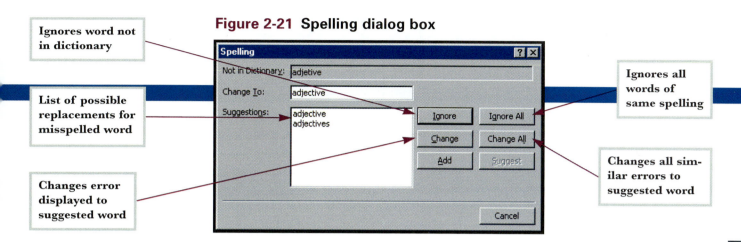

Figure 2-21 Spelling dialog box

- Ignores word not in dictionary
- List of possible replacements for misspelled word
- Changes error displayed to suggested word
- Ignores all words of same spelling
- Changes all similar errors to suggested word

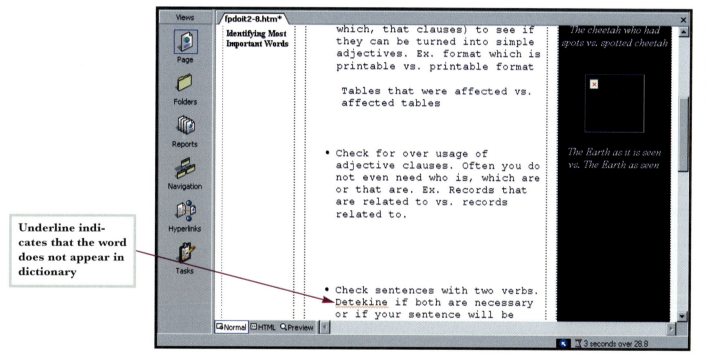

Figure 2-22 Misspelled word in page

- Underline indicates that the word does not appear in dictionary

Practice

Find and correct the spelling errors in fpprac2-8.htm. Save it as order_form.htm in the Caddy Shop Web.

skill Using the Find Command

concept

Quickly locating specific words or phrases can be difficult in a lengthy page or Web. The FrontPage Find and Replace commands enable you to search for and review or edit text quickly and accurately.

do it!

Use the Find command to locate a specific section of text on a particular Web page.

1. Open the Writing Tips page. Make sure your cursor is at the top left of the page.
2. Click Edit on the Menu bar, then click Find.
3. The Find and Replace dialog box opens, as shown in Figure 2-23.
4. In the Find what text box type adverb clauses.
5. Click [Find Next]. The Find command takes you to the first mention of adverb clauses.
6. Click [Find Next] again. The Find command takes you to the second occurrence of adverb clauses, as shown in Figure 2-24.
7. Click [Cancel].
8. Close the page.

more

The Replace command is also accessed from the Edit menu. The Replace tab is almost identical to the Find tab. The difference is that the Replace tab has an additional text box that enables you to enter replacement text. Two additional buttons enable you to replace a single instance, [Replace] or all instances of a particular word or phrase, [Replace All]. In the Search section options section, option buttons enable you to choose to search the entire document, selected page, or just the current page. In the Direction section, you can choose to search up or down the document or the entire document. You can use the Find and Replace commands in almost every view. You can also use them to find and replace text in HTML.

The Replace command may be on the extended Edit menu. Not all commands are visible on the primary menu. In Office XP, menus automatically expand after a few seconds. You can hasten the process by moving the pointer over the double arrows at the bottom of the menu. Primary menu commands will include commands you have recently used.

Figure 2-23 Find and Replace dialog box

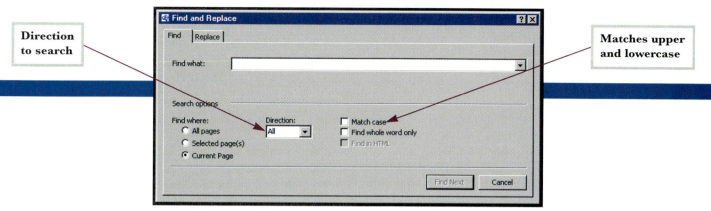

Figure 2-24 Text found in page

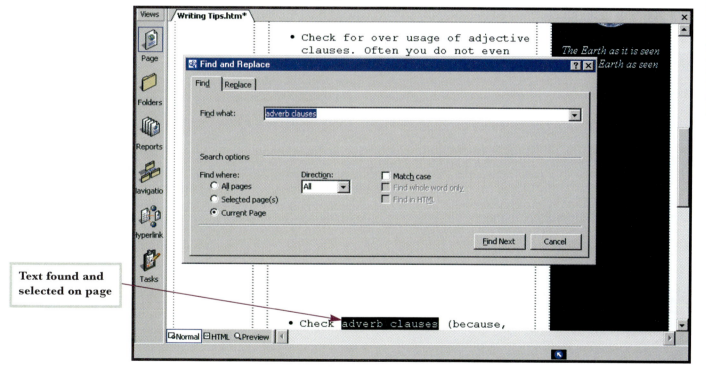

Practice

Open the order_form.htm and find a question that asks user to enter his or her age. View the question and close the file.

skill | Previewing a Web Page in a Browser

concept

FrontPage Webs will look exactly as you see them in Internet Explorer 4 or above, but may look very different in other browsers. Even simple Web pages will display differently depending on the browser used. The Preview tab in Page view, displays a Web as it will appear online. However, the Preview in Browser command will give you an even better idea of how your Web pages will look when published. A browser, as you will recall, is a program that enables you to view Web pages and HTML documents.

do it!

Preview your Web with a browser.

1. Open the Skydiver Web.
2. Open the Index page.
3. Click File on the Menu bar. Then click the Preview in Browser command. It may appear on the extended menu.
4. The Preview in Browser dialog box opens, as shown in Figure 2-25.
5. Click [Preview].
6. The browser opens with your page displayed, as shown in Figure 2-26. As long as they are in good working order, your hyperlinks will operate when you preview a page in your browser. You can link to other pages in a Web or to Web sites on the Internet.
7. Close the browser.
8. Close the Web and exit FrontPage.

more

If you click on a file directly from the folder it is in, rather than opening it in FrontPage, it will open in your default browser without going through the process of the Preview in Browser dialog box.

Figure 2-25 Preview in Browser dialog box

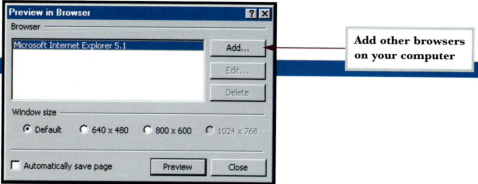

Add other browsers on your computer

Figure 2-26 Web page previewed in browser

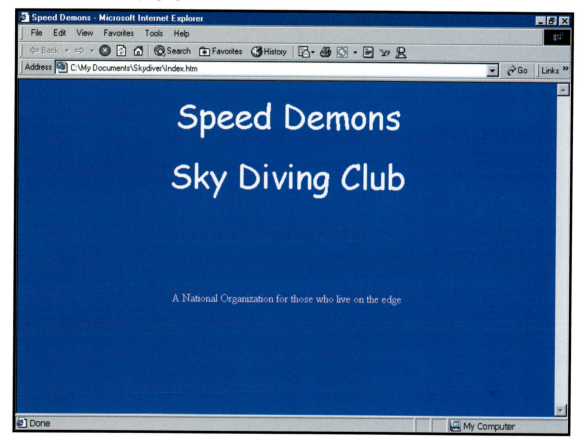

Practice

Open the Index page of the Caddy Shop Web and preview it in your browser. Close the file after previewing it.

shortcuts

Function	Button/Mouse	Menu	Keyboard
Create a New Page		Click File, then click New, then click Page or Web	[Ctrl]+[N]
Create a New Web		Click File, then click New, then click Page or Web	[Alt]+[F]+[N]+[P]
Preview in Browser		Click File, then click Preview in Browser	[Alt]+[F]+[B]
Find a section of Text		Click Edit, then click Find	[Ctrl]+[F]
Replace		Click Edit, then click Replace	[Ctrl]+[H]
Check Spelling		Click Tools, then click Spelling	[F7]

A. Identify Key Features

Name the items indicated by callouts in Figure 2-27.

Figure 2-27 Web page in FrontPage

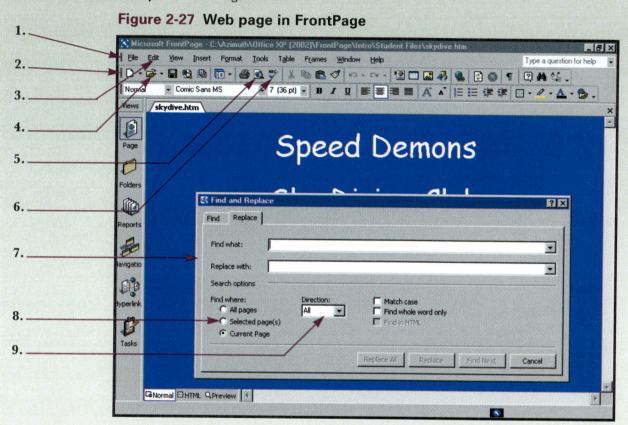

1.
2.
3.
4.
5.
6.
7.
8.
9.

B. Select the Best Answer

10. A series of dialog boxes that facilitate the creation of a Web page or an entire Web
11. A pre-constructed document that allows you to fill in your own content
12. Allows you to type text directly onto the page
13. This feature allows you to search by the casing of a letter in a word
14. A word will be flagged by the Spell Checker if it does not appear here
15. The first Web page you visit in a Web site
16. Allows you to view Web pages and HTML documents

a. Match case
b. Template
c. Browser
d. Dictionary
e. Wizard
f. Insertion point
g. Home page

quiz (continued)

C. Complete the Statement

17. If you open a file directly from a folder, rather than opening it in FrontPage:
    a. It will open in FrontPage anyway
    b. It will open in a Web editor
    c. It will open in a browser
    d. It will not open at all

18. When commands cannot be found on the regular menu sometimes, you must open:
    a. An extended menu
    b. A folder
    c. A wizard
    d. A keyboard shortcut

19. When you use either the Find or the Replace command, you have the option of searching a page:
    a. Left-to-right, right-to-left
    b. By the size of the word
    c. All, Up, or down
    d. By the verb tense

20. When creating a Web using the Import Web Wizard, you must select the folder to import using:
    a. The Find Folder command
    b. The File Open dialog box
    c. The Find Folder dialog box
    d. The Edit menu

21. If you misspell a word while typing, FrontPage alerts you:
    a. By highlighting the word
    b. By automatically changing the word
    c. By underlining the word in red
    d. By having a dialog box open automatically

22. The computer hard drive is usually marked by the letter:
    a. D
    b. E
    c. A
    d. C

23. If compared with the Find tab, the Replace tab has an additional:
    a. Button
    b. Textbox
    c. Option button
    d. Check box

24. FrontPage templates can come with:
    a. Option buttons
    b. Predesigned return forms
    c. Features to accommodate graphics
    d. All of the above

25. Every Web site contains:
    a. FrontPage-based templates
    b. Graphics and/or photographs
    c. A Home page
    d. All of the above

interactivity

Build Your Skills

1. Create a new Web page using a template:
    a. Click File, then click New. Click Page or Web from the submenu that appears.
    b. Select a template from the ones provided in the Page Templates dialog box.

2. Create a new Web with a template:
    a. Click File, then click New. Click Page or Web from the submenu that appears.
    b. Select the Personal Web wizard from the Web Site Templates dialog box.
    c. Save the Web as My Site.

3. Create a Web using a Web Wizard:
    a. Click File, then click New. Click Page or Web from the submenu that appears.
    b. Select Corporate Presence Wizard from the Web Site Templates dialog box.
    c. Create a Corporate Presence Web using the options provided.

4. Import a Web:
    a. Click File, then New. Click Page or Web from the submenu that appears.
    b. Select the Import Web Wizard.
    c. Create a Web called Water Taxi.
    d. Import the fpskill2 Web folder from the location where you have stored your Student Files to the Water Taxi Web.

5. Add and edit text:
    a. Fix the spelling error that occurs in the index.htm file of the Water Taxi Web.
    b. Place the insertion point at the end of the table. Press the [Enter] key until you are four lines below the table.
    c. Add the slogan for the Water Taxi service.

6. Preview a Web page in a browser:
    a. Make sure index.htm of the Water Taxi Web is open.
    b. Click File, then click Preview in Browser.
    c. Select a Web browser.
    d. Preview the file, close the browser, and then close FrontPage.

interactivity (continued)

Problem Solving Exercises

1. Use the Corporate Presence Wizard to create a Web site for Diggs & Associates. Name the Web folder Diggs and save it in your My Documents folder. Keep your earlier plans in mind. You can always add pages to a Web to accommodate your various ideas. Include a Products/Services page. Accept the default settings for the Products/Services page. Fill in the name of the company, Diggs & Associates, the address, 987 Park Lane, Thompson, MA 02411, and the telephone number, (502) 555-9043. The fax number is (502) 555-1649. Your e-mail address is the Webmaster's address. The general info address is: info@domain.diggs.com. Retain the default settings for everything else.

2. Your supervisors think you should add a product-ordering page. They have asked you to design a prototype for their review and comment. Use the Form Page Wizard, found in the Page Templates dialog box, to give them an idea of what a product-ordering page will look like. In the first dialog box, click Add to affix ordering information to the page. Retain the default settings for everything else.

3. Another Diggs employee is interested in previewing the Web site. He has asked you to create a blank Web using the Corporate Presence Wizard to give him a rough idea of the site structure. Change the options in various ways to create several versions to show him.

4. Create a personal Web site. Use a template or a wizard if appropriate. You can start with a blank page and write a short biography. Some topics for other pages might include Education, Hobbies, Sports, Favorite Books and CDs, and Future Plans. Develop each page as fully as you can.

Formatting and Adding Objects to Web Pages

- Creating Tables
- Formatting Tables
- Applying Themes to Webs
- Applying Custom Themes
- Applying Themes to Individual Pages
- Creating Text Hyperlinks
- Editing Hyperlinks
- Adding Images
- Formatting Images
- Image Mapping
- Creating a Hover Button
- Creating a Marquee
- Inserting Text Boxes
- Adding Check Boxes and Option Buttons
- Creating a Drop-Down List Box
- Creating a Push Button

Formatting to make your site both aesthetically pleasing and effective is a difficult task. Such formatting is crucial, however, in order to attract first-time visitors and to keep visitors coming back to your site. If you use a template, with preformatted text, you need not bother with formatting. However, as you become more skilled at creating your own Web pages, you will probably want to exert more control over the final product.

Of course, what makes for attractive design varies from person to person. Therefore, FrontPage offers many possibilities for designing Webs to suit various styles and sensibilities. Keep in mind, however, that in good Web design, form follows function. Styles and graphics should enhance a Web site's message, not detract from or overpower it. If a certain style or graphic seems excessive, don't add it.

Applying a theme is perhaps the easiest formatting method. The font or typeface, text color, background, bullet style, and graphics are chosen all at once. This saves time and you are able to choose various complementary elements at one go.

Adding objects takes practice and experience. Certain objects are more effective in specific situations. Lists, tables, hyperlinks, and images can be added to your pages and formatted to your specifications.

Forms can be added to Web pages or created as independent pages. Text boxes, option buttons, check boxes, and drop-down menus can be added to forms to gather information from Web site visitors.

After you add objects to a Web page, you must know how to reformat them, move them, change their colors, size, and borders, and even add animation.

Lesson Goal:

In this lesson, you will learn to create and format tables, apply themes and custom themes to Web or individual pages, create and edit hyperlinks, and add and format images. You will also learn to create an image map, hover buttons, a marquee, and add text boxes, check boxes, option buttons, drop-down boxes, and push buttons.

Creating Tables

concept

Tables are commonly used on Web pages to organize information in a structured and attractive way. To start with, all you need is a rough outline and a general idea of where you want to insert the table. Tables consist of cells containing text or numbers. Tables can be imported from Microsoft Word or Microsoft Excel, so that you can reuse existing tables from word processing or spreadsheet documents.

do it!

Insert a table into the Index page in the Skydiver Web.

1. Open the Index page from the Skydiver Web.
2. Place the insertion point halfway between the name of the club and the slogan for the club.
3. Click Table on the Menu bar. Then, click Insert and click Table from the submenu. This displays the Insert Table dialog box, as shown in Figure 3-1.
4. Click OK to accept the default settings.
5. A table is inserted with the insertion point in the first cell.
6. Type Organizational Goals. Press the [Tab] key.
7. Type Schedule of Events, Recent News, and Skydiving Near You, pressing the [Tab] key after each entry.
8. When you have finished entering the text, save the file. Your page should now look like Figure 3-2. You can create a table without borders by changing the Border size, Cell padding, and Cell spacing to 0 in the Insert Table dialog box.

more

The Insert Table button on the Standard toolbar can also be used to create a table. A drop-down menu appears in which you move the pointer to highlight the desired number of cells. If you want to change any of the cell properties, however, you should use the Table menu and go through the Insert Table dialog box. The number and size of the rows and columns does not have to be decided ahead of time. As you add content to your table, the rows and columns will expand. To add more rows to the table you just created, simply press the [Tab] key at the end of the text in the fourth cell. Another row with two cells will automatically be inserted.

If a table gets too large or becomes unnecessary, you can delete part or all of the table. To begin the process, you must be in Page View. Table 3-1 below explains how to delete tables or their elements.

Table 3-1 Deleting Table Elements

Action	Steps
Delete a table	Click anywhere in the table you want to delete, click Table, point to Select, click Table, right-click anywhere on the table, and click Delete Cells
Delete a cell	Click in the cell you want to delete, click Table, point to Select, click Cell, right-click on the cell, and click Delete Cells
Delete a row	Click in any cell in the row you want to delete, click Table, point to Select, click Row, right-click on the row, and click Delete Cells
Delete a column	Click in any cell in the column you want to delete, click Table, point to Select, click Column, right-click on the column, and click Delete Cell

INTERACTIVE COMPUTING FrontPage 2002 FP 3.3

Figure 3-1 Insert Table dialog box

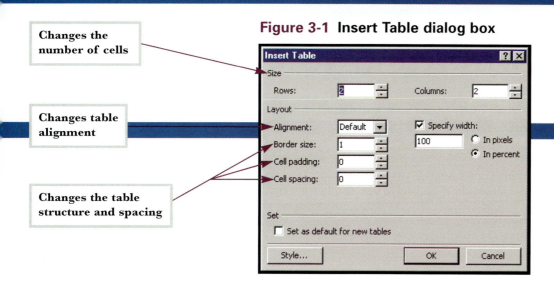

Changes the number of cells

Changes table alignment

Changes the table structure and spacing

Figure 3-2 Page with table inserted

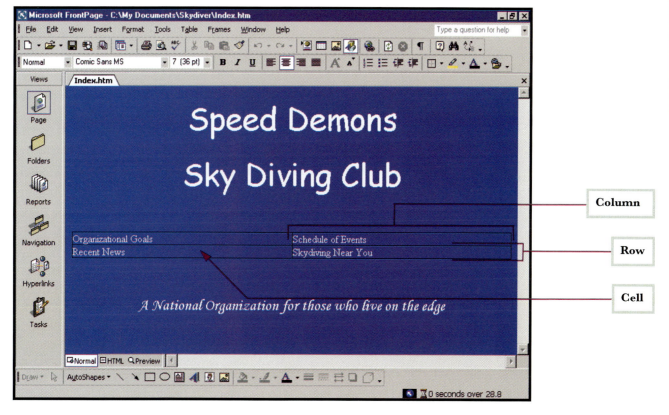

Column

Row

Cell

Practice

Insert a table in the Index page of the Caddy Shop Web. Add the following text; Sales, Products, Contact us, and Employment, into the four cells. Save the file.

skill | Formatting Tables

concept

Formatting can be applied to tables after they are created. Text formatting including font changes, underlining, and color can also be added. The Table Properties dialog box will enable you to add background colors, apply various borders, and adjust the spacing between cell contents and cell walls. Changes can be made to the entire table, individual cells or specific rows or columns.

do it!

Format the table you have created.

1. Right-click the border of the table.
2. Click Table Properties from the pop-up menu. The Table Properties dialog box opens.
3. Click the down arrow in the Color drop-down list box in the Borders section. Click the white color square.
4. Change the Light Border and Dark Border to white.
5. Change the Background Color to the same blue background as that of the page, as shown in Figure 3-3. Click Apply.
6. Click OK to close the Table Properties dialog box. Right-click the cell border. Click Cell Properties from the pop-up menu. The Cell Properties dialog box opens.
7. Click the down arrow on the Horizontal Alignment drop-down list box in the Layout section. Click Center from the drop-down list.
8. Click Apply and then OK. Notice that only one cell is affected. Click and drag to select the entire table. Reopen the Cell Properties dialog box and repeat the procedure to center the remaining cells. When you have finished, your page should look like Figure 3-4. If you click Font on the pop-up menu, the Font dialog box will open, allowing you to change the font, color, and other aspects of the text.

more

You can use the mouse pointer to resize a table. If you want to resize the table horizontally, move the pointer over a vertical border, and the pointer will turn into a horizontal resizing arrow ↔. If you want to resize the table vertically, move the pointer over a horizontal border and it will turn into a vertical resizing arrow ↕. Once the pointer has turned into a resizing arrow, simply click and drag the border until it is the size that you want.

To add rows or columns, drag to select the table. Click Tables on the Menu bar. Click Insert, then click Rows or Columns. Use the Insert Rows or Columns dialog box to insert the rows or columns you want. You can also insert rows and columns by right clicking the table and selecting Insert Rows or Insert Columns.

Figure 3-3 Table Properties dialog box

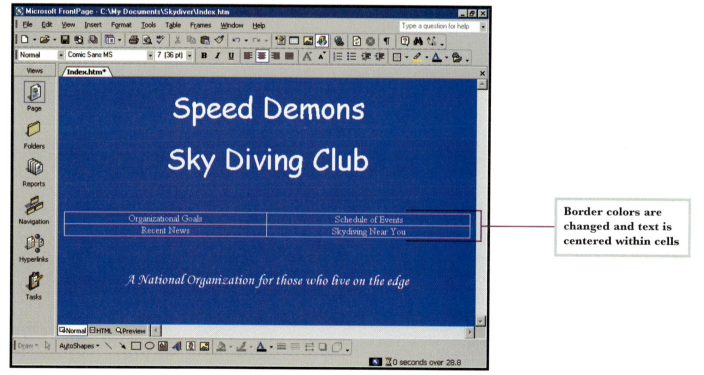

Figure 3-4 Formatted table on a page

Practice

Format the table on the Index page in the Caddy Shop Web so that the borders are of the same color, green, as the text. Save the file.

 **Applying Themes to Webs**

concept

A theme is a preformatted style that can be applied to a Web page or an entire Web. A set of formatting instructions control the background, fonts, colors, and button styles. Themes provide a fast method for designing Webs or applying a matching design to multiple pages.

do it!

Apply a theme to a Web in the Index page of the Skydiver Web.

1. Click Format on the Menu bar.

2. Click Theme. The Themes dialog box opens.

3. Near the top left of the dialog box, activate the All pages option button if it is not already selected. Click OK so the theme to be selected will apply to all pages of the Web.

4. In the list box on the left side of the dialog box, click the Blends theme to select it.

5. A warning message appears telling you that you will be permanently replacing the formatting information of the Web. Click Yes.

6. It takes FrontPage several seconds to apply the theme. When it does, your page should resemble Figure 3-6. Notice that the table text is not clearly visible since the background color of the table has been changed to blue.

7. If you open the organizational_goals page, you will notice the formatting has been applied to that page as well.

8. Save these changes.

more

You can apply a theme to one or more pages or to an entire Web site. If you apply a theme to all pages in a Web site, the theme becomes the default theme for that Web site. When you create new pages, the default theme is applied automatically.

A theme affects all the aspects of a page's appearance:

◉ Colors: A theme's color scheme specifies the color of body text, headings, hyperlinks, page banner text, link bar labels, table borders, and the page background. You can use normal or vivid colors.

◉ Graphics: Several page elements contain graphics, such as the background picture, the page banner, bullets, navigation buttons, and horizontal lines. You can use standard or active graphics. The active graphic set uses animated page elements such as hover buttons instead of plain buttons on link bars.

◉ Styles: A theme uses its own font styles and sizes for body text and headings.

Figure 3-5 Themes dialog box

Figure 3-6 Web with theme applied

Practice

Apply the Citrus Punch theme to the Caddy Shop Web.

 Applying Custom Themes

concept

One of the reasons themes are so useful is because they do not restrict the user to the preset format. Even though colors and fonts have already been selected, FrontPage allows you to make changes to these features. Knowing how to make these changes will enable you to work with existing themes to create a customized theme.

do it!

Customize an existing theme that you have applied to the Skydiver Web.

1. Click Format on the Menu bar, then click Theme. The Themes dialog box opens. Activate the All Pages option button.

2. Select the Vivid colors check box.

3. Click the Expedition theme to select it.

4. Click [Modify]. Several new buttons appear in the dialog box.

5. Click [Colors...]. The Modify Theme dialog box opens, as shown in Figure 3-7. You can apply any of the color schemes to the background of the current theme. Click [OK] to close the dialog box. You can use the Graphics button [Graphics...] to add background images to your Web.

6. Click [Text...]. The Modify Themes dialog box reopens. Body should be selected in the Item drop-down list box. In the Font list box, click the Comic Sans MS font to select it, as shown in Figure 3-8. Click [OK]. The text of the table will change to the selected font.

7. Click [Save As...] in the Themes dialog box. The Save Theme dialog box opens. Type New Theme in the Enter new theme title text box, as the title of the theme. Click [OK].

8. Click [OK] to close the Themes dialog box.

9. Save the changes. Your custom theme should look like Figure 3-9.

more

There are four additional options present in the Themes dialog box. These are:

Vivid colors: This check box enables you to use a bright color set for your theme.

Active graphics: This check box enables you to use a more elaborate and lively set of banners, buttons, bullets, and other graphical elements for your theme. The Active graphics check box is selected by default. To use the normal graphic set, clear the check box. The active graphic set uses animated page elements, such as hover buttons instead of plain buttons on link bars. Some theme elements do not contain any active graphics, so this check box may be unavailable by default.

Background picture: This check box enables you to use a picture as a background for your theme. This check box is selected by default. If you do not want to use it for your theme, clear the check box.

Apply using CSS: A Cascading Style Sheet, or CSS, is a document that contains style information that more than one Web page can reference. Such information defines the appearance and formatting of Web page content and gives authors more control over how Web browsers will display the content. Putting a check mark in the Apply using CSS check box applies a theme as a CSS, just linking the theme to the page rather than changing the actual HTML of the page. To apply a theme by changing the page's actual HTML code, clear the check box.

Figure 3-7 Modify Theme dialog box

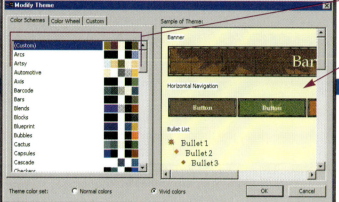

Figure 3-8 Text modification

Figure 3-9 New theme applied

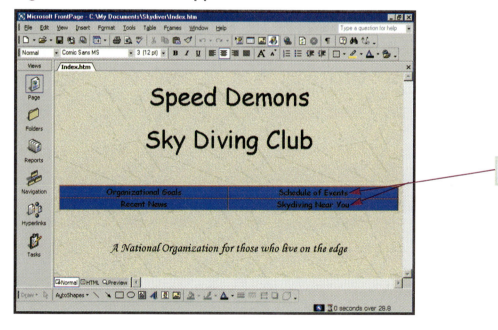

Practice

Add a customized theme to the Caddy Shop Web. Apply the Capsules theme and modify it using the Cactus color scheme. Change the font type to Garamond.

Applying Themes to Individual Pages

concept

In addition to applying themes to a Web, you can apply themes to selected pages. Once you apply a theme to a selected page, FrontPage makes this page different in appearance from the other pages of the Web. Applying themes to a selected page becomes handy when you want to make the Home page of a site different from other pages of the Web. You can use any of the following three views to apply a theme to a selected page: Page view, Folders view, and Navigation view. Remember, however, not to overuse different themes within a Web site. Consistency of themes helps viewers recognize they still are in the same site and reduces the chance that your Web site's message will become muddled under overly elaborate formatting.

do it!

Apply a theme to the Index page in the Page view

1. Click Format on the Menu bar.
2. Click Theme to display the Themes dialog box.
3. Ensure that the Selected page(s) option button is activated.
4. Click Industrial in the list below the option button, to select it. A preview of the theme is displayed in the Sample of Theme section, as shown in Figure 3-10.
5. Click OK . The theme will be applied to the Web page. Your page should resemble Figure 3-11.
6. Save the file. If you open the organizational_goals page, you will notice that this page does not have the Industrial theme applied to it.

more

You can remove a theme from a particular page or from an entire Web. To remove a theme from a particular page, open the page and access the Themes dialog box. Ensure that the Selected pages option is activated. In the themes list, click the No Theme option.

When you remove a theme from all pages in a web site, only those pages that were using the default theme are affected. If certain pages use a different theme, you must remove each of their themes individually.

Figure 3-10 Themes dialog box

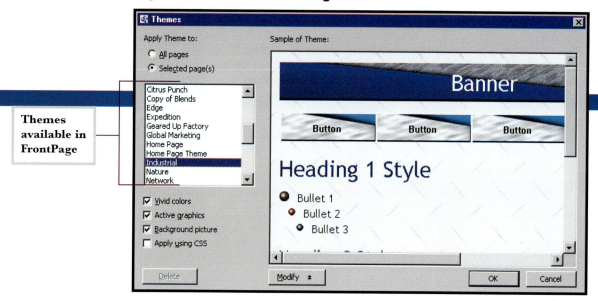

Themes available in FrontPage

Figure 3-11 New theme applied to the selected Web page

Practice

Apply the Citrus Punch theme to the Index page of the Caddy Shop Web and the Edge theme to the Order Form page of the Web. Save the files and close the Order Form page.

skill Creating Text Hyperlinks

concept

A hyperlink is an object in a Web page that connects a visitor to a file, to another Web page, or to another Web site. Hyperlinks can be designed to download files or start other operations. They can also link to e-mail addresses. Almost any object, word, or image can be used to create a hyperlink.

do it!

Create text hyperlinks in the Skydiver Web to link various pages in the Web.

1. Open the Index page in the Skydiver Web if it is not already opened.
2. Select Organizational Goals in the table.
3. Click Insert on the Menu bar, then click Hyperlink. The Insert Hyperlink dialog box opens.
4. Click organizational_goals in the list box, as shown in Figure 3-12.
5. Click [OK] to close the dialog box and create a hyperlink.
6. Select Recent News in the table. Click Insert, then click Hyperlink.
7. Double-click in the Address box and type recent_news.htm. Click [OK].
8. Follow the same procedure to create hyperlinks to the target URLs schedule_of_events.htm and skydiving_near_you.htm. Notice that the text that you have just changed to a hyperlink will change to blue and will be underlined. Since the background color is also blue, it might be difficult to read the text correctly. You need to change the color of the hyperlink text.
9. Select the Organizational Goals hyperlink.
10. Click [A] on the Formatting toolbar to display the drop-down palette.
11. Click the white color square that is second from left in the first row. The hyperlink color will be changed to white. The color in the Font Color button, on the Formatting toolbar, will be changed to white. You do not need to repeat the steps to change the hypertext color to white. Just select the text of the hyperlink and click [A].
12. Save the changes. Switch to the Preview view by clicking the Preview tab.
13. Notice that when you move the pointer over a hyperlink, it turns into a hand pointer, as it would in a browser.
14. Your page should look like Figure 3-13. Click the Organizational Goals hyperlink. The Organizational Goals page is displayed.
15. Close the Organizational Goals page.

INTERACTIVE COMPUTING   FrontPage 2002   FP 3.13

more

Four buttons are to the left of the URL list box. The Existing File or Web Page button enables you to use your Web browser to link to a selected page or file. The Place in This Document button enables you to link to a file on your computer. The Create New Document button creates a new page, then automatically links to that new page. The E-mail Address button enables you to create a link that sends e-mail. When users click the link, the default mail program opens to a mail-composing window with the specified e-mail address inserted.

You can create a hyperlink without choosing a specific word, phrase, or image on the Web page. Simply place the insertion point where you want to position the hyperlink. Access the Insert Hyperlink dialog box and locate the target page or file. When you create the link, the title of the target page will be inserted as the hyperlink text on the Web page. If there is no title, the URL will be inserted. The easiest way to create a hyperlink is to type the URL of the target page directly onto the Web page. FrontPage will automatically create a link to the specified Web address.

Figure 3-12 Insert Hyperlink dialog box

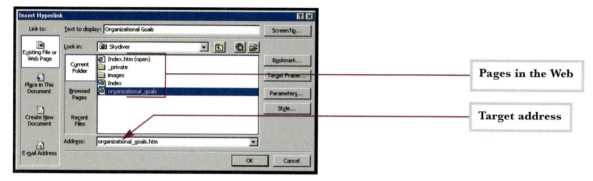

Figure 3-13 Hyperlinks on a page

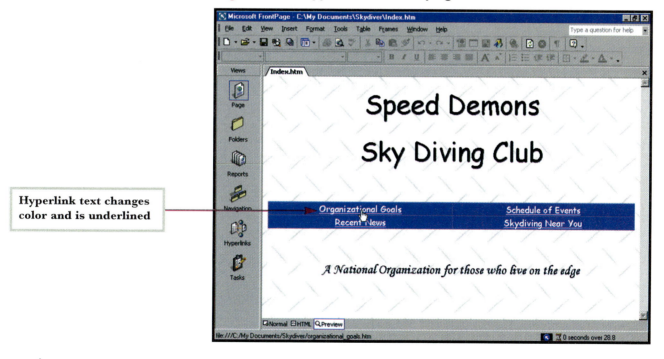

Practice

Create four hyperlinks for the four items in the table on the Index page in the Caddy Shop Web. The addresses are sales.htm, best_selling_items.htm (for Products) luckycaddy@domain.caddy.co, and the e-mail address luckycaddy@domain.caddy.com. Save the file.

skill Editing Hyperlinks

concept

It is necessary to edit hyperlinks when the page names or target addresses changes. You may want to switch from one kind of link to another, for example, change a URL link to an e-mail address link. Microsoft FrontPage 2002 makes it easy to change links after they have been inserted.

do it!

Make changes to hyperlinks you created earlier in the Index page of the Skydiver Web..

1. Right-click the Schedule of Events hyperlink.

2. Click Hyperlink Properties from the pop-up menu. The Edit Hyperlink dialog box opens.

3. Click the Create New Document button [Create New Document]. Type calendar.htm in the Name of new document text box, as shown in Figure 3-14.

4. Activate the Edit the new document later option button in the When to edit section and Click [OK] to close the dialog box.

5. Click File on the Menu bar, and select the Save As command. Change the title to Calendar by clicking [Change title...] to the right of the default page. Be sure to save it in the Skydiver Web. When you click [Save], the Microsoft FrontPage dialog box is displayed. Click [Yes] to save the changes.

6. Click the Index page to open it. Move the pointer over the Schedule of Events hyperlink. Hold [Ctrl] and click the hyperlink. The link takes you to the new page, calendar.htm.

7. Reopen the Index page and right-click the Skydiving Near You hyperlink. Follow the same procedure to name the new page local and change the title to Local. Repeat the procedure for the Recent News hyperlink. Click File and choose the Save As command to name the page news and change the title to News.

8. Close all the Web pages.

more

Changes can be made to hyperlink text in the same way that you make changes to regular text. You can use the Formatting toolbar to change the font, font color, font size, and font style of hyperlink text. If hyperlinks are in different locations on the page however, you will probably have to change each hyperlink individually. With the hyperlinks in the table structure, you can simply select the table and reformat it. To delete a hyperlink, select the hyperlink and access the Edit Hyperlink dialog box. Then click the [Remove Link]. The text that you used to activate the link will remain on your Web page. You can also delete the hyperlink text directly from the Web page.

If there is no theme applied, you can change the format of hyperlinks on a page by right-clicking the hyperlink, then clicking Page Properties in the pop-up menu, and then clicking the Background tab. The Background tab of the Page Properties dialog box is displayed in Figure 3-15. The Background tab enables you to add a picture as a background or format the hyperlinks. You can specify different colors for the visited and the unvisited hyperlinks. To change the text color of all the hyperlinks in a Web at once, access the Custom tab in the Color section of the Modify Theme dialog box. In the Item list box, select Hyperlinks and choose a color from the Color list box.

Figure 3-14 Edit Hyperlink dialog box

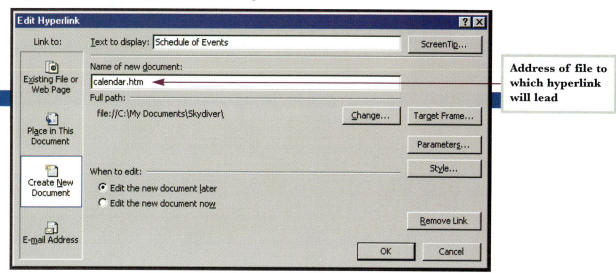

Address of file to which hyperlink will lead

Figure 3-15 Page Properties dialog box

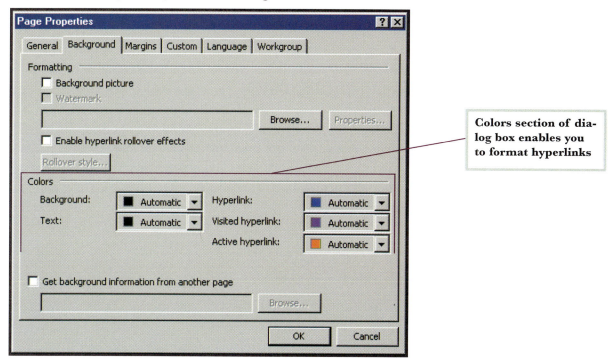

Colors section of dialog box enables you to format hyperlinks

Practice

Change the target URL of the first link to bestsales.htm in the Index page of the Caddy Shop Web. Title the page of bestsales.htm as Best Sales. Save them in the Caddy Shop Web.

 **Adding Images**

concept

Images can add informative content to a Web page or simply augment its style. You should keep in mind, however, that each picture lengthens the loading time of a page. The Microsoft Clip Art Gallery allows you to quickly add graphics and photos to your Web page.

do it!

Insert an image from the Microsoft Clip Art Gallery into the Index page of the Skydiver Web.

1. Open the Index page from the Skydiver Web.
2. Place the insertion point in the center of the line between the title of the club and the table.
3. Click Insert on the Menu bar. Point to Picture, then click Clip Art in the submenu that appears. The Insert Clip Art Task Pane is displayed.
4. Click in the Search text text box and clear the text box if required. Type airplane and press the [Enter] key. The results of the search are displayed as shown in Figure 3-16.
5. Click the first clip from the left.
6. The image is inserted as shown in Figure 3-17. Close the Insert Clip Art Task Pane. To insert a picture from your hard disk, you follow a similar procedure. Click Insert, point to Picture and click From File on the submenu. You will just have to locate the picture file on your computer.
7. Save the file. The Save Embedded Files dialog box will open. Click [OK]. This will save the image in the Skydiver Web. If the image is not saved with the Web, or is accidentally saved in a folder in another Web, it will not appear with the published Web.

more

Images are sometimes so large that they prevent a Web page from loading in a reasonable amount of time. Be sure to check the loading time on the Status bar.

The best formats to save images in are GIF (Graphic Interchange Format) and JPEG (Joint Photographic Experts Group). These formats compress large photographic files so that they do not take as long to load when published. Images you insert that are not in GIF or JPEG format will be automatically converted to GIF when FrontPage copies them to the Web page folder.

Figure 3-16 Clip Art search results in the Insert Clip Art Task Pane

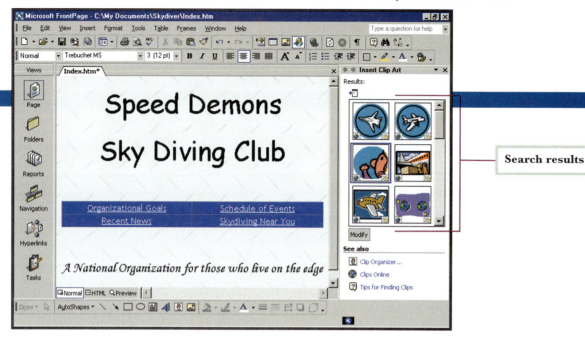

Search results

Figure 3-17 Image inserted in the Web page

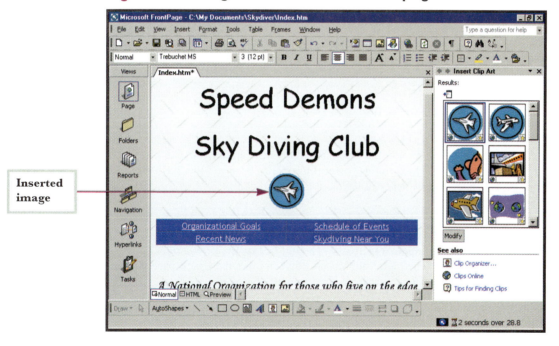

Inserted image

Practice

Search for a clip with the word cartoon. Insert the first clip into the Index page in the Caddy Shop Web. Insert it one line below the table and to the left side of the page. Save the file.

 **Formatting Images**

concept

FrontPage gives you the ability to easily format images once they are placed on the page. After you place images on a Web page it is often necessary to resize them, change their location, or alter their colors. There are many different formatting effects in FrontPage that you can choose from.

do it!

Format an image by resizing it and placing a border around it in the Index page from the Skydiver Web.

1. Click the image to select it. Sizing handles appear at the corners and on each side of the image. Move the pointer over the sizing handle at the lower-right corner of the image. The pointer turns into a resizing arrow.

2. Click and hold down the mouse button, drag it downward to increase the size of the image, as shown in Figure 3-18.

3. Right-click the image and click Picture Properties on the pop-up menu.

4. The Picture Properties dialog box opens. The Appearance tab is displayed by default. In the Border thickness spin box, type 3, as shown in Figure 3-19.

5. Click OK. The image now has a border around it.

6. Save the changes in the file.

more

Whenever you create a Web, FrontPage automatically creates an images folder. If you intend to use a lot of images, you should move them to this folder. Images can be saved there using the Save Embedded Files dialog box. This is a good file management practice that allows you to quickly locate the images.

You can resize an image horizontally or vertically using the midpoint sizing handles. Clicking and dragging the right or left midpoint sizing handle will adjust the image horizontally, while dragging the top or bottom midpoint sizing handle will adjust it vertically. While the image is selected, you can delete it using the [Delete] key on the keyboard. When you insert an image or click after it, a large insertion point is placed after the image. You can press the [Backspace] key to delete the image or align it left, right, or center using the corresponding buttons on the Formatting toolbar.

Formatting changes can also be made using the Pictures toolbar. The image can be rotated, flipped, cropped, beveled, and moved forwards or backwards. Text can be written over it, and contrast and brightness can be adjusted.

Figure 3-18 Resizing an image

Figure 3-19 Picture Properties dialog box

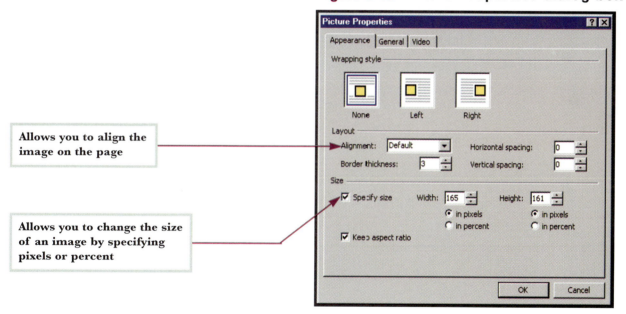

Allows you to align the image on the page

Allows you to change the size of an image by specifying pixels or percent

Practice

Resize the image on the Index page of the Caddy Shop Web so that it is larger and is centrally aligned. Save the file.

Image Mapping

concept

An image containing multiple links is called an *image map*. Creating a link between an image and another page is easy to accomplish. Image maps are also called *clickable images* or *hotspots*. Hotspots are invisible areas on a picture, each of which has a link attached to it. The Pictures toolbar contains three buttons for creating hotspots of different shapes.

do it!

Use the image you inserted in the Index page in the Skydiver Web to create a link to another page.

1. Click the image to select it.
2. Click View on the Menu bar and select Toolbars. Select Pictures on the shortcut menu. The Pictures toolbar appears.
3. Click the rectangular hotspot button [icon] on the Pictures toolbar. The Pictures toolbar is shown in Figure 3-20.
4. Use the pointer, which is now a pencil [icon] to draw a rectangle around the airplane, as shown in Figure 3-21.
5. The Insert Hyperlink dialog box opens. Click the Create new document button [icon].
6. Type Table of Contents.htm in the Name of new document text box. Click [OK].
7. Click the Preview tab. Notice that the pointer turns into a hand over the airplane as it would on any other hyperlink (Figure 3-22), but not when it is over part of the image that was not mapped. [icon] You can use the Circular Hotspot or the Polygonal Hotspot buttons on the Pictures toolbar to more precisely conform to the shape of the chosen area on the image.
8. Click on the image. The linked page opens.
9. Return to Normal view, save the changes, and close the file.

more

You can insert as many hotspots as will fit on an image, however, it is advisable to choose an image with easily distinguishable areas so that visitors can guess where the links are.

The entire image can also be a hyperlink. Simply click the image to select it and click Insert from the Menu bar. Then select Hyperlink and type in the URL, or locate the page or file you wish to link to in the Insert Hyperlink dialog box.

To change a hotspot's link, double-click the hotspot and change the URL or find a new page or file to link to in the Edit Hyperlink dialog box. To delete a hotspot, click once to select it and press the [Delete] key.

Figure 3-20 Pictures toolbar

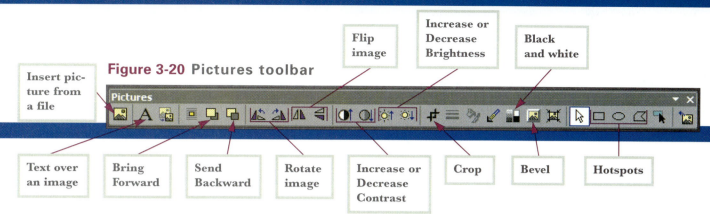

Figure 3-21 Creating a Hotspot

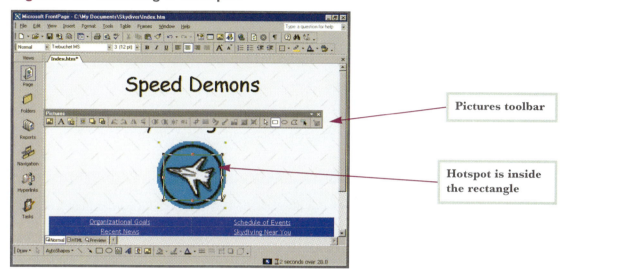

Figure 3-22 A Hotspot

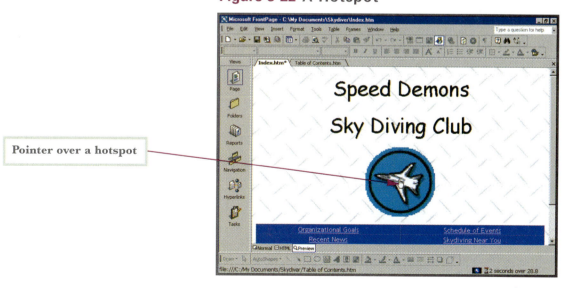

Practice

Create a hotspot on the Index page of the Caddy Shop Web. Link to a new file, frequently_asked_questions.htm. Save everything and close the file.

Creating a Hover Button

concept

A Hover button is a button whose appearance changes when you pass the pointer or hover over it. It is a Java applet, which means that its special effects will appear only on browsers that can read the Java programming language. The button may glow, change color or even appear to bend inward. Hover buttons are used as hyperlinks.

do it!

Create a Hover button on one of the Web pages in the Skydiver Web.

1. Open the organizational_goals page from the Skydiver Web.
2. Place the insertion point below the last line of text.
3. Click Insert and click the Web Component command. This displays the Insert Web Component dialog box.
4. Notice that the Dynamic Effects option is selected by default in the Component type section. Double-click the Hover Button option in the Choose an effect section. This inserts a hover button in the Web page and also displays the Hover Button Properties dialog box.
5. In the Button text text box, type Home. This word will appear inside the Hover button when viewed in Preview view.
6. Click [Browse...]. The Select Hover Button Hyperlink dialog box opens.
7. Click the Existing File or Web Page button [icon] if it is not already selected.
8. Click the Index page to link it to the organizational_goals page and click [OK].
9. Click the arrow of the Button color drop-down list box. Click the black square.
10. Click the arrow of the Effect color drop-down list box. Click the yellow square.
11. Click the arrow of the Effect drop-down list box and select Reverse glow.
12. The Hover Button Properties dialog box should now look like Figure 3-23.
13. Click [OK]. [icon] You can edit and make format changes to a Hover button by right-clicking it and selecting Hover Button Properties from the pop-up menu.
14. Save the file.
15. Switch to the Preview view.
16. Move the pointer over the Hover button, and it should glow in yellow color, as shown in Figure 3-24. If you click on it, it will take you to the Index page.
17. Close the file.

more

If a visitor does not have a Java-enabled browser, only the special effects will not function. The button will be present and the hyperlink will function, but the color change and glow will not occur.

Figure 3-23 Hover Button Properties dialog box

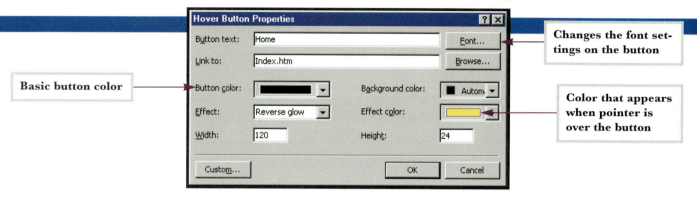

Figure 3-24 Hover button in Preview view

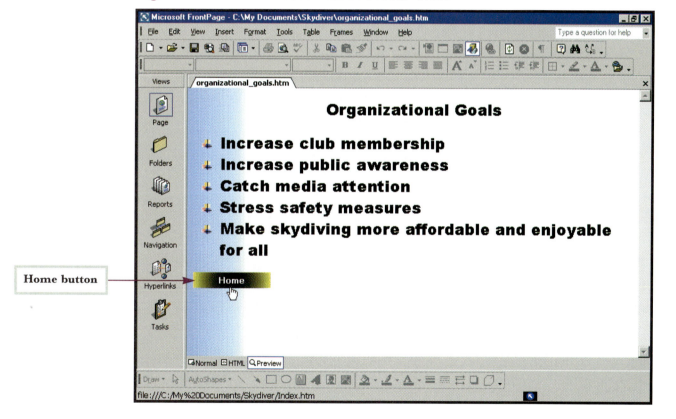

Practice

Add a Hover button with special effects to the best_selling_items.htm file of the Caddy Shop Web. Link this page to the Index page of this Web. Save and close the file.

skill  Creating a Marquee

concept

A marquee is a piece of animated text. Marquees grab people's attention as they scroll across the Web page. Scrolling marquees are supported by only Internet Explorer. Visitors who use Netscape Navigator will see only the marquee text.

do it!

Add a marquee to the Index page in the Skydiver Web.

1. Open the Index page in the Skydiver Web in the Normal view.
2. Place the insertion point in front of the S in Speed Demons.
3. Click Insert and click the Web Component command. This displays the Insert Web Component dialog box.
4. Notice that the Dynamic Effects option is selected by default in the Component type section. Double-click the Marquee option in the Choose an effect section.
5. The Marquee Properties dialog box opens. In the Text text box, type Come fly with us.
6. Activate the Alternate option button in the Behavior section as shown in Figure 3-25.
7. Click OK .
8. Save the changes.
9. Switch to the Preview view. The marquee moves around the screen, as shown in Figure 3-26.

more

Although marquees are typically placed at the top of a page, they can be placed wherever you wish. If you place the insertion point at the end of a line of text, the marquee will be inserted on the next line. As you saw in the exercise above, if you place the insertion point before a line of text, the marquee will be inserted one line above it. To format the marquee text; first, click the marquee text to select it. Sizing handles will surround the marquee. Either use the buttons on the Formatting toolbar, or click Format on the Menu bar and select Font, to open the Font dialog box.

Figure 3-25 Marquee Properties dialog box

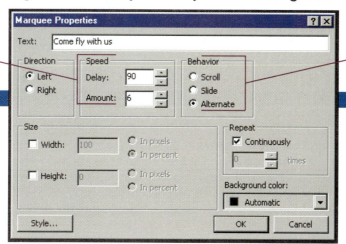

Figure 3-26 Marquee sliding and scrolling across the page

Practice

Place a marquee that says, **Lucky Caddy**, on the **Index** page of the **Caddy Shop** Web. Increase the speed and format it as per your requirements.

Inserting Text Boxes

concept

A text box is an area on a Web page where users can submit information back to the Web site. In FrontPage, a text box is called a form field. Often users are asked to complete registration forms before they can use a Web site. You can create these forms with the Form wizard. All forms contain a Submit and a Reset button. After you insert a form onto your Web page, you must determine the fields (or pieces of information) the visitor will be asked to submit.

do it!

Add a form page to the Skydiver Web. Then add form fields by inserting two text boxes and one text area box.

1. Switch to the Normal view.
2. Click File on the Menu bar, point to the New command, and click Page or Web. This displays the New Page or Web Task Pane.
3. Click the Blank Page hyperlink in the New section. This will display a new page.
4. Press the [Enter] key three times.
5. Click Insert on the Menu bar, point to the Form command and click Form in the submenu that appears. Two buttons appear. Place the insertion point before the Submit button and press the [Enter] key.
6. Place the insertion point one line above the buttons and type Name. Then click Insert, point to Form command, and click Text Box in the submenu. The text box is displayed in the form, as shown in Figure 3-27. Press the [Enter] key. You can click and drag a text box to reposition it in the form.
7. Type e-mail and insert a text box. Press the [Enter] key.
8. Type Describe your First Skydiving experience. Then click Insert, highlight Form, and click Text Area in the submenu. Press the [Enter] key.
9. Save the file as form.htm with the page title as Form.
10. Switch to Preview view. The form page should look like Figure 3-28. Close the Index page and leave the Form page opened.

To resize a text box, click it once to select it. Sizing handles will allow you to adjust its dimensions. If you right-click a text box, you can access many formatting options from the pop-up menu.

Figure 3-27 Form with text box inserted

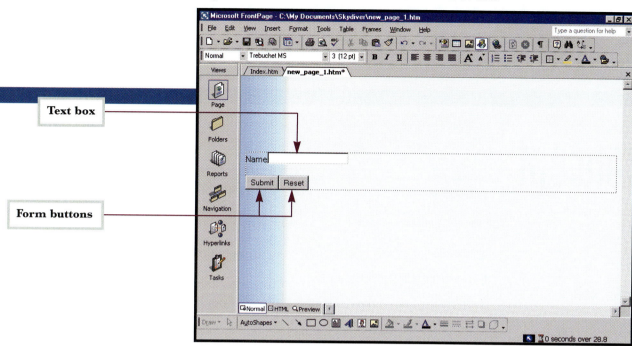

Figure 3-28 Form in Preview view

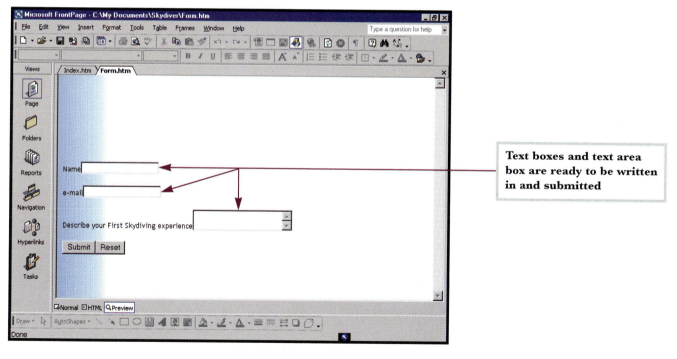

Practice

Create a new page in the Caddy Shop Web and insert a form into it. Create two text boxes for Name and e-mail, and one text area box with the text, Describe your requirements for your golf clubs. Save the file as form.htm and title the page as Form.

skill: Adding Check Boxes and Option Buttons

concept

Apart from text boxes, there are two other form fields, check boxes and option buttons. Check boxes are used to submit yes or no answers. Option buttons are generally created for questions where the answers have several options. These two form fields facilitate data entry by allowing visitors to answer questions with a click of the mouse.

do it!

Add a check box and option buttons to the Form page of the Skydiver Web.

1. Switch to the Normal view.
2. Place the insertion point before the word Name. Press the [Enter] key.
3. Place the insertion point one line above the Name text box.
4. Type Check the box if you have gone skydiving before.
5. Click Insert on the Menu bar, point to Form and click Check box from the submenu. A check box is inserted, as shown in Figure 3-29.
6. Press the [Enter] key.
7. Type If so how many times:. Press the [Enter] key again.
8. Click Insert, point to the Form command, and click Option Button from the submenu. An option button is inserted. Type: 1-10, then press [Tab]. Add another option button. Type 11-20. Press [Tab]. Add another option button, type 21 and over.
9. Save the changes.
10. Switch to the Preview view. Your page should look like Figure 3-30. When you switch to the Preview view, a message, This page contains elements that may need to be saved or published to preview correctly, may be displayed. Ignore it.

more

Option buttons and check boxes are similar in the sense that visitors can choose from one or more options. Option buttons offer a group of options from which one is chosen. Check boxes are generally used to answer yes or no questions but can also be created in situations where you want to allow multiple selections. Option buttons and check boxes cannot be resized or reshaped.

Figure 3-29 Form page with a check box

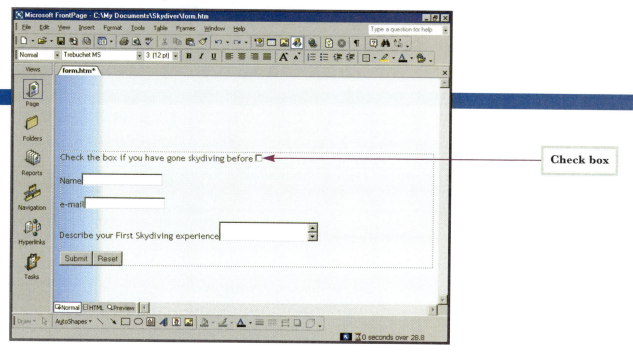

Figure 3-30 Form page with option buttons

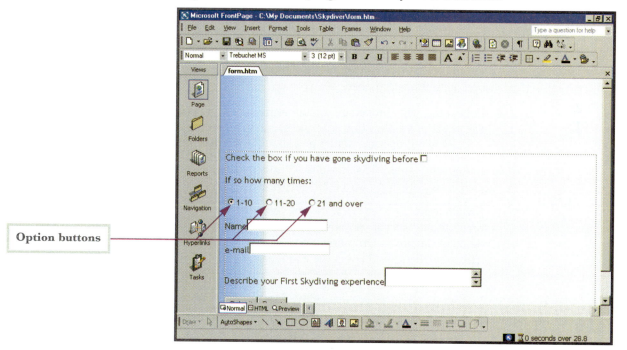

Practice

In the Form page of the Caddy Shop Web, create a check box with the text, Check the box if you already possess a golf club. Create four option buttons with the text, 1, 2, 3, and more than 3, respectively. Save the file.

skill  Creating a Drop-Down List Box

concept

Another form field that can be created is a drop-down box. After creating a drop-down box, you must add the selections from which the visitor will choose. Drop-down boxes are used when there are multiple selections. They simplify data entry and save space on the form.

do it!

Add a drop-down box to the Form page of the Skydiver Web that you have been working on.

1. Switch to the Normal view.
2. Place the insertion point after the scrolling text area box.
3. Press the [Enter] key.
4. Type What area of the country do you live in?
5. Click Insert on the Menu bar. Point to the Form command and click Drop-Down Box from the submenu. A drop-down box will be displayed on the page.
6. Double-click the drop-down box. The Drop-Down Box Properties dialog box opens.
7. Click Add... . The Add Choice dialog box opens. Type Northeast, as shown in Figure 3-31. Click OK . In the Initial State section, make sure the Not selected option button is activated.
8. Follow the same procedure to add Southeast, Midwest, South, Sunbelt, Rockies, North, Northwest, and West Coast. In the Name text box, type Area. When you are finished the Drop-Down Properties dialog box should look like Figure 3-32.
9. In the Allow multiple selections section, make sure the option button next to No is activated. Click OK . Save the changes.
10. Switch to the Preview view. When you click the down arrow of the drop-down box, the menu should appear, as shown in Figure 3-33. You might be wondering that if the name of the box is Drop-down box then why are the options displayed above the box? This is so, because there is not enough space on the page below the box to accommodate all the options.

more

In the example above, we left Not selected as the initial state for each option button. If you think most visitors will choose a particular answer, you can make one of the options appear preselected. If the user would have chosen that option, he or she can skip that field. The user can select another option if the default state is incorrect.

You can edit your entries using Modify... in the Drop-Down Box Properties dialog box. You can rearrange the list order using Move Up and Move Down . An option is also available for permitting visitors to make multiple selections from the list. Check boxes are probably a better choice when you want to allow multiple selections. Remove enables you to delete entries. Click Validate... to set data entry rules for the drop-down menu. You can stop a form from being submitted unless a menu item is selected, or you can disallow certain items from being selected. These options are available on all form controls.

Figure 3-31 Add Choice dialog box

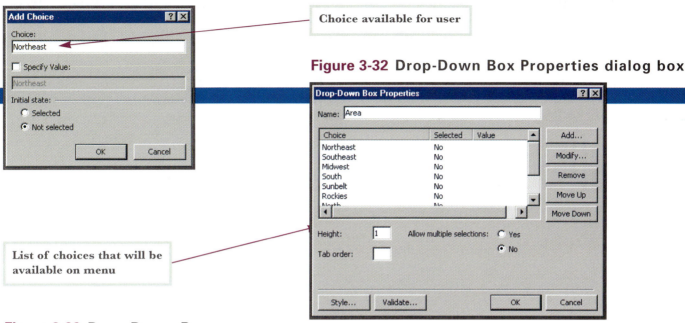

Figure 3-32 Drop-Down Box Properties dialog box

Figure 3-33 Drop-Down Box

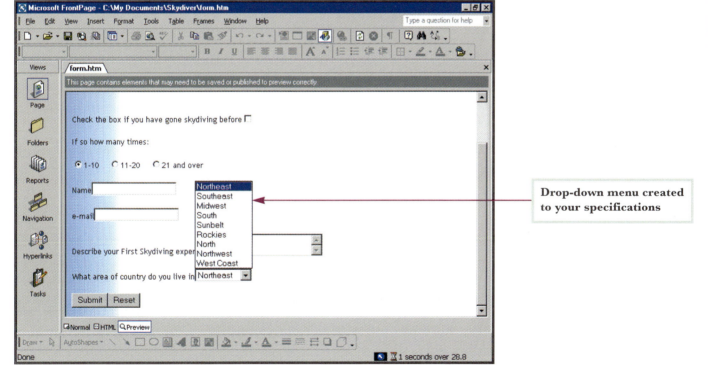

Practice

Create a drop-down box for Payment methods on the form page of the Caddy Shop Web. Your list should include cash, credit card, debit card, cash on delivery, and money order. Save the file.

skill Creating a Push Button

concept

Another form field is a **push button**. Most Web authors leave the **Reset** and **Submit** buttons at the bottom of the form page. However, sometimes it may be convenient to locate a Reset or a Submit button at some earlier point in the form. In these cases, a push button can be inserted. A push button can also be used to answer a yes or no question.

do it!

Create a push button that will reset the form in the **Form** page of the **Skydiver** Web, so that users do not have to scroll to the bottom of the form if they want to reset it.

1. Switch to the Normal view and place the insertion point after the check box at the top of the Form page of the Skydiver Web.

2. Press [Tab] five times.

3. Click **Insert**, point to the **Form** command, and click **Push Button** in the submenu. The button is created in the location you specified.

4. Double-click the button. The **Push Button Properties** dialog box opens.

5. In the **Value/label** text box, type **Reset**.

6. Activate the **Reset** option button in the **Button type** list. The Push Button Properties dialog box should now look like **Figure 3-34**.

7. Click [OK].

8. Save the changes.

9. Switch to the **Preview** view. Your form should now look like **Figure 3-35**.

10. Close the file.

more

To specify where a form is going to be submitted, right-click [Submit]. Then click **Form Properties** in the pop-up menu. Use the **Form Properties** dialog box to locate a file or folder, or an e-mail address where completed forms will be sent. You can also send forms to databases or to other types of files for storing data. Use the **Options** section of the Form Properties dialog box to specify what fields will be saved and where the data results will be saved once they are received.

Figure 3-34 Push Button Properties dialog box

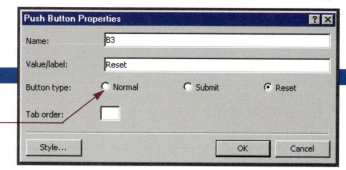

Normal button may be used to enter data, like a check box

Figure 3-35 Reset button in a form

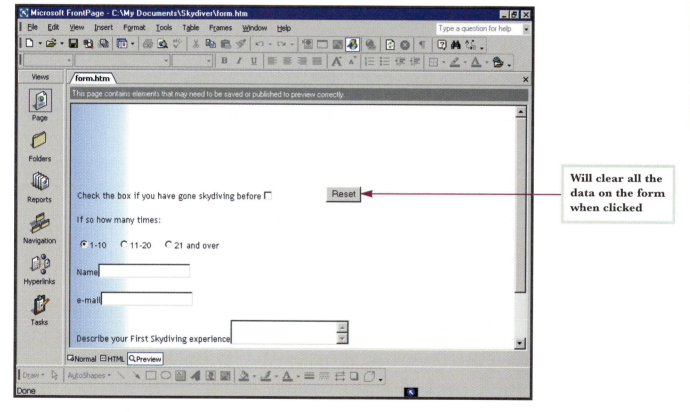

Will clear all the data on the form when clicked

Practice

Add a Reset button somewhere on the Form page in the Caddy Shop Web. Save and close the file.

shortcuts

Function	Button/Mouse	Menu	Keyboard
Bold	B		[Ctrl]+[B]
Italics	I		[Ctrl]+[I]
Underline	U		[Ctrl]+[U]
Center align			[Ctrl]+[E]
Align left			[Ctrl]+[L]
Align right			[Ctrl]+[R]
Insert Hyperlink		Click Insert, then click Hyperlink	[Ctrl]+[K]
Insert Web components		Click Insert, then click Web Components	
Insert table		Click Table, select Insert, then click Table	
Insert Bullets		Click Format, then click Bullets and Numbering	
Insert picture from file		Click Insert, select Picture, then click From File	
Decrease indents			[Ctrl]+[Shift]+[M]
Increase indents			[Ctrl]+[M]

INTERACTIVE COMPUTING | FrontPage 2002 | FP 3.35

A. Identify Key Features

Name the items indicated by callouts in Figure 3-36.

1. _____
2. _____
3. _____
4. _____
5. _____
6. _____
7. _____
8. _____
9. _____

Figure 3-36 Formatted Web page

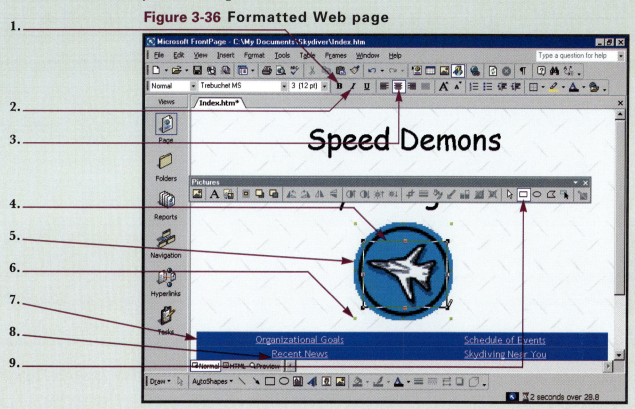

B. Select the Best Answer

10. Formats entire Web with similar fonts, color schemes, and other format options
11. Organizes information in a structured and attractive way
12. Creates a hyperlink over a specific area of an image
13. Creates a title for a page that scrolls or slides across the screen
14. Form field used for a yes or no question
15. Controls the typeface style on a page
16. The hotspot button is found here
17. The bold and italic buttons are found here
18. A button that creates an effect when the mouse pointer moves over it

a. Hotspot
b. Font list box
c. Marquee
d. Formatting toolbar
e. Pictures toolbar
f. Hover button
g. Table
h. Theme
i. Check box

quiz (continued)

C. Complete the Statement

19. When you move the pointer over the screen to enter text, the pointer turns into an:
    a. I-beam
    b. Insertion point
    c. I-point
    d. Insertion beam

20. You can change the properties of a numbered or bulleted list by:
    a. Double-clicking the list
    b. Right-clicking the list and selecting List Item Properties from the pop-up menu
    c. Right-clicking the list and selecting Number and Bullet Properties from the pop-up menu
    d. Double-clicking the list and selecting List Properties from the pop-up menu

21. You can perform every function from the Insert Hyperlink dialog box except:
    a. Color the hyperlink
    b. Link to a new page
    c. Create a link that sends an e-mail
    d. Search the browser for a page to link

22. The most efficient file formats for saving large images are:
    a. RIFF
    b. JIFF and TIFF
    c. GIF and JPEG
    d. TIFF and JPEG

23. A hyperlink over a specified area of an image is also called a:
    a. Linked map
    b. Warmspot
    c. Coolspot
    d. Hotspot

24. A Java applet, which is used to create a hover button is
    a. Named after a type of fruit
    b. Designed to run on all browsers
    c. A set of instructions written in the Java language
    d. Utterly useless without a plug-in

25. An alternative method of creating option buttons is:
    a. Using the Corporate Presence Wizard
    b. Using the Form Page Wizard
    c. Using the Submit Form Template
    d. Using the Option Button Properties dialog box

interactivity

Build Your Skills

1. Create and format a list:

   a. Open the **Water Taxi Web**.

   b. Create a new blank page in the Web, save it as **locations.htm**, and title it **Locations**.

   c. Create a bulleted list for the water taxi destinations: **Ocean Harbor, Lee Beach, Red Sands, Bay Sands, Cherry Road, Blue Birch,** and **Tom's Grand Cove**.

   d. Change the font of the list text to a font of your choice and save the page.

2. Insert a table:

   a. Create a new page called **Fees**. Title it as **Fees** and save it in the **Water Taxi Web**.

   b. Insert a table to organize the destinations listed above and their associated fees: **$3.50, $6.25, $4.75, $10.00, $5.25, $2.50,** and **$8.25**, respectively.

   c. Save the page.

3. Apply a theme to a Web:

   a. In the **Water Taxi Web**, apply the **Pixel** theme to the entire Web.

   b. Design a custom theme using the **Sumi Painting** theme. Name the new theme, **Customized theme**.

   c. Apply the custom theme to the **Index** page.

4. Create Hyperlinks:

   a. Create hyperlinks from the already existing text on the Index page of the **Water Taxi Web**. Create the new pages to which they will link. For example, create a link from the **Fees** link in the table to the newly created **Fees** page. Create a link from the Information link on the Index page to the newly created Locations page.

   b. For the rest of the links in the table, link them to a new page that you have titled and saved with the same name as the link. Create a **Staff** page, an **Employment** page, a **Weather** page, and a **Related Services** page.

   c. In **Preview View,** test all the links to make sure they work.

5. Add an image and create a hotspot:

   a. Create a new page, save it as and title it **Image**. Save it in the **Water Taxi Web**.

   b. Search the **Clip Art Gallery** using the word **water**. Select and insert the clip of a boat on the right.

   c. Create a hotspot somewhere on the image that links it to a new form page that you will create using the **Form Page Wizard**. Save and title the page **Form**.

interactivity (continued)

6. Create a hover button and a marquee:

    a. Open the Index page from the Water Taxi Web, if necessary.

    b. Create a scrolling marquee for the company name.

    c. Open the Locations page.

    d. Create a hover button with special effects that links to the Index page in the Water Taxi Web.

7. Add form fields to the Water Taxi Web form page:

    a. Open the Form page in the Water Taxi Web, if necessary.

    b. Add a check box at the top of the form that asks, Would you like to make reservations for a water taxi ride?.

    c. Type: How many people will be joining you?. Create three option buttons for the options: 1-4 persons, 5-8 persons, and 9-12 persons, with one option button for each option.

    d. Next type On what date will you be riding with us?. Add a one-line text box after the question.

    e. Type How did you hear about us?, and add a scrolling text box to the page.

    f. Type Where will you be going?. Create a drop-down menu that includes the list of locations that you entered on the Information page earlier.

Problem Solving Exercises

1. You have been doing a good job at Diggs & Associates, but the tough part has just begun. You must now format the Web to meet the tastes and the organizational needs of your employers. Insert a table with hyperlinks to each page in the Web. For example, create a cell that says Products and Services and link it to the Products and Services page. Design a conservative, professional-looking theme to apply to the Web. The Bold Stripes and Industrial themes are good places to start. Customize one of these two themes if you so desire. On the Products and Services page, create a products list including the categories: Fiction, Non-Fiction, How-To, Textbooks, Poetry, Drama, Biographies, Reference, and Children's. Create a marquee for the company name. At the bottom of the page, create a Hover button with the special effects and colors of your choice. Be sure to save after reformatting or adding objects to a page. Save the pages in the Diggs Web.

2. Create a form page using the Form Page Wizard. Select ordering information as the type of input to collect. Save the results to a text file. Keep the rest of the default settings. Add a one-line text box labeled Name. Insert a scrolling text box so users can describe how they heard of Diggs & Associates. Provide a check box for next day delivery. Create three option buttons to identify new customers, customers who have previously ordered from Diggs, and customers who have not ordered in a year. Create a drop-down menu list of Diggs' products that have been purchased before. Include None for new customers.

3. Begin formatting your personal Web site. You may want to begin by writing and formatting text. Change the font to set the tone for your site. Apply bold formatting, or underline or italicize your text. Align it left, right, or center. If you have digital camera photographs, or are able to scan photos, you can add these to your site. You can create text hyperlinks, image hyperlinks, and/or hotspots. You can create an image map to link to the other pages in your Web. If appropriate, organize information into a table or create a numbered or bulleted list. Decide if you want Hover buttons or a marquee for your Home page. Get out the list you created earlier and insert the elements you found appealing.

4. Create a form page either from scratch or using the Form Page Wizard. If you use the Wizard, you must determine what information to extract from the visitor. There are several types of inputs you can collect to get personal data. You can create option buttons or check boxes. If you do not use the Wizard, determine what information you want to gather and compose your questions. Create the appropriate form fields for each question. Some questions may require text boxes and others a drop-down menu. When you are finished, save the page as form and title it Form.

Publishing and Maintaining Web Pages

After you have designed and formatted your Web, you must maintain it. Hyperlinks might be broken, components may be malfunctioning, or new links may need to be created. Web site maintenance includes checking components, verifying that hyperlinks are targeted to the correct locations, and ensuring that visitors can easily navigate the site.

Other basic tasks you need to learn are, how to import Office documents and how to use the Office Clipboard. FrontPage Web pages can be created quickly by importing Word documents. Entire documents can be inserted, or portions of documents can be cut and pasted onto a Web page.

After you have previewed and tested your Web, it will finally be time to publish it. Viewing it over the Internet is after all, the final goal. Updating your Web after a period of time is as easy as publishing it.

Lesson Goal:

In this lesson, you will learn to create a Web hierarchy, add a navigation bar, view and print the Web structure, organize files in the Folders view, verify hyperlinks, and rename Web pages. You will also learn to change page titles in banners and buttons, open an Office document in a Web, use the Office Clipboard, create and print reports, and publish a Web.

- Creating a Web Hierarchy
- Adding a Navigation Bar
- Viewing and Printing the Web Structure
- Organizing Files in Folders View
- Verifying Hyperlinks
- Renaming Pages and Changing URLs
- Changing Page Titles in Banners
- Opening an Office Document in a Web
- Using the Office Clipboard
- Creating and Printing Reports
- Publishing a Web

Creating a Web Hierarchy

concept

Creating a Web hierarchy will help you in organizing your links. When the structure or hierarchy of your site has been defined, FrontPage will be able to create Navigation bars to connect the Web pages. A Web hierarchy, also called a tree diagram, is created in the Navigation view. When you create a Web using a Web Wizard, the tree diagram is automatically constructed.

do it!

Use the Navigation view to create a Web hierarchy or tree diagram for the Skydiver Web site.

1. Open FrontPage, if it is not already opened.

2. Click the Navigation button on the Views bar. The Navigation view should resemble Figure 4-1. The Navigation view shows the icon of the Speed Demons page, which is the Index page, in the right-hand section of the screen and a list of files on the left-hand section called the Folder List.

3. In the Folder List, drag organizational_goals.htm so that it is underneath the Speed Demons page. When you release the mouse button, the Organizational Goals page is linked to the Index page as shown in Figure 4-2. The Organizational Goals page is now a child page of the Index page and the Index page is the parent page of the Organizational Goals page.

4. Click and drag News.htm page so it is underneath the Index page and next to the Organizational Goals page. It is thus a child page of the Index page and on the same level as the Organizational Goals page.

5. Follow the same procedure until the Local, Table of Contents, and Form pages are all child pages of the Index page.

6. Click and drag the Calendar page so that it is underneath the News page. Thus, the Calendar page will be a child page of the News page. The tree diagram or Web hierarchy is shown in Figure 4-3. If you create a form page and save the results to a text file, it will be included in the Folder List. Do not add it to the hierarchy. It will still be part of the Web.

more

A Web hierarchy organizes the links in a Web. It is a prerequisite to creating Navigation bars. Navigation bars are rows of buttons or text that link to the other pages in the Web following the tree diagram. Navigation bars will be created to link the parent page, Index, to every other page except the Calendar page. Conversely, each of the child pages will link back to the Index page. The Calendar page will link to its parent page, News. Most Web pages have lowercase file names. Lowercase names refer to files, while uppercase names refer to page titles. Notice that the file names in the Folder List are lowercase and the page titles in Navigation view are uppercase.

To reorganize the tree, click and drag a page to a different position in the hierarchy. Observe the line that appears as you drag, and position the page to create the desired relationship. There is no need to save a hierarchy. FrontPage will reopen a Web with the last tree diagram you created before exiting the program.

Figure 4-1 Page in the Navigation view

Figure 4-2 Parent page and child page

Figure 4-3 Web hierarchy

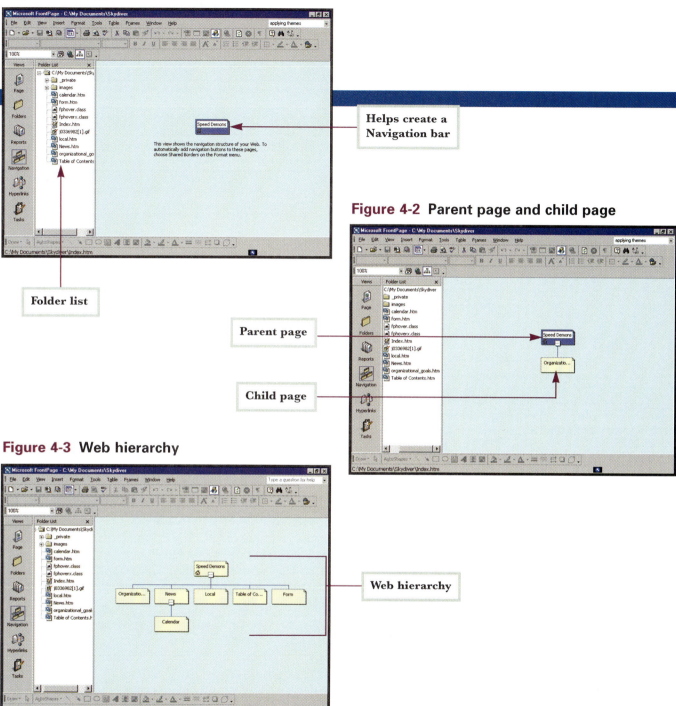

Practice

Create a hierarchy of the Caddy Shop Web so that the Employment, Best Selling Items, Form, and Sales pages are child pages of the Index page. Make the Table of Contents page a child page of the Best Selling Items page.

skill Adding a Navigation Bar

concept

Navigation bars are rows of text or buttons that allow you to navigate through a Web. When you create Navigation bars, the links behind them are automatically created. Navigation bars can be formatted to enhance the Web site's attractiveness.

do it!

Add Navigation bars to a Web site.

1. Open the Index page of the Skydiver Web and switch to Navigation view.

2. Click Format on the Menu bar (you may have to access the extended menu). Then, click Shared Borders. The Shared Borders dialog box opens.

3. Make sure that the All pages option button is activated.

4. Select the Left check box, then select the Include navigation buttons check box. The dialog box should now look like Figure 4-4.

5. Click [OK]. Switch to the Preview view. Hyperlinks appear on the left of the Index page. When you move the pointer over one of these links it turns into 🖑.

6. Switch back to the Page view and double-click one of the links. The Link Bar Properties dialog box opens.

7. Make sure that the Child level option button is activated. Also, make sure that the Home page and Parent page check boxes are selected. Your dialog box should look like Figure 4-5.

8. Click [OK]. Save the Index page in a folder called _borders using the Save As command. Switch to the Preview view. Your page should look like Figure 4-6. Hyperlinks change color after they have been clicked. Hyperlink text colors can be modified by accessing the Background dialog box from the Format menu. You cannot access this feature however, if a theme is applied.

9. Close the file.

more

You can test the Navigation bars by previewing the Web in a browser. After opening the Web in your browser, click the hyperlinks on the Navigation bars to verify that the target pages open.

Not all pages will link to each other. The child pages of the Index page link back to their parent, which is the Index page. The News page links to its parent page, Index, and its child page, Calendar.

A Navigation bar can also be inserted by clicking Insert, on the Menu bar and selecting the Navigation command. The properties are then set in the Navigation Bar Properties dialog box.

Figure 4-4 Shared Borders dialog box

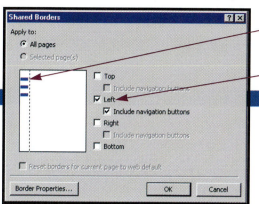

Preview of where the Navigation bar will appear

Creates a vertical Navigation bar at the left of the page

Figure 4-5 Link Bar Properties dialog box

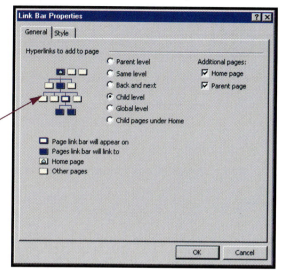

Preview of the pages containing hyperlinks

Figure 4-6 Page with Navigation bar

Navigation bar with hyperlinks

Practice

Create a Navigation bar in the Caddy Shop Web. Make it a horizontal bar and save the changes.

Viewing and Printing the Web Structure

concept

When you are in the process of designing a Web, having a hard copy of the site structure can sometimes be useful. If you are creating a site for someone else, an outline of the proposed structure can demonstrate the progress you are making or serve as a visual aid in presentations. FrontPage enables you to print the tree diagram directly from the Navigation view.

do it!

View the hierarchy of a Web in the Navigation view and print a hard copy.

1. Open the Index page of the Skydiver Web.
2. Click the Navigation button on the Views bar.
3. Click the minus sign at the bottom of the Speed Demons page in the Navigation view. The hierarchy collapses, as shown in Figure 4-7.
4. Click the plus sign to expand the hierarchy.
5. Click File on the Menu bar, then click Print.
6. The Print dialog box opens, as shown in Figure 4-8.
7. Make sure you have the correct printer selected. Click OK. Click Properties, in the Print dialog box to change everything from page orientation to graphical resolution.
8. A copy of the navigation structure is printed.
9. Save any changes to the print settings you might have made. Exit the application.

more

The Print Preview command is also found on the File menu. You may have to access the expanded menu to find it. The Print Preview command enables you to view the tree diagram as it will look when printed. Once you know the parameters of a tree diagram, you can make the necessary changes to ensure that it prints properly. You can change the page orientation to Landscape by clicking Properties and accessing the Layout tab from the Properties dialog box. This may be necessary to ensure that the page fits on one page. You can also return to the Page view and select the Page Setup command from the File menu.

Figure 4-7 Web hierarchy collapsed

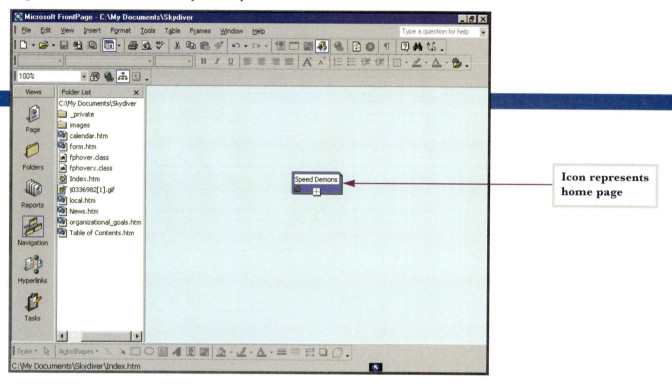

Figure 4-8 Print dialog box

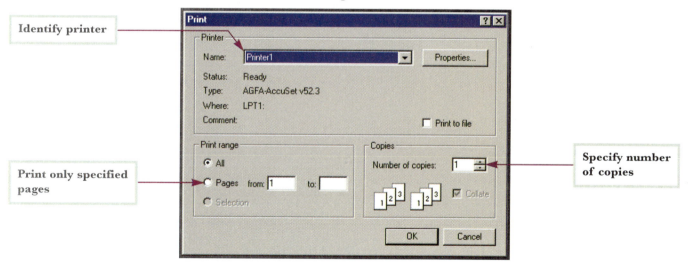

Practice

Print two copies of the navigation structure of the Caddy Shop Web.

skill | Organizing Files in Folders View

concept

As additional files and folders increase the size of your Web, some basic organizational skills become essential. Some file organization can be done in the Navigation view, but the majority is done in the Folders view. These basic skills include moving, renaming, and sorting files.

do it!

Move a file to a subfolder from your Web site into a folder, rename a file, and sort the files by size.

1. Open the Index page of the Skydiver Web.
2. Click the Folders button  on the Views bar.
3. Click and drag the jo336982[1].gif image file from the Contents window to the images folder in the Folder List section of the screen, as shown in Figure 4-9. To view the contents of a folder in the Folder List, click the plus sign ⊞ next to that folder.
4. Right-click the file fphoverx.class. This is one of the Hover button files. Click Rename in the pop-up menu.
5. The file name is selected. Type hoverbutton.class and press the [Enter] key. A dialog box appears, prompting you to update the hyperlinks affected by the name change, as shown in Figure 4-10. Click Yes.
6. Click the column heading Size in the Contents window. The files will be sorted in descending order. Click the Size column heading again. The files will now be sorted in the ascending size order, as shown in Figure 4-11.
7. Save the changes.

more

You can view and modify file properties by right-clicking a file and selecting Properties from the pop-up menu. The Properties dialog box allows you to change page titles, view the size and modification dates of a file, add comments to the file, and assign the file to a workgroup.

Figure 4-9 Folders view

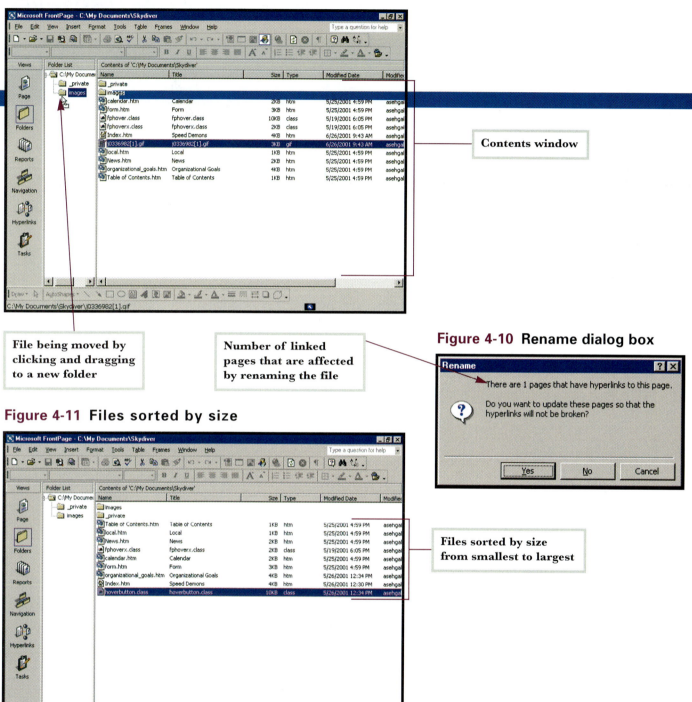

Figure 4-10 Rename dialog box

Figure 4-11 Files sorted by size

Practice

In the Caddy Shop Web, rename the image file you inserted earlier to caddy.gif. Then, move it to the images folder. Finally, sort the files by the Modified Date.

skill | Verifying Hyperlinks

concept

Hyperlinks are one of the most important elements in a Web. If hyperlinks are malfunctioning, Web visitors will be unable to navigate the site. A broken hyperlink will prevent a user from viewing the page they require. Incorrect target names, changed file names, or changed or incorrect URLs can cause broken hyperlinks. There are several ways to verify hyperlinks. Earlier, we tested them in a browser. Now, we will use the Reports view and the Hyperlinks view to verify hyperlinks.

do it!

Verify that all of the hyperlinks in the Web are inserted and working properly.

1. Click the Reports button on the Views bar.
2. The Site Summary opens, as shown in Figure 4-12. If the Site Summary does not appear, click the View menu, point to Reports, and click Site Summary.
3. If you notice any unlinked file, double-click the Unlinked files row in the Site Summary section to know the details of the unlinked file.
4. Click the Hyperlinks button on the Views bar. This displays the tree diagram of the links to and from the Index page.
5. Click the Index page in the Folder List. All of the hyperlinks to and from the Index page are displayed, as shown in Figure 4-13. Links to the page you are viewing appear on the left and links from that page appear on the right.
6. Click the News page in the Folder List. There are two links from the Index page and one link from the Calendar page. The News page links to the Index page and the Calendar page.

more

Hyperlinks can be repaired manually by opening the pages containing the faulty hyperlinks. They can be repaired using the Recalculate Hyperlinks command in the Tools menu. The Recalculate Hyperlinks dialog box informs you that the command will repair the hyperlinks in your Web, update the components, including shared borders and Navigation bars, synchronize Web data, database information, and categories.

Figure 4-12 Reports view

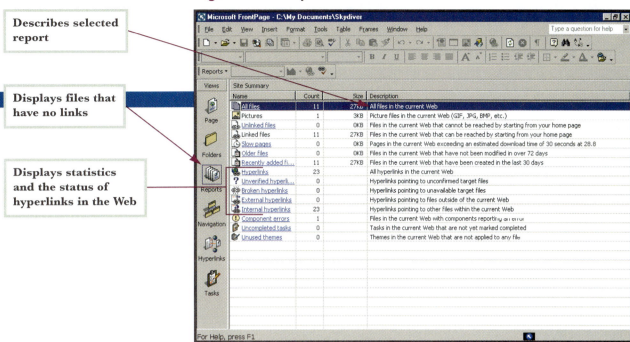

- Describes selected report
- Displays files that have no links
- Displays statistics and the status of hyperlinks in the Web

Figure 4-13 Hyperlinks view

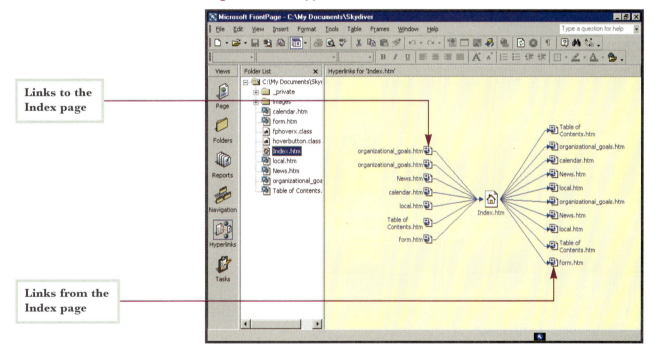

- Links to the Index page
- Links from the Index page

Practice

Verify that all of the hyperlinks in the Caddy Shop Web are functional. Repair them if necessary.

skill Renaming Pages and Changing URLs

concept

Two other important file management tasks are renaming pages and changing URLs. Earlier, we changed the file name of a page but not its title. In this skill, we will change the page title and the URL. Distinctive titles are important for both the Web author and the Web site visitor. If page names are too similar, distinguishing between them can become problematic. In the Skydiver Web, the Index page should be given a distinctive title so that the Web designer does not make errors creating links and the Web site visitor is able to navigate to the correct page.

do it!

Rename one of the pages in the Skydiver Web to improve the site's structure.

1. Click the Navigation button on the Views bar.

2. Right-click the Speed Demons page icon and click Rename in the pop-up menu.

3. The title is selected. Type Home and press the [Enter] key.

4. Right-click the Index page in the Folder List and click Rename in the pop-up menu.

5. The file name is selected. Type home.htm and press the [Enter] key. Click Yes in the Rename dialog box to update the pages so that links will not be broken. You can access the Rename and Properties commands to make changes to the URL or page title by right-clicking the file icon or the page icon in any of the different FrontPage views.

6. Right-click the Home page icon again. Click Properties in the pop-up menu. The Properties dialog box appears, as shown in Figure 4-14. The Properties dialog box displays the path and the description of the Home page.

7. Click OK to close the Properties dialog box.

8. In the Navigation view, the Home page should now look like Figure 4-15.

9. Return to the Page view and save the changes.

10. Close the file.

more

You can also change the URL in the Page view. Right-click an empty area on the page and click Page Properties from the pop-up menu. Type the desired URL in the Base location text box in the Page Properties dialog box. This is not necessary in the exercise above because changing the file name will change the URL. You should check the files of the Web in the Reports view after changing a URL to verify that no hyperlinks were broken.

If you save a file under a new name, the old file will still exist. If the file is not deleted, it can disrupt file management. Both file names will be in your Folder List and you may accidentally create a link to the obsolete version.

Figure 4-14 Properties dialog box

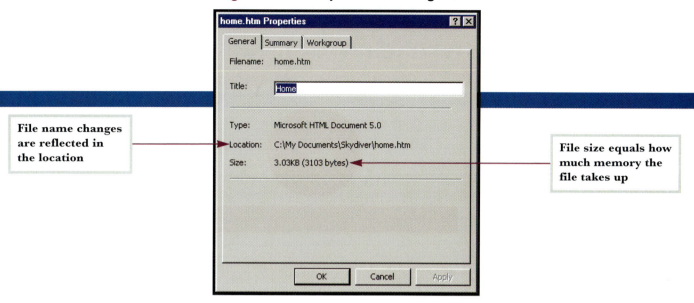

File name changes are reflected in the location

File size equals how much memory the file takes up

Figure 4-15 Change reflected in the Navigation view

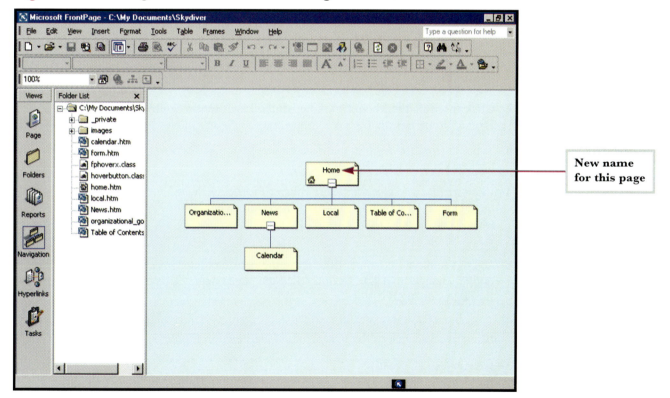

New name for this page

Practice

Change the title and file name of the Index page in the Caddy Shop Web to Home and home.htm, respectively.

Changing Page Titles in Banners

concept

A page banner is a feature of FrontPage, which enables you to quickly add titles to your Web pages. If you have applied a theme to your Web page, the page banners use the styles, formatting, and graphics of the corresponding theme. Otherwise, the page banners are displayed as plain text, which you can format later. To use page banners, you first need to set the navigation structure of your Web in the Navigation view. A page banner will only be visible on a page if the page is included in the navigation structure. Page banners use the page titles from the Navigation view, so if you change the page title, its page banner label will also change and vice versa. After you add a page banner to a page, you can change the text that is displayed on it and you can specify whether to display a graphic or just text. In case you choose to display a graphic as a page banner, the picture that will be displayed will be the one associated with the theme for that particular page.

do it!

Create a graphical page banner and change its title.

1. Open the Form page of the Skydiver Web. The insertion point is displayed in the first line of the page by default.

2. Click Insert on the Menu bar and click the Page Banner command. This displays the Page Banner Properties dialog box. Notice that the Picture option button is already selected.

3. Type Registration form in the Page banner text box. The Page Banner Properties dialog box should now look like Figure 4-16.

4. Click [OK] to close the Page Banner Properties dialog box and display the graphical page banner, as shown in Figure 4-17. If you switch to the Navigation view, you will notice that the page title of form.htm has changed and is now the same as the page banner, Registration form.

5. To change the page banner title, place the mouse pointer over the page banner. The mouse pointer changes to a [icon]. Double-click the page banner. This displays the Page Banner Properties dialog box.

6. Type Register with us! in the Page banner text box. Click [OK]. The title of the page banner will change to Register with us! as shown in Figure 4-18.

7. Save and close the file.

more

To format the text of the page banner, right-click the page banner and select Font in the pop-up menu. This displays the Font dialog box. You can modify the font using this dialog box. To change a graphic page banner to a textual page banner, switch to the Page view, if required, and double-click the page banner. This displays the Page Banner Properties dialog box. Activate the Text option button and click [OK]. This will change the page banner. Click anywhere in the screen to deselect the page banner. Your screen should now resemble Figure 4-19.

To quickly format the textual page banner, select the page banner and format it using the formatting options such as Font, Font size, and Font color, available on the Formatting toolbar.

Figure 4-16 Page Banner Properties dialog box

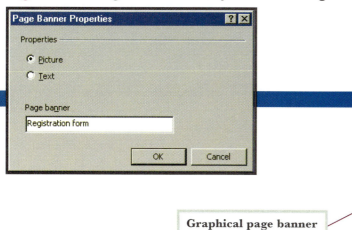

Figure 4-17 Graphical page banner

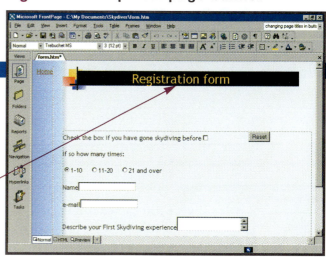

Graphical page banner

Figure 4-18 Modified graphical page banner

Graphical page banner with the modified text

Figure 4-19 Textual page banner

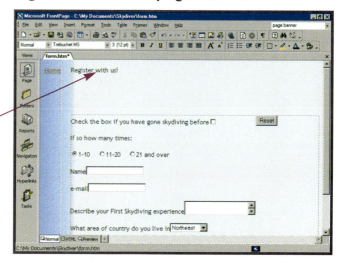

Textual page banner

Practice

Create a textual page banner in the Form page of the Caddy Shop Web and format the page banner in the way you like.

skill: Opening an Office Document in a Web

concept

Many Microsoft Office programs allow you to save documents in HTML format and open pages in your default browser. Office documents can be imported and published in a Web. Almost all Microsoft created documents can be imported into a FrontPage Web.

do it!

Open a Microsoft Office document, in this case a Microsoft Word document, in FrontPage.

1. Begin with a blank page in the Skydiver Web.
2. Click Insert, then click File. The Select File dialog box opens.
3. Click the arrow in the Files of type drop-down list box and click Word 97-2002 (*.doc), as shown in Figure 4-20.
4. Navigate to the location where you have stored the student files and click fpdoit4-8.doc.
5. Click . You may have to install this feature, of opening an office document in a Web, from your Office 2002 CD-ROM.
6. The Word document opens as a Web page, as shown in Figure 4-21. When the document opens in FrontPage, it has been converted to HTML and is now a Web document.
7. Save the page in My Documents as wordfile.htm and close the file.

more

You may have noticed when you accessed the Files of type drop-down list box, that Word documents are not the only files that can be inserted into a Web Page. You can insert Rich Text Format (RTF) documents, Plain text (TXT or ASCII) files, Excel worksheets, or Lotus1-2-3 worksheets, WordPerfect 5.x and 6.x, Works 4.0, Word for Macintosh, and HTML documents.

Instead of cutting and pasting or re-entering data, importing allows you to take previously saved documents in various formats and convert them to HTML.

Figure 4-20 Select File dialog box

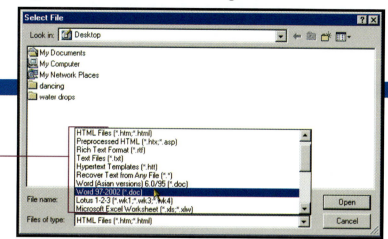

Lists the formats that can be inserted into FrontPage Webs

Figure 4-21 Word document in FrontPage

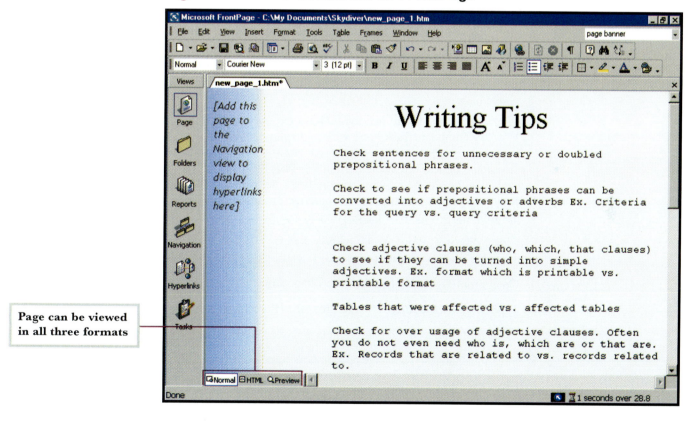

Page can be viewed in all three formats

Practice

Open fpprac4-8.doc from the location where you have stored the Student Files in FrontPage. Save the file as insertword.htm and close the file.

skill Using the Office Clipboard

concept

The Office Clipboard enables you to save up to twenty four pieces of data from any Office program to the clipboard. Clipboard items can be pasted into other programs or used within a single application. Data is sent to the clipboard using the Cut and Copy commands. After it is saved to the clipboard, the Paste command is used to insert it into the various programs. Using the Office Clipboard, you can copy and paste the portions of a document you need, rather than importing the entire document.

do it!

Copy and paste data from another program to FrontPage with the aid of the Office Clipboard.

1. Open fpdoit4-9.doc.
2. Microsoft Word opens to a meeting agenda.
3. Scroll down the document until you reach the Agenda section of the document. Select the entire Agenda section beginning with Ad Campaign and ending with President Maria Fragen.
4. Click Edit on the Menu bar, then click Copy. If you click the Copy command twice, the 1 of 24 - Clipboard Task Pane will be displayed. The section of the text that you have copied is sent to the Office Clipboard, as shown in Figure 4-22. 1 of 24 in the Clipboard Task Pane indicates that the item in the Task Pane is the first item to be pasted. 24 indicates that the Clipboard can carry up to 24 items to be pasted. You can also cut, copy, and paste data within the FrontPage program. If you place something incorrectly or put it on the wrong Web page, you can cut it and paste it to the correct location.
5. Close Microsoft Word. You may be asked if you want the data on the clipboard to be available for use in other programs. If so, click Yes.
6. Open FrontPage and open the News page from the Skydiver Web.
7. Type Monthly Meeting Agenda. Press the [Enter] key.
8. Click Edit on the Menu bar, then click Paste.
9. Save the changes. This page should now look like Figure 4-23.
10. Close the file.

more

There is also a Paste Special command in the Edit menu of the FrontPage, although you may have to access the extended menu to view it. The Paste Special command enables you to paste data onto the clipboard in different formats. You can paste it as one paragraph, break it into several paragraphs, turn it into formatted paragraphs, add line breaks, or simply treat the data as HTML.

Figure 4-22 Clipboard Task Pane

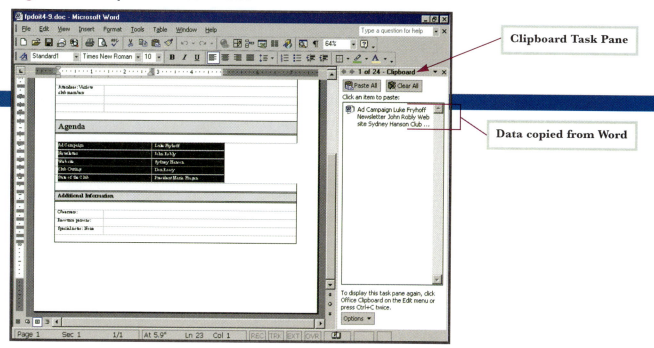

Figure 4-23 Data pasted into FrontPage

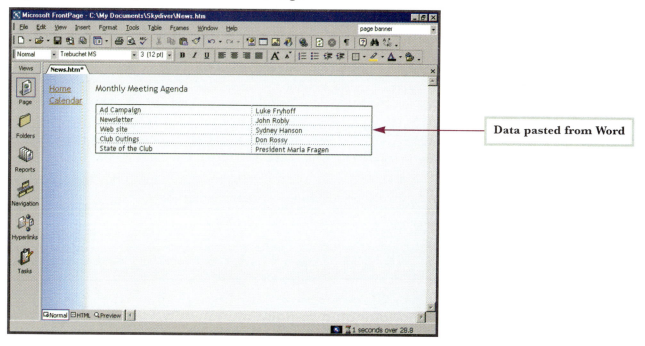

Practice

Open fpprac4-9.doc. There is only one line of text. Copy it from Word and paste it at the bottom of the Home page in the Caddy Shop Web.

skill Creating and Printing Reports

concept

Reports enable you to analyze and summarize a wide range of Web site information. Reports enable you to:

- View a Web site summary. You can get general information about the content in your Web site, such as a summary of the number and types of files or a listing of the number of hyperlinks contained in your Web site.
- View maintenance problems. Reports can list maintenance problems, such as which pages have a large file size (and will download slowly as a result) or contain broken hyperlinks.
- Manage workflow. Reports can also help you manage your workflow by displaying the status of your Web pages. Files in your Web site can be categorized, assigned to different authors, and checked in and out using source control—all of which you can monitor using reports.
- Monitor Web site usage. Using reports, you can track data such as frequently visited pages and the Web browsers used to visit your site.

do it!

Display the All Files and the Component Errors reports.

1. Click View on the Menu bar, point to Reports, point to Files, and then click the All files command (see Figure 4-24). The All Files report appears, as shown in Figure 4-25.
2. To display the Component Errors report, click View on the Menu bar, point to Reports, point to Problems, and then click the Component Errors command. The Component Errors report appears, as shown in Figure 4-26. This report shows that the form.htm file has an error.
3. Expand the Errors column to read the description of the error.
4. Save as componenterrorsreport.htm and close the file.

more

The Site Summary report displays an overview of the vital statistics of a Web site such as the number and sizes of files and pictures, and the number and types of hyperlinks.

The Files reports display an overview of the age of files, the authors working on them, and the modification dates of the files. The different kinds of File Status reports are All Files, Recently Added Files, Recently Changed Files, and Older Files.

The Problems reports list the problems with your Web site, including broken links, component errors, and files that take too long to download. The different kinds of Maintenance Problem reports are Unlinked Files, Slow Pages, Broken Hyperlinks, and Component Errors reports.

The Workflow Status reports indicate the status of the files and assignments in your Web site, including the review status, the authors of the files, and whether it has been checked out using source control. The different kinds of Workflow Status reports are Review Status, Assigned To, Categories, Publish Status, and Checkout Status reports.

The Usage reports display information about the visits to your Web site, including page hits, and browsers used by site visitors. The different kinds of Site Usage reports are Usage Summary, Monthly Summary, Weekly Summary, Daily Summary, Monthly Page Hits, Weekly Page Hits, Daily Page Hits, Visiting Users, Operating Systems, Browsers, Referring Domains, Referring URLs, and Search Strings reports.

Figure 4-24 All Files command of the Files report

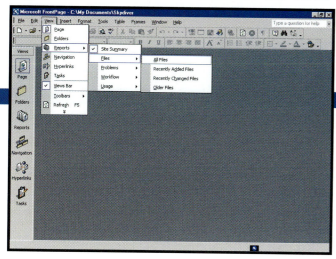

Figure 4-25 All Files report

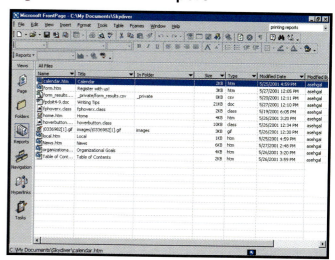

Figure 4-26 Component Errors report

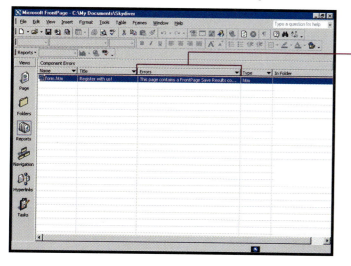

Expand the Errors column to read the description

Practice

Display the All Files report of the Caddy Shop Web.

Publishing a Web

concept

When you create a Web site, the goal is to get it published. You can publish directly to a Web server using FrontPage. New pages can be published and existing ones can be changed with ease. If you find mistakes or have a page that requires continuous updating, just edit your original files and republish. The changed files will automatically replace the existing ones.

do it!

Publish your Web so that it can be viewed as a Web site.

1. Open fpdoit4-11.htm in FrontPage from the location where you have stored the student files. Save it as table_of_contents.htm in your Skydiver Web. When a dialog box prompts you to replace the file of the same name, click Yes.

2. Click File on the Menu bar and click the Publish Web command; you may have to access the extended menu to find the Publish Web command. The Publish Destination dialog box opens.

3. Type C:/My Documents/Published Skydiver Web in the Enter publish destination text box, as shown in Figure 4-27.

4. Click OK. This displays the Microsoft Information window that prompts you to create the Published Skydiver Web folder.

5. Click OK. This displays the Publish Web dialog box with all the related files of the Skydiver Web listed in a list box, as shown in Figure 4-28.

6. Click Publish.

7. The files are copied to the necessary folder, as shown in Figure 4-29. If a warning message about FrontPage Server Extensions appears, consult the More section below on how to handle this situation.

8. When all the files are copied, a dialog box opens telling you that your Web has been published successfully, as shown in Figure 4-30.

9. Click the link that says Click here to view your published web site. Your default Web browser will open, displaying your published Web site; all objects and links should work properly now that the Web is published. Review the Web site, then close the browser.

10. In the FrontPage application, click Done, then close FrontPage.

more

Before you publish your Web with a server, you will need several pieces of information. You will need to get the address of your Web server and an assigned name for your Home page. You will also need to find out if the server has FrontPage extensions. In some cases, in order to be viewed, components require that your server have this special Microsoft software installed. If your server does not have FrontPage extensions, you may be able to get the address of an FTP or File Transfer Protocol server to circumvent this problem.

Your Web server will also give you folder information, such as what folder the server wants you to upload to and how the server wants your Web files to be organized. Once you have published the Web, you can publish individual pages or the entire Web again to continually update it. Many Web servers require that you join their online communities and choose a user name and password. You will be required to enter this information when you publish your Web.

Figure 4-27 Publish Destination dialog box

Figure 4-28 Publish dialog box

Figure 4-29 Publish a Web

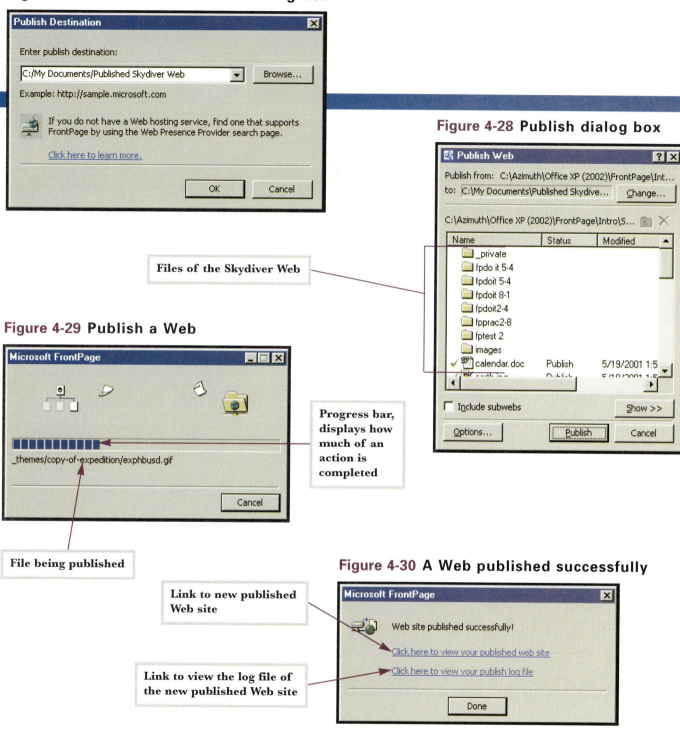

Figure 4-30 A Web published successfully

Practice

Publish the Caddy Shop Web to C:/My Documents/Caddy Shop Web Final.

shortcuts

Function	Button/Mouse	Menu	Keyboard
Copy		Click Edit, then click Copy	[Ctrl]+[C]
Cut		Click Edit, then click Cut	[Ctrl]+[X]
Paste		Click Edit, then click Paste	[Ctrl]+[V]
Print		Click File, then click Print	[Ctrl]+[P]
Publish Web		Click File, then click Publish Web	[Alt]+[P]
Page View		Click View, then click Page	
Folders View		Click View, then click Folders	
Reports View		Click View, then click Reports	
Navigation View		Click View, then click Navigation	
Hyperlinks View		Click View, then click Hyperlinks	

INTERACTIVE COMPUTING | FrontPage 2002 | FP 4.25

A. Identify Key Features

Name the items indicated by callouts in Figure 4-31.

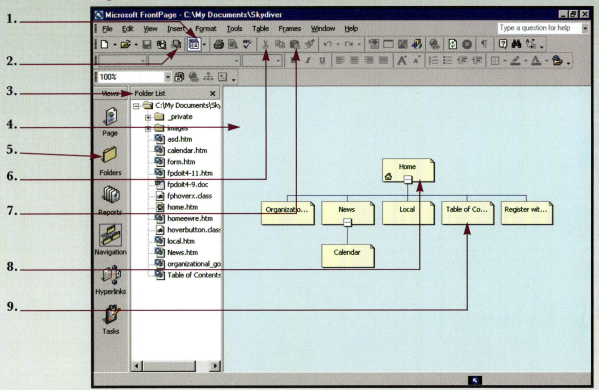

Figure 4-31 Skydiver Web in FrontPage

B. Select the Best Answer

10. A Web hierarchy is also known as
11. You can add a Navigation bar to your Web pages using this command
12. A printed reproduction of a computer screen
13. When your hyperlinks are broken use this command
14. A Web address
15. The view you should use to make sure all your files and links work properly
16. This holds up to 24 pieces of data
17. Access this menu to open an Office document in FrontPage
18. Allows you to view what a page will look like when it is printed

a. Shared Borders
b. Reports
c. Office Clipboard
d. Recalculate hyperlinks
e. Insert
f. Hard copy
g. Print Preview
h. Tree diagram
i. URL

quiz (continued)

C. Complete the Statement

19. You must use this view to create a Web hierarchy:
    a. Reports
    b. Hyperlinks
    c. Tasks
    d. Navigation

20. A list of files appears in the:
    a. Tasks view
    b. Folder List
    c. Reports view
    d. Hyperlinks view

21. When you insert a file from another program, you must use this dialog box:
    a. Insert Document
    b. Select File
    c. Insert Data
    d. Insert

22. To prevent people from sabotaging sites that are not theirs, most Web servers require:
    a. A user name and password
    b. A computer ID number
    c. A coded entry language
    d. A keyword or secret phrase

23. One method you can use to format hyperlinks is to access the:
    a. Hyperlinks menu
    b. Background dialog box
    c. Foreground dialog box
    d. Page Properties dialog box

24. You can use these two commands to take data from one document and insert it into another:
    a. Copy and Insert
    b. Cut and Insert
    c. Cut and Place
    d. Copy and Paste

25. Once an Office document has been opened in FrontPage, it is converted to:
    a. FrontPages
    b. Java
    c. HTML
    d. Applet

26. Clicking the plus sign in the Navigation view and the Hyperlinks view performs this function:
    a. Expands the diagrams
    b. Contracts the diagrams
    c. Expands the menu
    d. Contracts the window

Build Your Skills

1. Create a Web hierarchy:
    a. Open the Water Taxi Web.
    b. Switch to the Navigation view. Drag all the files except form.html from the Folder List so that they become child pages of the Index page.
    c. Make the Form page in the Water Taxi Web a child page of the Fees page.

2. Create a Navigation bar:
    a. Create a Navigation bar on the Index page that links to all of its child pages.
    b. Make sure there is a link from the child pages back to the Index page.
    c. Make the links in the Navigation bar text rather than buttons.

3. Print a Web structure:
    a. Open the Water Taxi Web in Navigation view.
    b. Print the structure of the Web.

4. Verify your hyperlinks:
    a. Open the Water Taxi Web in the Reports view.
    b. If there are broken hyperlinks, repair them with the Recalculate Hyperlinks command.
    c. Make sure that you have linked the necessary files.
    d. View the Web in the Hyperlinks view to make sure that all of the pages are linked properly.

5. Open an Office document in a Web:
    a. Open fpskill4.doc in FrontPage.
    b. Save it as Resume.htm.

6. Publish a Web:
    a. Open the Water Taxi Web.
    b. Publish the Web to C:/My Documents/Watertaxiweb.
    c. After publishing the Web, view it, close it, then close FrontPage.

interactivity (continued)

Problem Solving Exercises

1. Your work at Diggs & Associates is almost finished. Your job does not include composing all the text. You are to train a group of Diggs' employees to finish creating the site and maintain it. They will complete any additional pages following the design, theme, color scheme, and style you have devised. Before you are finished, you must create a Web hierarchy and Navigation bars. The Index page, of course, will be at the top of your hierarchy. The Search, Feedback, Contents, and all other pages will be child pages of the Index page. After you have completed the tree diagram, create Navigation bars. Use button hyperlinks for your Navigation bars. They should link from the Index page to each child page, according to the hierarchy you created. Each child page should in turn, link back to the Index page. Demonstrate your progress to Diggs' executives by printing several copies of your Web structure. View the Web in the Folders view and if necessary, move image files to the image folder and rename files.

2. Verify the hyperlinks in the Diggs Web. First view the Web in the Reports view. Make sure none of the necessary files are unlinked. Also, make sure there are no broken hyperlinks. If any of the hyperlinks are broken, use the Recalculate hyperlinks command to fix them. Rename all of the pages so that they are easier to organize. Rename any similarly titled pages. For example, the Services pages need distinct names rather than Service 1, Service 2, etc. This will enable Diggs' employees to locate particular pages for editing.

3. Continue working on your personal Web. First, create a Web hierarchy. If you used a wizard to create your personal Web, this was done automatically. If you have added pages to a Home page or formatted several pages and linked them together however, you will need to either edit or create a tree diagram. If you decide to add Navigation bars, make sure they complement your chosen style. Print the Web structure and view the Web in the Folders view. Reorganize files and folders, if necessary.

4. View the Web in the Reports and Hyperlinks views to verify the hyperlinks. Thoroughly navigate your Web as a final check that all links are functional. Make sure all file names, URLs, and page names are correct. If you want to put poetry or fiction that you have written, or a resume on your site, import the documents from your word processing program. If you promote it, prospective employers or publishers might discover and view your Web site. Use the Office Clipboard to insert a table or a block of text from another program. Remember to save imported documents and make sure they are linked to your site. Finally, publish the Web. If you have a URL and a Web server, and are confident that your site is ready, you can publish it with your Web server. If not, publish it to C:/My Documents/Diggsweb, following the instructions on publishing a Web that are found in Lesson 4.

Advanced Formatting

- Importing Text
- Importing Web Pages
- Importing Images
- Advanced Image Formatting
- Editing Graphics on Web Pages
- Placing Text over an Image
- Using the Format Painter
- Inserting a Hit Counter
- Inserting a Time Stamp
- Creating a Search Form
- Formatting Web Page Transitions
- Using Style Sheets

Formatting Web pages includes more than formatting text, changing colors, applying themes, and adding hyperlinks. You will want to control many other variables, as you become more comfortable with creating Webs. FrontPage includes many components you can add and features you can use to make your Web pages both visually intriguing and functional.

You can import an Office document in FrontPage so that it inherits the style and theme of your Web. You can also import Web pages and images. Imported Web pages are also automatically converted to the style and theme of your Web. When you import images and save them in your Web, they are converted to one of the two image file formats supported by most browsers. You can format your images to add to the aesthetic appeal of your Web. You can add a three-dimensional effect called a bevel to an image. You can also add text over an image.

It can become counterproductive to make multiple formatting changes to many different blocks of text. Instead, you can use the Format Painter to copy all paragraphs and character formatting from one paragraph to another. In a few short steps, you can easily create uniform paragraphs or identically formatted blocks of text.

FrontPage also enables you to add features that will make your Web more functional and informative. Among these are hit counters and search forms. You can also apply special effects that run as one page disappears and another loads. You can use a powerful formatting tool, cascading style sheets, to position elements on your Web page. Experienced Web authors believe that cascading style sheets will eventually replace tables as the layout device of choice for HTML pages.

Lesson Goal:

In this lesson, you will learn to import text, images, and Web pages, format an image using the advanced features of FrontPage, place text over an image, and use the Format painter. You will also learn to insert a hit counter and time stamp on a Web page, create a search form on a Web page, format Web page transitions, and use style sheets.

skill | Importing Text

concept

You can import many different types of files into your Web. Imported text is automatically converted to HTML. You can use documents you have already created to easily construct Web pages. Importing text is easier than copying and pasting full documents. Furthermore, unlike inserted documents, imported documents are converted to the style and theme of your Web.

do it!

Import a schedule of events into the Calendar Web page of the Skydiver Web.

1. Open the Calendar page in the Skydiver Web.

2. Click File on the Menu bar and click the Import command on the File menu. The Import dialog box opens.

3. Click [Add File...]. The Add File to Import List dialog box opens.

4. Locate the folder where you have stored the student files. Click the calendar.doc file.

5. Click [Open]. The file appears in the Import dialog box, as shown in Figure 5-1. The documents and file types that can be imported are: HTML, MS Word, RTF (Rich Text Format) documents, TXT (plain text or ASCII) files, worksheets from MS Excel and Lotus 1-2-3, and WordPerfect documents.

6. Click [OK]. The file has been imported into your Web.

7. Click Insert on the Menu bar and click the File command. The Select File dialog box opens. Locate the Skydiver Web. Double-click to place it in the Look in list box.

8. Click the arrow next to the Files of type text box. Scroll to the top of the drop-down menu and click All Files.

9. Click the calendar.doc file to select it.

10. Click [Open]. The text is converted to HTML format. It is also converted to the style and theme of your Web. The imported document is displayed in Figure 5-2.

11. Save and close the Web page.

more

You can also import files and link them to a Web page, rather than inserting a file on a page. Simply create a hyperlink on your Web page. The target of the hyperlink will be the name of the file. If the file to which you are linking has been imported to your Web folder, the link will work properly. To quickly import a file or a selection of files, you can drag them to the Folder List from the Windows Explorer program.

Figure 5-1 Import dialog box

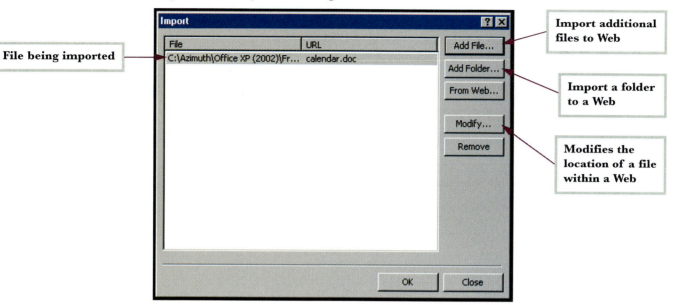

Figure 5-2 Imported text converted to HTML

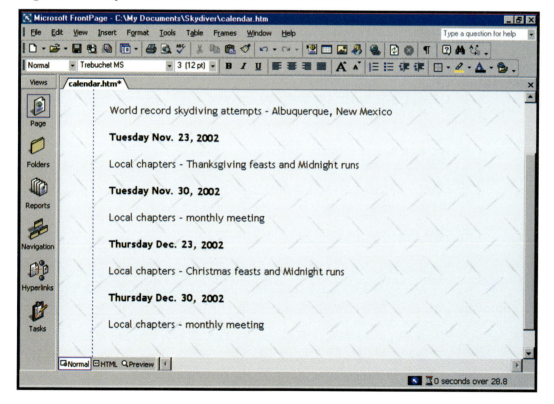

Practice

Import the MS Word document fpprac5-1.doc to the Caddy Shop Web. Insert the text from that document at the bottom of the Home page.

FP 5.4 LESSON FIVE Advanced Formatting

skill | Importing Web Pages

concept

If you have already created or have access to finished Web pages, you can easily import them. Importing will convert the Web pages to the style and theme of the current Web. You can import individual pages or entire Web folders that are stored on your computer, LAN, or the World Wide Web. This is particularly useful for a company that uses the same Web page on several different sites.

do it!

Import an existing skydiving FAQ Web page into the Skydiver Web.

1. Open the Home page from the Skydiver Web.
2. Click File on the Menu bar. Click Import on the File menu. The Import dialog box opens.
3. Click [Add File...] to open the Add File to Import List dialog box.
4. Locate the folder where you have stored the student files. Open the fpdoit5-2 folder. Click faq.htm to select it.
5. Click [Open]. The FAQ page is added to the Import dialog box as shown in Figure 5-3.
6. Click [OK]. The file has been imported.
7. Open the FAQ page. This is displayed in Figure 5-4.
8. Right-click faq.htm in the Folder List. Select Properties on the shortcut menu. Type FAQ, to replace the selected default text in the Title text box. Click [OK].
9. Click the Navigation button on the Views bar. Drag faq.htm from the Folder List to the tree diagram. Place it below the Table of Contents page. Return to the Page view.
10. Save and close the FAQ and Home pages.

more

You can import Web pages directly from the Internet by clicking [From Web...] on the Import dialog box. This opens the Import Web Wizard. You will be required to enter the Web site address of the page you want to import. You can also import a published Web from your local network with the Import Web Wizard. After specifying the address, you can control how much information you download and how long it will take. When you finish, the Web page will be imported to your Web. You can click [Add Folder...] to add an entire folder to your Web. This is useful for adding a folder of images or other files to your Web.

It is important to note that although you can easily import Web pages that others have created, to your own Web, you should not do so unless you have their permission. Otherwise you may violate copyright law.

Figure 5-3 Import dialog box

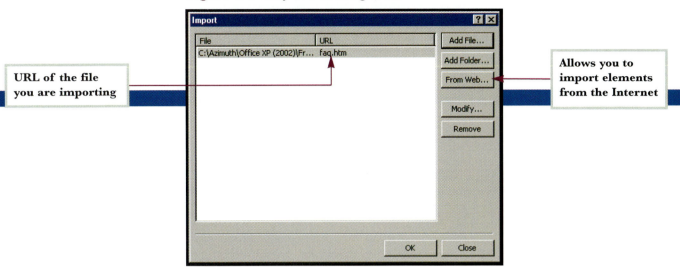

Figure 5-4 Imported page converted to your Web style

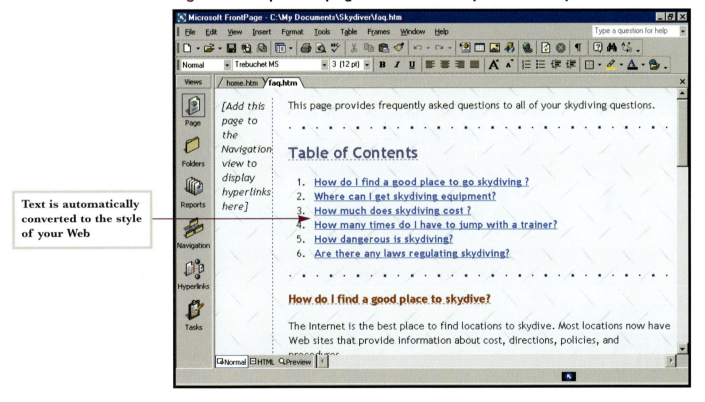

Practice

Import a page of your choice from the Skydiver Web to the Caddy Shop Web.

skill | Importing Images

concept

You can import images to a Web that you have stored on your computer. When you import images, store them in the images folder. This way they will be in a central location where you can easily use them more than once. This will be convenient for graphics such as logos that you will use on multiple pages.

do it!

Import an existing image from another and store it in the images folder in the Skydiver Web.

1. Open the News page in the Skydiver Web.
2. Click File on the Menu bar. Click Import on the File menu. The Import dialog box opens.
3. Click [Add File...] to open the Add File to Import List dialog box. Navigate to the location of the student files.
4. Double-click to open the fpdoit5-3 folder. Open the images folder. Select plane.wmf as shown in Figure 5-5.
5. Click [OK]. The plane image is added to the Import dialog box.
6. Click [OK]. The file is imported to your Web. Importing images does not automatically add them to your Web page. It simply means you are getting them onto your site so you will be able to easily access them. You must insert images to place them in your pages.
7. Click Insert on the Menu bar. Move the mouse pointer over the Picture command on the submenu and click From File on the submenu.
8. The Picture dialog box opens. Locate the student files and double-click plane.wmf to insert the image, as shown in Figure 5-6.
9. Save the News page.

more

You can click [Modify...] to change the location to which the file will be imported. Enter a new file location within your Web, or rename the file in the Edit URL dialog box. You may want to change the file name or store imported files with similar names in different folders to avoid confusion. Another advantage of importing and inserting an image is that it will be converted to GIF or JPEG format. When you format the image (as you will see in the next skill), you will have to save the embedded file. The image you just inserted will be converted to GIF format.

You can also create a thumbnail or small version of your image. With the image selected, click the Auto Thumbnail button on the Pictures toolbar. The thumbnail replaces the full-sized image on the Web page. Visitors can click the thumbnail to view the full-sized image.

Figure 5-5 Add File to Import dialog box

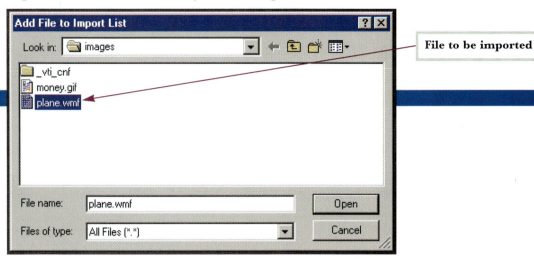

Figure 5-6 Imported image inserted into a Web page

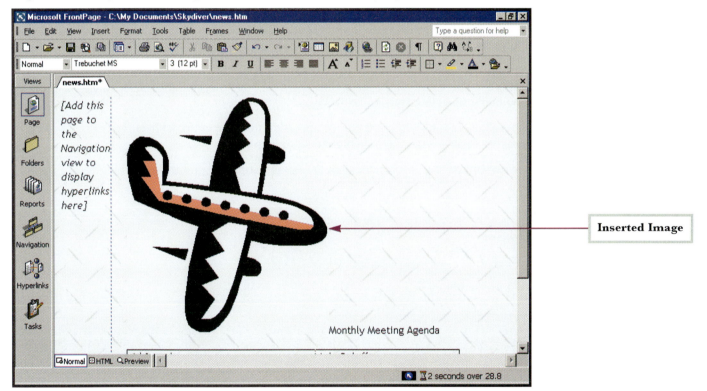

Practice

Import money.gif from the fpdoit5-3 folder on any page of the Caddy Shop Web.

Advanced Image Formatting

concept

You can apply many different effects to your pictures, including beveling. Beveled borders give images an elevated, three-dimensional appearance. You can also resize your graphics to tell the Web browser how to display them. These image formatting tools will help you to design lively Web pages.

do it!

Resize a graphic and use the Bevel command to create a three-dimensional frame effect around the image.

1. Click the image of the plane in news.htm page. The image is selected and surrounded by sizing handles. The Pictures toolbar opens. If your Pictures toolbar does not open, click the View menu, point to Toolbars to display the Toolbars submenu, and then click the Pictures command.

2. Move the pointer over the sizing handle on the lower-right corner of the image. The pointer turns into a resizing arrow.

3. Drag the bottom-right corner to the upper-left until the entire table at the bottom of the page is visible. Your page should now look like Figure 5-7.

4. With the image still selected, click the Bevel button on the Pictures toolbar.

5. The image has been beveled, as shown in Figure 5-8.

6. Click the Save button to save the News page. The Save Embedded Files dialog box opens.

7. Click OK to save the embedded image.

8. Close the file.

more

You can make modifications to the bevel effect on the image. Clicking the Bevel button multiple times will add depth to the frame. You can continue to click the Bevel button until you get the effect you want. If you do not like the depth of the frame, use the Undo button to reverse the effect you have just applied. You can click the arrow next to the Undo button to access a list of your most recent actions. You can undo multiple actions back to, and including the first action you performed.

When you resize graphics, use a corner sizing handle to maintain the proportions of your image. If you use a side handle, the image will be distorted. When you decrease the size of an image, it will take up a smaller area in the browser window, but the file size and download time will not be changed. To decrease the file size, click the Resample button on the Pictures toolbar after you have resized the image. The file size will be reduced to match the smaller image size.

Figure 5-7 A resized image in FrontPage

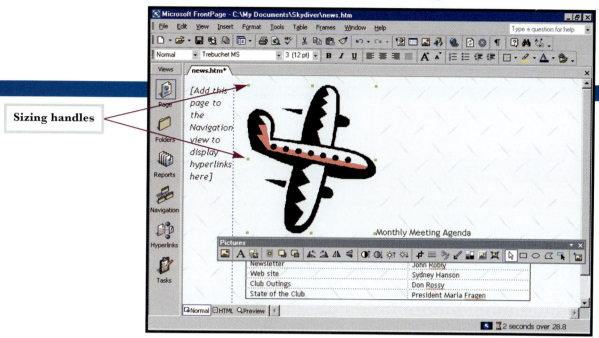

Figure 5-8 A beveled image in FrontPage

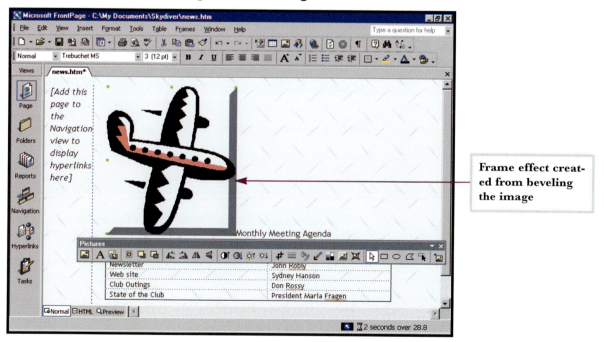

Practice

Insert the fpprac5-4.gif from the student files on one of your pages in the Caddy Shop Web. Resize until you like the size. Then, bevel the image. Click the Bevel button until you get the effect you like. Then save the page.

skill: Editing Graphics on Web Pages

concept

In addition to resizing the graphics, you can edit the graphics present on the Web page. FrontPage enables you to edit the graphic in the graphic editor of your choice, such as Adobe PhotoShop, MS Paint, and Microsoft PhotoDraw. To edit a graphic, you first must specify a graphic editor for the graphic files, such as BMP, JPG or GIF files.

do it!

Edit a graphic on the Table of Contents page of the Skydiver Web, using MS Paint, a graphics editing program installed by default as part of your Windows operating system.

1. Open the Table of Contents page of the Skydiver Web.

2. Place the insertion point on the first line of the page.

3. Click Insert on the Menu bar, then point to the Picture command and click From File. The Picture dialog box appears.

4. Navigate to the folder in which you have stored your Student Files and click the file named airplane.bmp.

5. Click [Insert] to insert the picture in the Web page. The Web page should now look like Figure 5-9.

6. Click Tools on the Menu bar and then click the Options command. The Options dialog box appears.

7. Click the Configure Editors tab to activate it.

8. Click [Add...]. The Add Editor Association dialog box appears.

9. Type bmp in the File type text box and MS Paint in the Editor name text box. Then click [Browse...]. The Browse dialog box opens.

10. Locate the Mspaint.exe file from the Look in list box. (This file probably is located in the Accessories subfolder of the Program Files folder, which is present on the C: drive.)

11. Double-click the Mspaint.exe file. The path for MS Paint is displayed in the Command text box on the Add Editor Association dialog box. The Add Editor Association dialog box should now look like Figure 5-10.

12. Click [OK]. Scroll down till the end of the list box on the Configure Editors tab of the Options dialog box. You will see that bmp is displayed in the Type column and MS Paint (Mspaint.exe) is displayed in the Editor column, as shown in Figure 5-11. Leave the default setting as it is.

13. Click [OK].

(continued on FP 5.12)

Figure 5-9 Picture inserted in the Web page

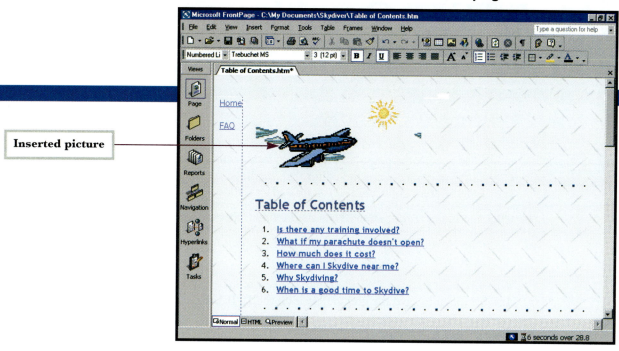

Figure 5-10 Add Editor Association dialog box

Figure 5-11 Options dialog box

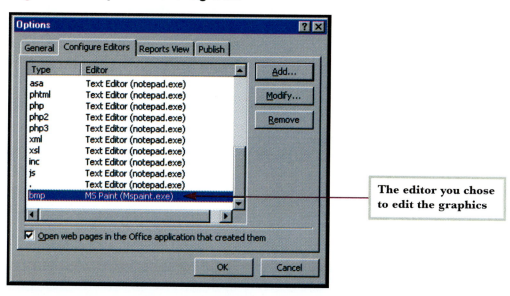

skill | Editing Graphics on Web Pages (continued)

do it!

14. Right-click the graphic you inserted in the page. Click Edit Picture from the shortcut menu. This opens the graphic in MS Paint, as shown in Figure 5-12. For animated GIF files, FrontPage opens the editor that you have set for standard GIF files. You cannot specify a different application for animated GIF files.

15. Click the Eraser Tool button on the toolbox. This tool enables you to erase a graphic.

16. Erase the clouds and the sun in the graphic by clicking the left mouse button and dragging the eraser over them, as shown in Figure 5-13.

17. When you have erased the clouds and the sun in the graphic, click the Save command on the File menu to save the graphic, then close MS Paint.

18. The graphic on the Table of Contents Web page is edited exactly in the way you have edited it in MS Paint (see Figure 5-14).

19. Save the Web page and the graphic and close the Web page.

more

MS Paint is a relatively simple editing program, but it does have the advantage of being installed by default with the Windows operating system. For more advanced graphics editing, you may wish to purchase and install a more sophisticated editing program.

Once you have specified a graphics editor for a particular graphic file, you can edit that type of graphic file throughout your Web. If you want to edit graphics files such as GIF or JPG files, for example, you need to specify the graphic editor separately for each type of file. If you have previously specified a graphic editor for JPG files, then want to edit GIF files, you will not be able to do so until you associate a graphic editor for those GIF files.

Figure 5-12 Graphic from FrontPage displayed in MS Paint

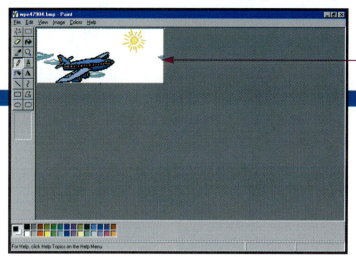

Graphic from FrontPage

Figure 5-13 Erasing parts of a graphic

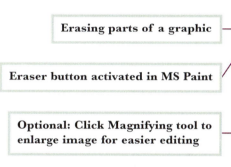

Erasing parts of a graphic

Eraser button activated in MS Paint

Optional: Click Magnifying tool to enlarge image for easier editing

Figure 5-14 Edited graphic

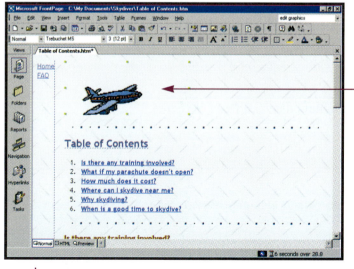

Parts of the graphic are deleted

Practice

Insert the student file, fpprac5-5.gif, in one of the pages of Caddy Shop Web and delete any portion of the image that you like.

skill  Placing Text over an Image

concept

You can also insert text over the top of an image. Placing text over an image allows you to label your graphics or add a title to give an image a magazine-cover look. A graphical table of contents, image map, product advertisement or logo may also benefit from the merging of text and images.

do it!

Place text over the image you inserted previously on the News page.

1. Open the News page of the Skydiver Web and access the Pictures toolbar.
2. Click the image to select it.
3. Click the Text button **A** on the Pictures toolbar. A text box appears at the center of the image.
4. Type Skydiver News. Your page should look like Figure 5-15.
5. Close the Pictures toolbar.
6. Click the arrow next to the Font Color button on the Formatting toolbar. Click the black square in the Standard Colors palette if the text is not already black in color.
7. Click in the center of the text box and drag it to the upper-left corner of the page until it will not go any further.
8. Move the pointer over the right midpoint-sizing handle, so the pointer turns into a horizontal resizing arrow ↔. Drag to the left until only the word Skydiver is visible.
9. Next, move the pointer over the bottom midpoint-sizing handle, so the pointer becomes a vertical resizing arrow ↕.
10. Drag the vertical resizing arrow ↕ until the word News is visible.
11. Click outside the image to deselect the text box. Your page should look like Figure 5-16.
12. Save the News page and close it.

more

If the image you inserted is in GIF format, the text box will immediately open in the center of the image. If the image is in JPEG format, FrontPage will prompt you to convert it to GIF. Text is not supported in the JPEG format. Click OK to convert the image to GIF. If the image is in a different format such as BMP or WMF, you will be prompted to save it as a GIF when you save the page.

You can format text over an image the same way you format any other text. You can use the Formatting toolbar to change the alignment, color, size, font, and other attributes of the text. If you increase the size of the text placed over an image, you will be required to increase the size of the text box. You can do this by dragging the sizing handles until all the text is visible.

Figure 5-15 Unformatted text placed over an image

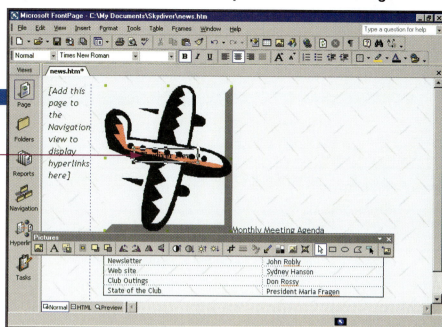

Text is unformatted and barely visible over the image

Figure 5-16 Text placed over an image and formatted

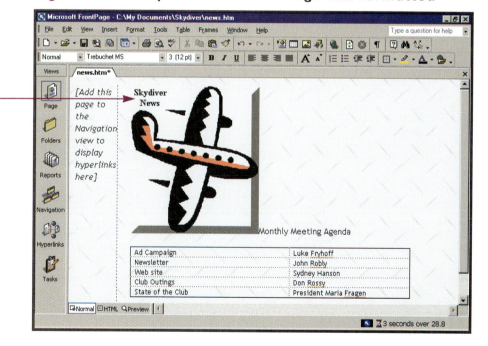

Formatted text is visible and fits the image

Practice

Insert the leopard.jpg file in one of the pages of Caddy Shop Web and place a text of your choice over it.

skill | Using the Format Painter

concept

You can format large blocks of text quickly and easily using the Format Painter. You can make multiple formatting changes with just a few clicks of the mouse. Rather than selecting many different formatting commands to achieve a uniform result, you can copy all the character formatting from one block of text and apply it to another.

do it!

Use the Format Painter to change the formatting of sections of text on a Web page.

1. Open the Home page of the Skydiver Web.
2. Select the text, A National Organization for those who live on the edge, as shown in Figure 5-17.
3. Click the Format Painter button on the Standard toolbar.
4. Click the Navigation button on the Views bar. Double-click the Calendar page to open it.
5. Move the pointer to the beginning of the first date listed, Monday Nov. 1, 2002. The I-beam changes to a Format Painter I-beam.
6. Select the date. The format of the text has been changed to the format you copied from the home page.
7. With the first date still selected, click the Format Painter button again.
8. Now, select the next date, Thursday Nov. 18, 2002.
9. Follow the same procedure to format all the dates on the page. When finished, your Calendar page should resemble Figure 5-18. To copy the desired format to several locations, double-click the Format Painter button. When you have finished pasting the desired format to different pieces of text, click the Format Painter button again to deactivate the Format Painter.
10. Save and close the Calendar page.

more

You can also use the Format Painter to copy and paste a hyperlink. To copy multiple links from one hyperlink, simply select the desired hyperlink. Then, double-click the Format Painter button and select all the pieces of text, which you want to link to the original target. Both the format and the target of the hyperlink will be copied to the selected pieces of text.

You can also copy all paragraphs formatting including style, alignment, and indent from one paragraph to another. When you select a paragraph and click the Format Painter button, both the paragraph and character formatting are copied. You can quickly create identical paragraphs on your Web pages.

Figure 5-17 Select the format to be copied

Format painter icon

Once the desired format is selected, click the Format Painter button

Figure 5-18 Copied format pasted to another Web page

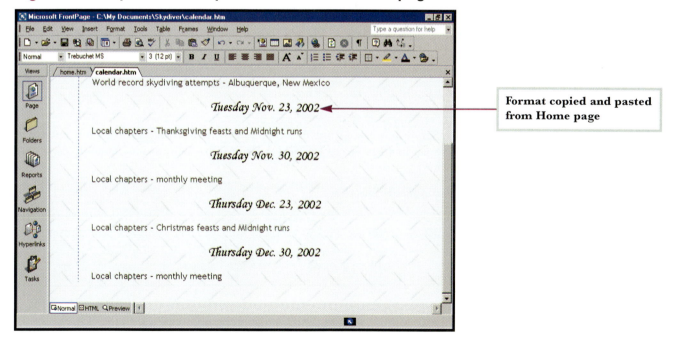

Format copied and pasted from Home page

Practice

Use the Format Painter to copy the format from text on one Web page and paste it to another page in the Caddy Shop Web.

skill: Inserting a Hit Counter

concept

One fun element you can add to your Web site is a hit counter. A hit counter is an interactive tool that is used to track the number of visitors to your site. Web masters often use hit counters to maintain a record of how many hits a Web site receives over a certain period of time.

do it!

Add a hit counter to the Home page of the Skydiver Web.

1. Place the insertion point at the end of the word edge in the last line of text at the bottom of the Home page. Press the [Enter] key.

2. Type You are visitor number. Then, press the [Enter] key.

3. Click Insert on the Menu bar. Click the Web Component command. The Insert Web Component dialog box appears.

4. Click the Hit Counter option in the Component type list box. Various hit counter styles appear in the Choose a counter style list box.

5. Double-click the second style. The Hit Counter Properties dialog box appears, as shown in Figure 5-19. This dialog box displays various hit counter styles and enables you to specify the reset counter value and the number of digits you want to appear in the hit counter.

6. Leave the default values selected and click OK.

7. If you publish your Web with the Microsoft Personal Web Server or with a server that has FrontPage Server Extensions, it will look like Figure 5-20. You must publish your Web to a server that has FrontPage Server Extensions for your hit counter to be visible on the Internet.

8. Save and close the Home page.

more

The Microsoft Personal Web Server for Windows NT and Windows 95 can be downloaded from the Microsoft Web site. If you are using Windows 98, you can install it from your program CD-ROM. To install it, click Start and select the Run command. In the Open list box, type E:\add-ons\pws\setup.exe (where E is the letter of your CD-ROM drive).

Next, you will have to install the FrontPage Server Extensions onto the Personal Web Server. Close FrontPage. Click Start and select Programs. Select Microsoft Office Tools and click Server Extensions Administrator to open the Microsoft Management Console. Close the Tip of the Day. Click the plus signs in front of FrontPage Server Extensions and your computer name. If anything is listed in front of your computer name, right-click it and select Task. Click Remove Server Extensions. Leave the check on Preserve Meta information. Right-click your computer name and select New. Click Web to open the Server Extensions Configuration Wizard. If you are asked to choose, select Microsoft Personal Web Server and click Next. When you are asked for your SMTP server, either use your real information or enter the TCP/IP loop back address, 127.0.0.1. Complete the steps of the wizard and click Finish. Close the console and save the settings when prompted.

Open FrontPage. Open the File menu and open the Web. In the Folder name list box, type http://localhost. Click Open. You should now be on the Personal Web Server and have full functionality.

Figure 5-19 Hit Counter Properties dialog box

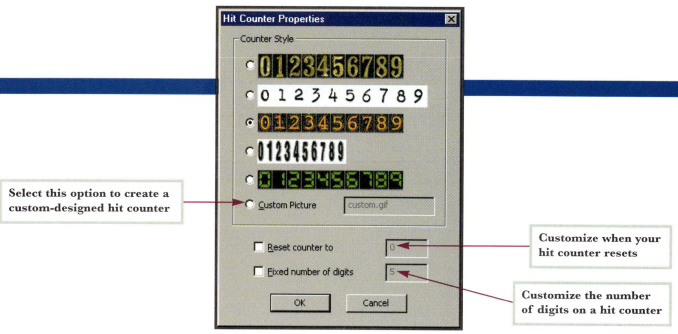

Select this option to create a custom-designed hit counter

Customize when your hit counter resets

Customize the number of digits on a hit counter

Figure 5-20 Hit counter on a Web page

Hit counter

Practice

Add a hit counter to the Home page in the Caddy Shop Web.

skill | Inserting a Time Stamp

concept

You may want the visitors of your Web site to know the date when you have last updated or modified the Web site or a particular Web page. For instance, when you have created a Web page that displays the latest news or information about something, you would want the users to know that the information they are going through, is the latest information for that particular product. For this, you can insert a time stamp in the Web page. A time stamp enables you to display either the time or the date, or both, that the page was created or last modified. A time stamp lets site visitors know whether the information on your site has changed since their last visit.

do it!

Insert a time stamp to the News page of the Skydiver Web.

1. Open the News page of the Skydiver Web.

2. Place the insertion point below the table and press [Enter]. Type This page was last edited on:.

3. Click Insert on the Menu bar and click the Date and Time command. The Date and Time dialog box opens.

4. Leave the Date this page was last edited option button selected.

5. Click the Date format list box and select the second last option.

6. Click the Time format list box and select the last option. The Date and Time dialog box should resemble Figure 5-21.

7. Click OK . A time stamp is inserted in the Web page (see Figure 5-22). This time stamp will tell the user when the Web page was last updated or edited.

8. Save and close the Web page.

more

The Date and Time dialog box enables you to display the date and time in various different formats. For instance, if you want to display the date in the mm/dd/yyyy format, you can select the second option from the Date format list box, which is 08/09/2002. If you want to display the name of the week day, name of the month, date, and the year, you can choose the third format from the Date format list box, which is Thursday, August 09, 2002. Similarly, if you want to display the time in hours:minutes:seconds AM/PM format, you can choose the second option from the Time format list box, which is 10:24:40 AM. If you want to display the time in the hours:minutes format, you can choose the third option from the Time format list box, which is 10:24. The date and time displayed in the Date and Time dialog box corresponds to the date and time set on your system.

Figure 5-21 Date and Time dialog box

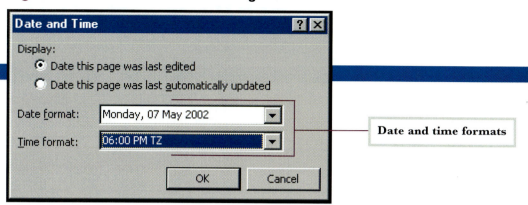

Figure 5-22 Date and time inserted in a Web page

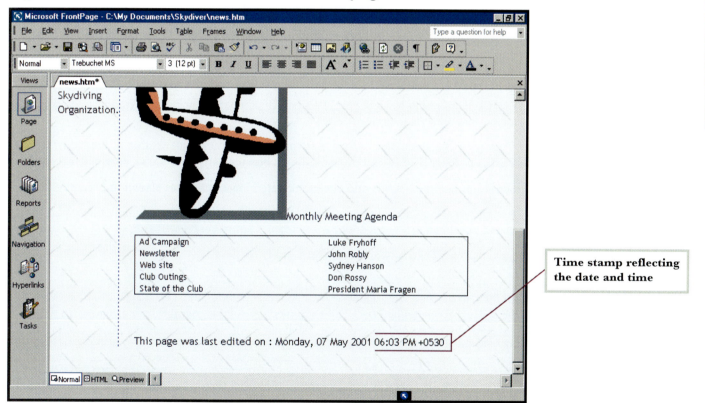

Practice

Insert a time stamp in the Home page of the Caddy Shop Web. Choose a location of your choice to display the date and time.

skill Creating a Search Form

concept

Visitors to your site may want to quickly access a specific piece of information. You can create a search form to help them find what they want. The user types a word or phrase into a text box, clicks the Search button, and a list of items that match the topic appears. The easiest way to create a search form is to create a new page based on the FrontPage Search Page template. You can customize the template with your own introductory text, copyright information, and button labels. Search forms are most useful on large Web sites where related information is found on many different pages.

do it!

Add a search form to your Home page so visitors can locate specific information in your Web.

1. Open the Home page of the Skydiver Web.
2. Click File on Menu bar and point to New. Then, click New Page or Web from the shortcut menu. The New Page or Web Task Pane appears.
3. Click the Page Templates hyperlink in the New form template section of the New Page or Web Task Pane. The Page Templates dialog box appears, with the General tab activated.
4. Scroll through the list box and click the Search Page option, as shown in Figure 5-23.
5. Accept the default settings and click [OK]. The Web page containing the search form opens, as shown in Figure 5-24.
6. Save the Web page as search form.htm and close the file.

more

A search form, like many FrontPage components, must be published with a FrontPage compliant server. You can publish your Web with the Personal Web Server to test it on your local computer. When the search form is published, users can type keywords and the server will return a list of pages. Each item on the list will be a hyperlink to a page containing a match to the keyword.

On the Search Results tab in the Search Form Properties dialog box, you can select the Display score check box to include the score for each match with the list of hyperlinks. A higher score will indicate a closer match.

You can make the one-line text box on a search form longer or shorter. Right-click the search form and click Search Form Properties on the shortcut menu. Change the number in the Width in characters text box. The visitor can still type as many characters as necessary. The extra characters will scroll off the left end of the text box, but the complete text will be submitted to the server.

Figure 5-23 Page Templates dialog box

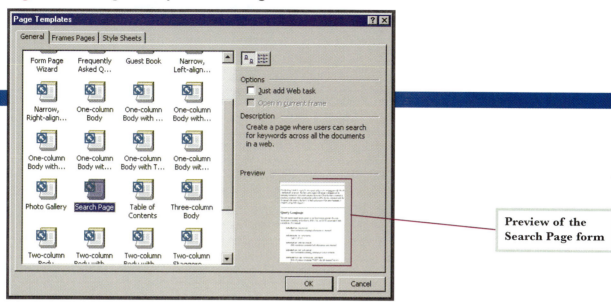

Figure 5-24 Search form

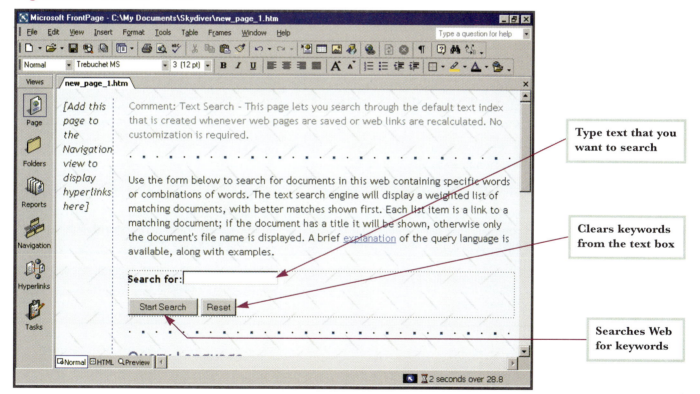

Practice

Add a search form to the Home page in your Caddy Shop Web.

skill: Formatting Web Page Transitions

concept

FrontPage also includes special effects you can add as one page disappears or another page loads. Page transitions will make your Web site resemble a PowerPoint slide show. These animations can add spark to your site. Attractive page transitions will impress your visitors as they enter and leave your Web pages.  FrontPage prohibits the use of page transition effects unless the Dynamic HTML option is active. To activate it, click Tools, click Page Options, and click the Compatibility tab in the Page Options dialog box to bring the tab forward. In the Available Technologies section near the bottom of the tab, make sure a check mark appears in the Dynamic HTML check box.

do it!

Format the page transitions on the Home page of the Skydiver page.

1. Click Format on the Menu bar. Click Page Transition on the Format menu. You may have to open the extended menu to find the Page Transitions command. The Page Transitions dialog box opens.

2. Click the Event list arrow. Click Page Exit to select it.

3. In the Duration (seconds) text box type 3. You must make the duration long enough that the effect is visible but short enough that it doesn't bore visitors. If you leave the Duration text box blank, FrontPage will used a default duration of 1 second.

4. In the Transition effect list box, click Wipe right to select it. The Page Transition dialog box should look like Figure 5-25.

5. Click OK. Save the Home page.

6. Switch to the Preview mode. You can view the page transition on the Preview tab only if you have Internet Explorer 4.0 or above installed on your computer. If you do not have IE 4.0 or above, preview the page in a Web browser that supports DHTML.

7. Click one of the hyperlinks in the table on the Home page. For three seconds the home page will slide to the right as the new page enters. This transition is displayed in Figure 5-26.

8. Save and close the Home page.

more

Some page transition effects are created using Dynamic HTML (DHTML). Unfortunately, Internet Explorer 4 and above and Netscape Navigator 4 and above use two different forms of DHTML. Special effects you create using FrontPage DHTML may not appear in Netscape Navigator. To add a page transition effect to a specific page element, select the page element and open the Format menu. Click the Dynamic HTML Effects command. On the DHTML toolbar, select Page load in the On list box. Select the animation effect and setting in the Apply and Effect list boxes.

Figure 5-25 Page Transitions dialog box

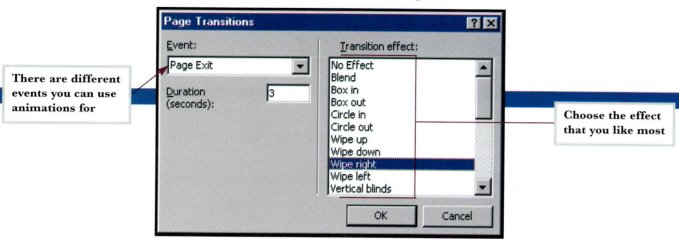

Figure 5-26 A Page transition in effect

Practice

Open the Home page in your Caddy Shop Web. Create a page transition for exiting pages in your Web. Make sure the duration is long enough that the effect will be visible.

skill Using Style Sheets

concept

The W3C or World Wide Web Consortium, which is responsible for the official HTML standards, developed the Cascading Style Sheet system. Cascading Style Sheets (CSS) enable you to position the Web page elements and design page layouts. A style sheet is a collection of style rules that allow you to precisely fine-tune how your pages will look. As older browsers become obsolete, Web designers believe CSS, which separates the HTML content of a page from its presentation, will become the standard in Web page design.

do it!

Use a style sheet to arrange items on the News page of the Skydiver Web.

1. Open the News page in the Skydiver Web.

2. Right-click the image on the page. Click Picture Properties on the shortcut menu. The Picture Properties dialog box opens. Access the General tab of the Picture Properties dialog box.

3. Click [Style...]. The Modify Style dialog box opens.

4. Click [Format ▼]. Click Position on the menu. The Position dialog box opens.

5. In the Wrapping style section, click the Right icon.

6. In the Positioning style section, click the Relative icon. The dialog box should look like Figure 5-27.

7. Click [OK] to close the Position dialog box. Click [OK] twice to close the Modify Style and Picture Properties dialog boxes.

8. The style sheet has rearranged the location of items on the Web page, as shown in Figure 5-28. In the past, you had to write the style sheet code. Using FrontPage 2002, you can apply absolute or relative positioning using the familiar Windows interface, and FrontPage will create the style sheet code for you.

9. Save the News page and close FrontPage.

more

There are two types of style sheet positioning: Relative and Absolute. When you use absolute positioning, you place an element at an exact location on the page. You designate the (x, y) coordinates of the top left corner of the element relative to the top left corner of the page (0, 0) to position the element. When you use absolute positioning, elements are not part of the text flow. Instead, they will appear in front of or behind the text flow.

Do not use absolute positioning with DHTML because you may not be able to control the results. Relative Positioning places elements at a fixed point within the text flow. The element is moved the designated distance down and to the right from where it would normally appear on the page, rather than from the edge of the page.

With relative positioning, the position of the element will adjust to the flow of the rest of the page. You can use style sheets to position any element on a Web page including tables lists, and graphics. Style sheet rules, including positioning, are not supported by older browser versions. For a cross-platform, cross-browser layout, use tables to position your page elements.

Text wrapping can also be modified with style sheets

Figure 5-27 Position dialog box

Specific coordinates and dimensions are used for absolute positioning

Figure 5-28 Items reconfigured with style sheets

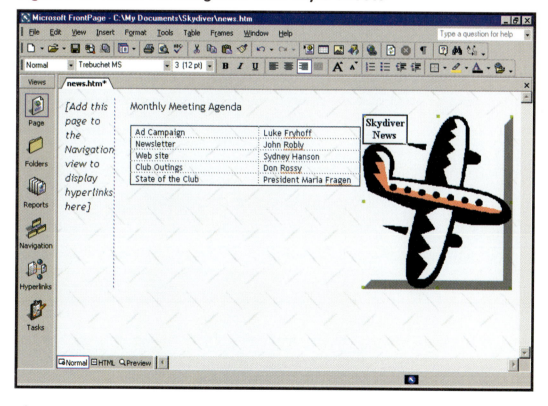

Practice

Use style sheets to modify the page where you inserted the money.wmf image earlier. Change the positioning, and the way the text is wrapped around it.

shortcuts

Function	Button/Mouse	Menu	Keyboard
Format Painter			
Undo last action		Click Edit, then click Undo	[Ctrl]+[Z]
Apply Font Color		Click Format and click Font	[Alt]+[O], [F]
Insert Component		Click Insert and then click Web Component	[Alt]+[I], [W]
Page Transition		Click Format, then click Page Transition	[Alt]+[O], [A]

A. Identify Key Features

Name the items indicated by callouts in Figure 5-29.

Figure 5-29 Using style sheets in FrontPage

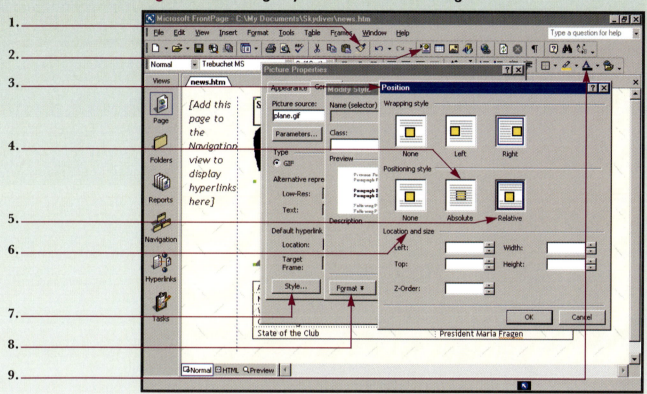

1. _____
2. _____
3. _____
4. _____
5. _____
6. _____
7. _____
8. _____
9. _____

B. Select the Best Answer

10. Allows you to format large blocks of text quickly and easily
11. One of two types of positioning with style sheets
12. This is used to create some page transition effects
13. Search form looks for these on a Web site
14. Tracks how many visitors have been to your Web site
15. A special effect that makes an image appear as if it is in a frame
16. The command buttons to bevel an image and place text over it are found here

a. Bevel
b. Dynamic HTML
c. Format Painter
d. Hit Counter
e. Keywords
f. Pictures toolbar
g. Relative

quiz (continued)

C. Complete the Statement

17. One of the advantages of importing text from another document rather than simply opening it in a Web page is:
    a. Imported text is automatically linked to the document it is imported from
    b. Imported text is automatically converted to the style of your Web
    c. Imported text is more fun than opening an office document
    d. Importing text takes up less memory

18. To import a Web page from the Internet you must first:
    a. Click Add File in the Import dialog box to open the Add File dialog box
    b. Click Open in the Import dialog box to open the Open File dialog box
    c. Click From Web in the Import dialog box to open the Import Web Wizard
    d. Click From Web on the File menu to open the From Web Wizard

19. When you click Modify in the Import dialog box:
    a. You will erase all the files you are importing
    b. The Edit URL dialog box opens
    c. All files are converted to HTML format
    d. All files are converted to JPEG format

20. Clicking the Bevel button on the Pictures toolbar multiple times will:
    a. Undo the bevel effect
    b. Open the Bevel dialog box
    c. Make no changes
    d. Add depth to the frame

21. The essential function of the Format Painter is to:
    a. Copy and paste the format of a block of text
    b. Copy and paste a block of text
    c. Move a block of text
    d. Erase a block of text

22. In order for hit counters and search forms to be visible on your Web pages, you must:
    a. Make sure the HTML code is correct
    b. Publish them to a server which is FrontPage compliant
    c. Make sure you have the Windows NT Personal Web Server
    d. Publish them to a Windows NT Server

23. The two types of style sheet positioning are:
    a. relational and fixed
    b. relative and absolute
    c. temporary and permanent
    d. none of the above

24. The Date and Time dialog box enables you to:
    a. display date and time in differing formats
    b. display the date in mm/dd/yyyy format
    c. display the time in hours:minutes format
    d. all of the above

25. When you import text into a FrontPage Web, the imported text:
    a. automatically requires reformatting with the Format Painter
    b. automatically converts to HTML
    c. both (a) and (b)
    d. none of the above

interactivity

Build Your Skills

1. Import text to your Web site:

    a. Open the Information page in the Water Taxi Web.

    b. Open the Import dialog box from the File menu.

    c. Open the Add File to Import List dialog box.

    d. Import the MS Word document, Water Taxi Calendar.doc, to your Web from the location of your Student Files.

    e. Use the Select File dialog box to insert the Water Taxi Calendar.doc on the Information page. Save your changes to the Information page.

2. Import Web pages to your Web site:

    a. Open the Import dialog box from the File menu of the Water Taxi Web.

    b. Open the Add File to Import List dialog box.

    c. Import the fpskill5.htm Web page to your Web from the location of your Student Files.

    d. Rename fpskill5.htm to faq.htm. Change the page title to FAQ. Add it to the Web hierarchy underneath the Information page.

3. Import an Image to your Web site:

    a. Open the Import dialog box from the File menu on the Information page of the Water Taxi Web.

    b. Open the Add File to Import List dialog box.

    c. Import the boats1.bmp image from the location of your Student Files. Insert the image on the Index page between the table and the slogan. Center align the picture.

    d. Save your changes to the Index page.

4. Use advanced formatting tools to format an image:

    a. Open the Index page in the Water Taxi Web.

    b. Click the plane.gif image to select it and open the Pictures toolbar.

    c. Click the Bevel button three times. If you don't like this effect, click the Undo button to reverse it.

    d. Save your changes.

interactivity (continued)

Build Your Skills (continued)

5. Increase the contrast and brightness of an image:

    a. With the Index page still open and the image still selected, click the More Contrast button.

    b. Click the More Brightness button several times. Then, use the Less Brightness button to get the desired effect.

    c. Resize the image in any way you want.

    d. Switch to Folders view and move all the images to the images folder.

6. Use the Format Painter to format text:

    a. Open the Index page in the Water Taxi Web and open the Calendar page in the Skydiver Web.

    b. Use the Format Painter to copy the format of the text in the first cell of the table on the Calendar page. Paste the format to all the hyperlinks on the Index page in the Water Taxi Web. Double-click the Format Painter button so you can easily format the text in both the table and the navigation bar in the left shared border.

    c. Save your changes.

7. Insert a hit counter:

    a. Use the Web Component button on the Standard toolbar to insert a hit counter on your Index page in the Water Taxi Web.

    b. In the Hit Counter Properties dialog box, select a style of hit counter, how many digits will be on the hit counter, and when it will reset.

    c. If you have installed the Microsoft Personal Web Server, publish this Web to test the hit counter and save the changes.

8. Create a search form:

    a. Create a search form using the Search Form wizard.

    b. Accept the default settings.

    c. If you have installed the Microsoft Personal Web Server, publish this Web to test the search form.

    d. Save the form as Search.htm.

9. Apply the page transition:

    a. Open the Page Transitions dialog box using the Format menu.

    b. Select Page Exit in the Event list. Type 3 for the duration. Select your own transition effect.

    c. Preview the transition to make sure it works correctly.

    d. Save your changes.

interactivity

Problem Solving Exercises

1. Create a new Web and name it as River Rafting. Create two Web pages, Index and Home. Use style sheets to arrange the elements on your pages. Open the Index page. Insert a table. Use the Table Properties dialog box to access the Position dialog box. Use relative positioning to position the elements on your page. Regardless of the changes you make to the page above or below them, the layout of the positioned elements will stay the same.

2. Use your advanced formatting skills to format all the pages in the River Rafting Web site. First, find and insert a clip art image related to river rafting. Bevel the image. Click the Bevel button several times to add depth to the frame. If you don't like it, use the Undo command. Place the text River rafting is fun, over the image. Locate a block of text with character formatting you like, and use the Format Painter to copy the formatting to a block of text on the Index page. Save this page as rafting.htm Create a Search form on the Index page. If you have installed the Microsoft Personal Web Server, publish the Web locally to show your friends. Save all your changes.

3. Use some of the advanced formatting techniques you just learned on your personal Web site. Begin by adding a hit counter to your Index page. Remember to choose a hit counter from the Hit Counter Properties dialog box that fits with the general theme and style of your Web. Some hit counters may not look good with the colors you may have chosen. If you have many pages in your Web, add a search form to help visitors find information on your site.

4. Use the Page Transition command to format the page transitions for your Web. Either choose an effect that can be viewed by multiple browsers or one that fits your target audience. Do not create an effect that does not fit the style and theme of your Web. For example, a Web site dealing with a serious topic should not have frivolous effects. On the other hand, if your Web is geared towards adventure sports, choose an effect that will impress users.

Modifying Tables

As you have seen, tables can be easily added to Web pages and are perfect for organizing and presenting information in a visually attractive and organized way. Innovative Web designers have learned to use tables to expand the page layout possibilities. You can modify, format and integrate text and images in tables to create sophisticated Web pages.

Before you can design novel page layouts using tables, you must learn some basic tasks. You need to know how to draw a table directly onto your Web page. Then you can use the menu commands or the new Tables toolbar to adjust and format it to meet your specifications. You can insert rows or columns to add information to your table, delete unnecessary cells, divide cells in half, or combine selected cells and merge them into a single cell.

You can also create special borderless cells that extend the entire width of a table. These cells, called captions, can provide a heading for your table or an instructive note at the bottom of a table. Captions share the background color you have applied to your table and are generally used to provide a descriptive title. A caption can tell visitors to your site how to use the table and the data it contains.

You can also convert the text you have already composed and formatted, into a table. Tables give structure to an existing page. You can then split or merge cells, equalize the width and height of selected rows or columns, or change the size of certain cells to design a truly innovative page. You can also remove a table format and convert a table back to text if it will improve your page design.

skills

- Deleting Table Rows and Columns
- Drawing Table Rows and Columns
- Resizing Table Cells
- Merging Table Cells
- Converting Text into a Table
- Inserting Captions

Lesson Goal:

In this lesson, you will learn to draw and delete rows and columns, resize and merge table cells, convert text into a table, and insert captions.

skill: Deleting Table Rows and Columns

concept

You may have to modify a table after it has been created. One way to modify a table is to delete rows and columns. You can delete rows and columns to delete information from a table, save space, or enhance the appearance of your Web pages.

do it!

Delete a row from the table on the Home page in the Skydiver Web.

1. Open the Home page of the Skydiver Web in FrontPage. Scroll down until the table is visible.

2. Move the pointer over the left border of the table, so it becomes a right-pointing selection arrow ➡ pointing to the second row of the table.

3. Click to select the second row. Your table should look like the one in Figure 6-1.

4. Click Table on the Menu bar.

5. Click Delete Cells on the Table menu.

6. The cells are deleted, as shown in Figure 6-2.

7. Click the Undo button. You can also use the Delete Cells button on the Tables toolbar to delete a single cell. First, select the cell using the Cell command on the Select submenu and then click the Delete Cells button.

8. Save the Home page.

more

To delete a column rather than a row, move the pointer over the top border of the table until it becomes a down-pointing selection arrow ⬇. Make sure it is pointing at the column you want to delete. Click to select the column, then click Delete Cells on the Table menu, as you learned earlier. You can also add and delete single cells from your table. This can produce an unusual visual effect for data that is not strictly tabular in nature. Above or below the single cell there will be an odd-looking blank space that is neither a cell nor available space. By default, cells are added to the right of a left-aligned table and to the left of a right-aligned table. To insert a single cell in a left or center-aligned table, click in the cell that you want to be on the left of the new cell. Open the Table menu, select Insert and click the Cell command.

Figure 6-1 A selected table row

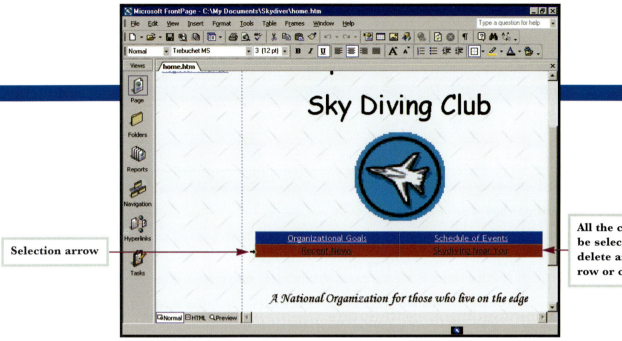

Selection arrow

All the cells must be selected to delete an entire row or column

Figure 6-2 A table after a row is deleted

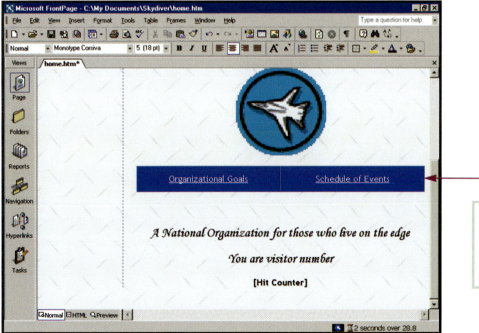

The space and alignment on the page is altered by the deletion of rows and columns

Practice

Delete the right column of the table on the Home page in the Caddy Shop Web. When you have finished, undo the action and save the page.

skill: Drawing Tables and Columns

concept

You can also customize tables by drawing rows and columns. Drawing rows and columns in a table enables you to create uneven spacing in your tables. You can use the Draw Table pencil and the Eraser tool to experiment with unusual page layout designs.

do it!

Expand the table on the Home page of the Skydiver Web to include enough cells to accommodate links for the rest of the pages in the Web.

1. Scroll down until the table is visible in the Home page.

2. Click View, point to Toolbars and click Tables. The Tables toolbar opens. You may find the tools on the Tables toolbar, displayed in two rows.

3. Using the horizontal resizing arrow, ↔, drag the toolbar to the left side, so that it resembles Figure 6-3.

4. Click the Draw Table button. The pointer has turned into a pencil.

5. Move the pointer near the top border of the table, at the end of the words Organizational Goals.

6. Drag down until you reach the bottom of the table. A dotted line appears to display where the new cell borders will be. This process is shown in Figure 6-4.

7. The column that existed before is moved to the left of the new column.

8. Repeat the same procedure with the column on the far right of the table. Your table should now look like the one in Figure 6-5.

9. Close the Tables toolbar and save the changes to the Home page.

more

To deactivate the Draw Table function, click the Draw Table button on the Tables toolbar. The pointer will return to normal. The Eraser button will activate the eraser tool, which you can use to remove any unwanted borders between cells. You can also use the Draw Table feature to create a table from the beginning. Simply drag the pointer to create a table, which has the dimensions you want. This will simply create a large table with one cell. Follow the steps outlined above to add cells to the table.

To draw a row in a table, draw a line where you want the cell border to be, vertically rather than horizontally. Clicking the Insert Rows button and Insert Columns button on the Tables toolbar automatically inserts rows and columns evenly. Use one of these commands if you want all the cells to have an equal amount of space. To automatically fit tables and rows in relation to one another after you have drawn them, use the AutoFit to Contents button on the Tables toolbar.

Figure 6-3 Tables toolbar

- Draw Table & Eraser buttons
- Insert Rows, Insert Columns, & Delete Cells buttons
- Merge Cells & Split Cells buttons
- Align Top, Center Vertically, & Align Bottom buttons
- Distribute Rows Evenly, Distribute Columns Evenly, & AutoFit to Contents buttons
- Fill Color, Table AutoFormat Combo, & Table AutoFormat buttons
- Fill Down & Fill Right buttons

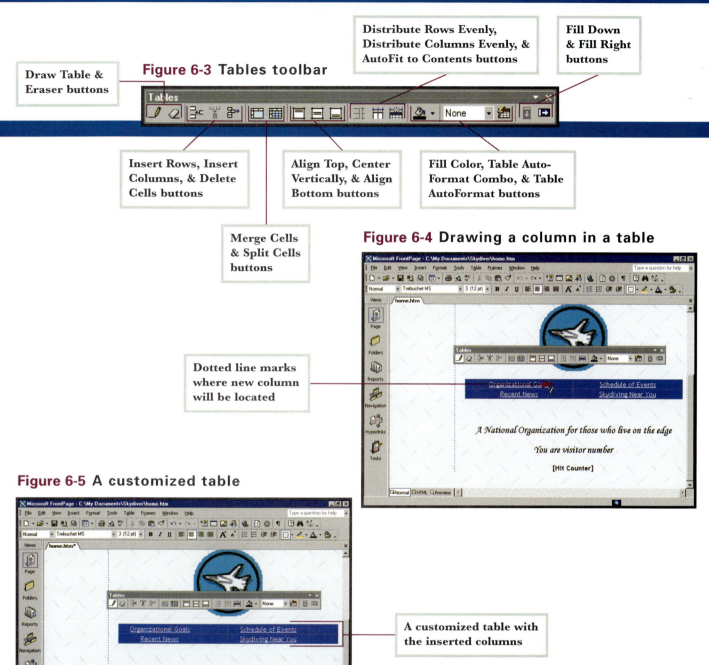

Figure 6-4 Drawing a column in a table

Dotted line marks where new column will be located

Figure 6-5 A customized table

A customized table with the inserted columns

Practice

Add a row to the table on the Home page in the Caddy Shop Web. Make the new row border run through the top row of the table. Save your changes to the Home page.

skill: Resizing Table Cells

concept

As you learned earlier, cells automatically expand as you add content. If you want cells to occupy a certain percentage of the table, you can define the size of your cells. You can specify how many rows or columns a cell will span. You can also set the width and height of cells in pixels or as a percentage of the table. These are excellent tools for emphasizing or de-emphasizing certain cells in a table.

do it!

Resize the cells in the table on the Home page.

1. Right-click in the cell that contains the words Organizational Goals. Click Cell Properties on the shortcut menu that opens. This opens the Cell Properties dialog box.
2. In the Columns spanned spin box, click the up arrow once to change the number to 2. The selected cell will now span 2 columns instead of one.
3. In the Rows spanned spin box, click the up arrow button once. This will change the number in the text box to 2.
4. Double-click in the text box under the Specify width check box to select its contents.
5. Type 25. This will increase the width of the cell. The Cell Properties dialog box should resemble Figure 6-6. Leave the default settings selected.
6. Click OK.
7. Save the changes to your Home page. Your table should look like the one in Figure 6-7. To even out the available space between rows or columns, use the Distribute Rows Evenly button and Distribute Columns Evenly button on the Tables toolbar. To reopen the Tables toolbar, open the View menu, point to Toolbar and click Tables.
8. Save the Home page.

more

You can also use pixels to specify the cell width. Click the In pixels option button next to the Specify width: text box. This allows you the maximum control over the width of the cell. Pixels are units that are used to form images. They are the smallest units of a video display such as the display on a computer monitor. Specifying a measurement in pixels specifies the area an object will occupy on your computer display.

If you size a cell in pixels, the cell size will not change regardless of the size of the table. If you set the width and height of a cell as a percentage of the overall table, the cell size will change in accordance with the size of the table. If you would rather have the cells automatically size themselves depending on the content, remove the check from the Specify width check box.

To change the dimensions of the entire table, right-click the cells to open the Table Properties dialog box. If you set table size as a percentage of page size, the table dimensions will change according to the size of the browser window. If you set the width and height in pixels, the size of the table will not change with the page size.

Figure 6-6 Cell Properties dialog box

Specify the dimensions of a cell by making it span multiple rows or columns

Resized width of a table cell

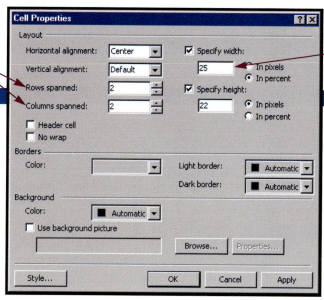

Figure 6-7 A resized table cell

Cell has more than doubled in size by spanning 2 rows and 2 columns

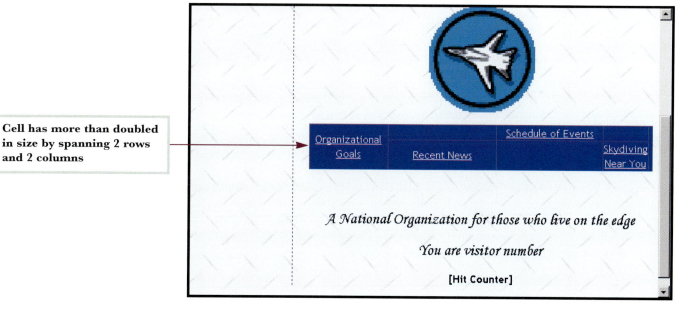

Practice

Select one cell from the table on the Home page in the Caddy Shop Web. Use the Cell Properties dialog box to manipulate the size of that cell. Once you have found a size you like, save the changes.

skill | Merging Table Cells

concept

You can use the Merge Cells command to combine two or more adjacent cells. You can merge cells to create larger available spaces to insert graphics or simply to eliminate empty cells. You can merge several cells in one column and leave the cells in the other columns divided to create an attractive table design.

do it!

Merge cells in the table on your Home page.

1. Click in the cell that contains Recent News and drag the mouse pointer up so both the bottom and top cells are selected. Use the [Shift] key while dragging, if you are not able to select both the cells.

2. Click Table on the Menu bar.

3. Click Merge Cells on the Table menu. The cells are merged, as shown in Figure 6-8.

4. Follow the same procedure for the next two columns. When you are finished your table should look like the one in Figure 6-9. To organize your table more efficiently, you may want two blocks of text to share the same cell. Two cells that contain text can also be merged.

5. Save the changes you made to the Home page and close the page.

more

You can also use the Tables toolbar to merge cells. Select the cells you want to merge just as you did in the exercise. Then click the Merge Cells button on the Tables toolbar.

There is also a command on the Tables toolbar that allows you to split cells rather than merge them. Splitting the cells divides single cells into multiple cells. You can split cells into multiple rows or columns. Select the cell(s) in the table you want to split. Click the Split Cells button on the Tables toolbar. This opens the Split Cells dialog box, shown in Figure 6-10. Choose whether to split the cells into rows or columns. Use the Number of columns spin box to set the number of times to split the cell and click OK.

Figure 6-8 Two cells merged into one

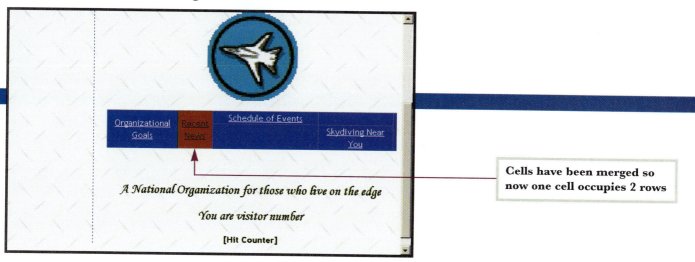

Cells have been merged so now one cell occupies 2 rows

Figure 6-9 Merging cells in a table

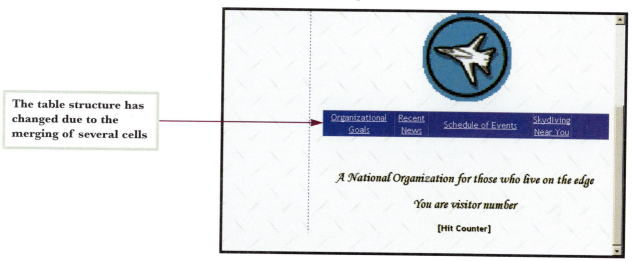

The table structure has changed due to the merging of several cells

Figure 6-10 Split Cells dialog box

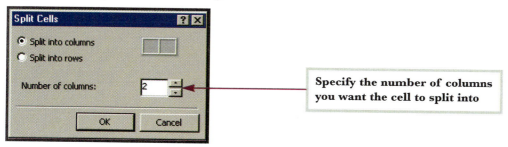

Specify the number of columns you want the cell to split into

Practice

Merge the cells that contain text with the ones next to them that are empty, on the Home page in the Caddy Shop Web.

skill: Converting Text into a Table

concept

You can also convert text you have already inserted and formatted, into a table. The text must be delimited or separated using characters such as commas and paragraph markers. FrontPage will format the table so that all the text fits properly. You can use this feature to create interesting page layouts including one-celled tables that contain various blocks of text on a page.

do it!

Convert the text on the Calendar page into a table.

1. Open the Calendar page in the Skydiver Web.
2. Click at the top of the page and drag down the mouse pointer until all the text is selected.
3. Click Table on the Menu bar.
4. Point to Convert on the Table menu.
5. Click Text To Table on the submenu that appears.
6. The Convert Text To Table dialog box opens.
7. Click the Commas option button to select it, as shown in Figure 6-11. This will specify how your table is organized.
8. Click [OK].
9. The text is converted into a table. Separate cells are created at each comma. Your table should now look like the one in Figure 6-12.  To create a one-celled table, click the None (text in single cell) option button in the Convert Text To Table dialog box.
10. Save your changes to the Calendar page and close the page.

more

You can also convert a table to text. Click anywhere in the table and open the Table menu. Move the pointer over Convert and click Table To Text on the submenu. You can perform this procedure on any table or use it to reverse a text-to-table conversion.

HTML does not directly support tab characters, so you might run into problems if you use them as your text delimiter. If your text does not contain separator characters, you will have to type them in where you want to divide your text into columns. When you use any delimiter other than paragraph to separate the text, a new column is created at each separator character and the paragraph markers automatically signal the end of each row. If you separate the text at each paragraph, a new row will be created at each paragraph marker and there will be only one column.

Figure 6-11 Convert Text To Table dialog box

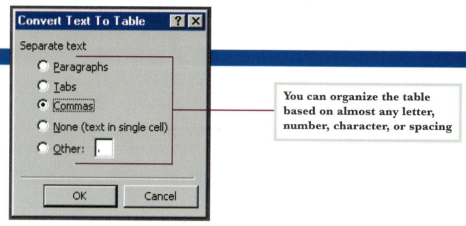

You can organize the table based on almost any letter, number, character, or spacing

Figure 6-12 Text converted into a table

Monday Nov. 1	2002
Annual National Skydiving Conference - New Paltz	N.Y.
Thursday Nov. 18	2002
World record skydiving attempts - Albuquerque	New Mexico
Tuesday Nov. 23	2002
Local chapters - Thanksgiving feasts and Midnight runs	
Tuesday Nov. 30	2002
Local chapters - monthly meeting	
Thursday Dec. 23	2002
Local chapters - Christmas feasts and Midnight runs	
Thursday Dec. 30	2002
Local chapters - monthly meeting	

A new column has been created at each comma and a new row at each paragraph marker

Practice

In Lesson 5, you inserted text at the bottom of the Home page in the Caddy Shop Web. Convert this text into a table. Use whichever setting will make the table most attractive and organized. Save your changes once you are satisfied.

skill Inserting Captions

concept

You can use captions, which are borderless cells, to add a descriptive title to your table. Captions can also be used to explain the relevance of certain data, the contents of the table or to provide instructions on how to use the table. You can use them to add a disclaimer or simply to leave a message for your visitors.

do it!

Add a caption to a table to explain its contents.

1. Open the Home page in the Skydiver Web. Scroll down until the table is visible.
2. Click anywhere inside the table.
3. Click Table on the Menu bar.
4. Point to Insert on the Table menu.
5. Click Caption on the Insert submenu.
6. This process is displayed in Figure 6-13.
7. Type Click on a link to read more information about skydiving and the Speed Demons National Skydiving Organization. Your table should resemble the table in Figure 6-14.
8. Save the changes to your Home page.
9. Close the Home page and FrontPage.

more

A caption can be displayed above or below a table and can be formatted just like any other text. To place the caption below the table, right-click the caption and select the Caption Properties command on the shortcut menu. The Caption Properties dialog box opens. Click the Bottom of table option button, as shown in Figure 6-15. Click OK. To change the alignment of a caption, select the caption and click either the Align Right button or Align Left button on the Formatting toolbar. To quickly select a lengthy caption to apply formatting changes, press the [Alt] key and click the caption. The entire caption will be selected.

Figure 6-13 Inserting a caption on top of a table

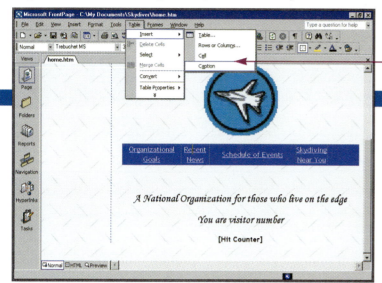

Figure 6-14 A caption for a table

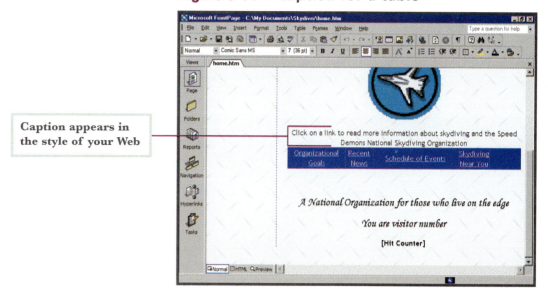

Figure 6-15 Caption Properties dialog box

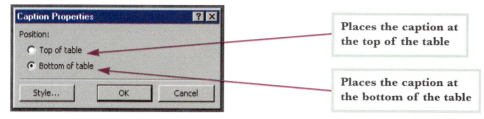

Practice

Add a caption to the first table on the Home page in the Caddy Shop Web. Position the caption at the bottom of the table. Make sure the caption accurately describes the information contained in the table.

shortcuts

Function	Button/Mouse	Menu	Keyboard
Draw Table		Click Table, then click Draw Table	[Alt]+[A], [I], [T]
Erase			
Insert Rows		Click Table, then move pointer over Insert, then click Rows or Columns	[Alt]+[A], [I], [N]
Insert Columns		Click Table, then move pointer over Insert, then click Rows or Columns	[Alt]+[A], [I], [N]
Delete Cells		Click Table, then click Delete Cells	[Alt]+[A], [D]
Merge Cells		Click Table, then click Merge Cells	[Alt]+[A], [M]
Split Cells		Click Table, then click Split Cells	[Alt]+[A], [P]
Distribute Rows Evenly		Click Table, then click Distribute Rows Evenly	[Alt]+[A], [N]
Distribute Columns Evenly		Click Table, then click Distribute Columns Evenly	[Alt]+[A], [Y]
AutoFit to Contents		Click Table, then click AutoFit to Contents	[Alt]+[A], [F]
Undo		Click Edit, then click Undo	[Ctrl]+[Z]

A. Identify Key Features

Name the items indicated by callouts in Figure 6-16.

1. _____
2. _____
3. _____
4. _____
5. _____
6. _____
7. _____
8. _____
9. _____

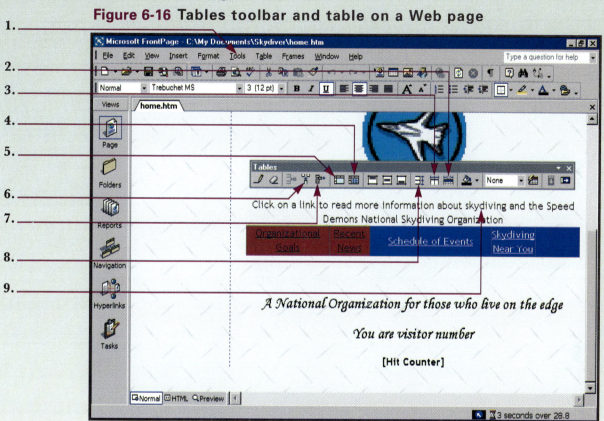

Figure 6-16 Tables toolbar and table on a Web page

B. Select the Best Answer

10. Many commands necessary to draw and modify a table appear here
11. Use this to resize a cell in your table
12. This feature allows you to leave visitors a message about your table
13. This command breaks a cell into two equal cells
14. This command combines two adjacent cells
15. A feature used to separate text in a table by paragraphs, tabs, or commas, etc.

a. Merge Cells
b. Split Cells
c. Tables Toolbar
d. Caption
e. Cell Properties dialog box
f. Convert Text to Table dialog box

quiz (continued)

C. Complete the Statement

16. The first thing to do to delete a column or a row is:
    a. Click Table on the Menu bar
    b. Click Delete Cells on the Table menu
    c. Select the cells you want to delete
    d. Click the Undo button

17. When you use the Draw Table command to create a new table, the new table will have:
    a. 1 cell
    b. 2 cells
    c. 3 cells
    d. 4 cells

18. Rather than specifying the dimensions of a table using percentage, you can use:
    a. Inches
    b. Thumbnail
    c. Picas
    d. Pixels

19. A pixel is:
    a. A type of table that is created using the Draw Table command
    b. A computer display
    c. A unit of measurement that is the smallest unit of a video display
    d. The width of a cell

20. You can only merge cells if:
    a. The cells are not next to each other
    b. You only select one cell
    c. You select cells that are next to each other
    d. You select cells from different tables

21. The Split Cells command:
    a. Combines cells that are next to each other
    b. Divides a cell into multiple cells
    c. Cannot be used unless you buy a special plug-in
    d. Is not very useful

22. Converting text into a table and converting a table into text:
    a. Is simple using the Convert submenu on the Table menu
    b. Are both impossible to do
    c. Are only useful in other MS Office programs
    d. Should only be used in emergencies

23. The text used to create a caption:
    a. Must be imported from somewhere else
    b. Cannot be formatted after it is inserted
    c. Can only be a certain length
    d. Can be formatted just like any other text

24. Modifying table format includes all of the following except:
    a. Deleting rows or columns
    b. Using the AutoFit to Contents button
    c. Resizing cells
    d. Changing font color

25. The Cell Properties dialog box contains all of the following sections except:
    a. Cell Features
    b. Layout
    c. Borders
    d. Background

Build Your Skills

1. Delete table rows and columns:

    a. Open the Fees page in the Water Taxi Web.

    b. Delete the first row from the table.

    c. Undo the previous action.

2. Draw a table row and column:

    a. On the Fees page, draw two columns at the far right of the table.

    b. Draw a row at the bottom of the table.

    c. Save your changes to the Fees page.

3. Resize table cells:

    a. On the Fees page, select one cell in the table.

    b. Resize that cell so it takes up one more row and one more column than it previously did. (Hint: Open the Cell Properties dialog box.)

    c. Save your changes to the Fees page.

4. Merge table cells:

    a. On the Fees page, locate a table cell that has text in it next to an empty cell.

    b. Select both the cells.

    c. Merge the two cells so they become one.

    d. Repeat steps (a) through (c) until all of the empty cells in the table are gone. You can use the Select Cell and Delete Cells commands to delete any extra cells.

    e. Close the Web page.

interactivity (continued)

Build Your Skills (continued)

5. Convert text to a table:

   a. Open the **Information** page. It contains the **Water Taxi Calendar** you inserted in the previous lesson. Select the text.

   b. Open the **Table** menu, select **Convert**, and click the **Text to Table** command.

   c. Choose **commas** as your delimiter. Click the **OK** button to close the **Convert Text to Table** dialog box.

   d. Format the text in the table. Adjust the cell and table properties in any way you choose.

   e. Close the Web page.

6. Insert a caption:

   a. Open the **Fees** page in the **Water Taxi** Web.

   b. Insert a caption on the table.

   c. The caption should read **Fares represent the one-way charge per person. Tipping is customary.**

   d. Format the caption text any way you choose. Save the changes to the Fees page.

Problem Solving Exercises

1. Create a Web named **Practice**. Insert the tables on each page of the Practice Web and then modify them. Begin with the **Index** page. First, use the **Draw Table** command to add two rows and columns to every table. For now these tables will have empty cells, but you will modify that later. Next, go to all the other pages except the Index page. Make the cell that contains the link to the Index page larger than all the other cells in each table. After you have resized the Index link cell, remove the empty cells in the tables. You can either merge cells or delete them, but make sure the cell with the link to the Index page remains larger than the other cells in the tables.

2. Next, create the **Feedback** page and type some text into it. Convert the text on this page into a table. For large amounts of text it is advisable that you do not use commas to separate the cells in the table. First separate the text at the paragraph markers. If this makes the table look awkward, use a different method. You may have to create more paragraphs to add rows and use another delimiter to separate the text into columns. When you have achieved a suitable table format, add a caption and insert hyperlinks to every page in the Web. Add a second caption to summarize the data in the table and inform visitors that the links will take them to the other pages in the Web.

Problem Solving (continued)

3. Now you will make the necessary modifications to the pages in your personal Web. If you have not created a table, convert a block text on one of the pages into a table. Even if you think a table is not necessary, just try it. A table will make your Web pages more organized and attractive. Also, as you learned in the previous chapter, you can use tables and style sheets to position elements on the Web. If you have any text that may be better served as a table, convert it now. You should also add a caption to any table you create. This can be invaluable to site visitors.

4. Finally, make any necessary modifications to the tables on your Web pages. You may need to delete cells to eliminate unnecessary space. You can also do this by merging cells. Take advantage of the versatility of the table format to organize your page layout. You can merge two adjacent cells containing data to make the information on your page tighter. You may decide to do the opposite and create more cells. If so, drawing a new column or row will give you the maximum control over the final product. You can also use the Split Cells command to divide any cells containing too much data in half.

Advanced Web Management and Design

skills

* Using Global Find and Replace
* Checking the Spelling of a Web
* Using Shared Borders
* Adding and Modifying Banners
* Using Dynamic HTML Effects
* Inserting an ActiveX Control
* Add a Photo Gallery
* Reaching a Target Audience
* Creating Frames Pages
* Saving Frames Pages
* Manipulating Frames Pages
* Creating No-Frames Pages

Since text usually carries the main content of Web pages, two Web management tools you will want to use fully are the global spelling check and global find and replace feature. You can use these tools to perform routine maintenance and to ensure that your content is accurate, well phrased, and professional.

Another management tool you should become familiar with is compatibility targeting. You can target your Web for compatibility with specific browsers, browser versions, or technologies. However, if you try to target the widest possible audience by making your Web compatible with older browsers, you may not be able to use some of the more advanced features of FrontPage, such as Dynamic HTML effects and ActiveX controls. As a result, you may want to set the compatibility of your Web to a higher level, such as browser versions 4 or above. At the same time, it would probably be wise to use advanced special effects sparingly so that users with older browsers can still enjoy your site.

FrontPage also includes tools for organizing the content of your Web. Two more layout and design options you can choose are shared borders and frames. You can add effects, text, or images that will be shared by all the pages in your Web. Frames allow visitors to view multiple documents in the same window. You are probably familiar with the frames pages used by most search engines. The search form generally appears in one frame and the results in another. Web designers often put a multimedia file, Java applet, or inline video clip in a separate frame. Even Web pages with borderless frames are very recognizable. You click a hyperlink and part of the page changes while the rest stays the same. Frames are most often used to construct a functional navigation scheme. Generally, a Table of Contents occupies the left frame and the target of each hyperlink opens in the center frame. You can also create a no-frames page for your visitors who cannot view frames.

Lesson Goal:

In this lesson you will be able to globally use the find and replace command in your Web, spelling check a Web, use shared borders use dynamic HTML effects, insert an ActiveX control, and add a Photo Gallery. You can also reach a target audience, create and save frame pages, manipulate frame pages and create no-frame pages.

skill Using Global Find and Replace

concept

Global find and replace simply means using the Find and Replace commands to change text throughout your Web. For example, you may have to change the company name, a product name, or an employee's name that appears on multiple pages in your Web. The global Find and Replace command makes it easy to perform wholesale text changes and is a great time-saving device. It prevents you from having to change every instance of the word individually.

do it!

Use the global Find and Replace feature to capitalize all instances of the word sky in your Web.

1. Open the Home page in the Skydiver Web, in FrontPage.
2. Click Edit on the Menu bar.
3. Click Replace on the Edit menu. You may have to access the extended menu to find the Replace command. The Find and Replace dialog box opens.
4. Click the All pages option button in the Find where section.
5. Select the Match case check box in the Search options section.
6. Type sky, in the Find what text box. Type SKY, in the Replace with text box. The Find and Replace dialog box should look like Figure 7-1. You can select the Up or Down options from the Direction section of the Find and Replace text box to specify the direction in which every page will be checked, before you select the All pages option. You can check from the top to the bottom or from the bottom to the top.
7. Click [Find In Web]. The Find and Replace dialog box displays a list of pages and the number of times the word occurs per page, as shown in Figure 7-2. Double-click the first page in the list box to begin editing.
8. Click [Replace All]. FrontPage makes the replacement. The Microsoft FrontPage dialog box appears that prompts you to continue with the replace operation.
9. Click [Yes]. The Web is edited and all the occurrences of sky are changed to SKY. Notice that in the status section, the red circles have been changed to yellow circles and has a word Edited displayed with them, as shown in Figure 7-3.
10. Close the Find and Replace dialog box.

Figure 7-1 Find and Replace dialog box

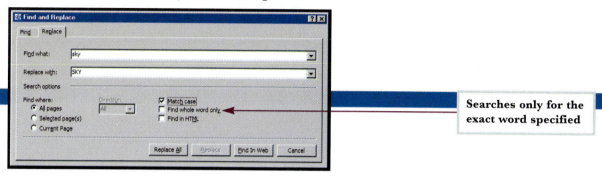

Searches only for the exact word specified

Matches uppercase and lowercase in selected text

Allows you to find and replace text in the HTML code

Red circles mark the pages that have not been edited

Figure 7-2 Pages with selected text are listed

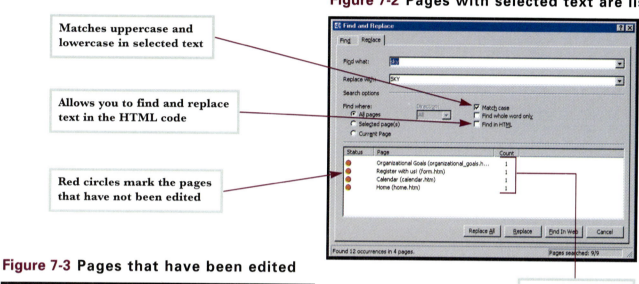

Specifies number of times selected text was located

Figure 7-3 Pages that have been edited

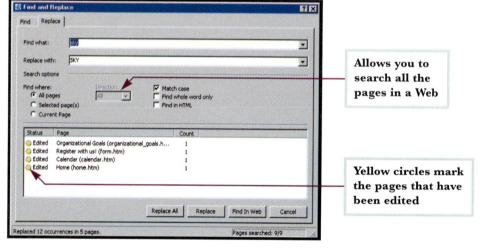

Allows you to search all the pages in a Web

Yellow circles mark the pages that have been edited

Practice

Use the Find and Replace command to make sure all instances of the word Caddy are capitalized. If FrontPage does not find any corrections that need to be made simply close the Find and Replace dialog box.

skill: Checking the Spelling of a Web

concept

When you work with many pages in a Web, checking the spellings one at a time is no longer time efficient. You can use FrontPage to run a spelling checker on an entire Web. Like the global Replace command, the global spelling checker will create a list of each page with an editing task. It will also display how many misspelled words were found on how many pages. You can easily view each page and correct the errors to ensure that your site looks more professional.

do it!

Check the spellings across the entire Skydiver Web and correct the errors.

1. Click the Navigation button  on the Views bar to open the Navigation structure.
2. Click the Spelling button on the Standard toolbar. The Spelling dialog box opens.
3. Make sure the Entire Web option button is selected, as shown in Figure 7-4.
4. Click Start. The Spelling dialog box displays the pages with misspellings, the misspelled words, and how many misspellings are on how many pages. This is shown in Figure 7-5.
5. Double-click the Calendar page. The Spelling dialog box changes to the dialog box displayed in Figure 7-6.
6. Click Add to add the word to the dictionary. The word will be added into the dictionary. Keep adding the words when you reach the end of the document.
7. At the end of the document, a Continue with the next page dialog box will open, which will prompt you to move to the next page. Click Next Page.
8. The next page is opened and the spelling checker takes you through the misspelled words. Check the spellings and add the words in a similar manner.
9. When you reach the end of the page, a dialog box appears prompting you to continue checking the spellings on the next page. Close the dialog box.
10. Close the Spelling dialog box.
11. Save the Home page.

more

Clicking Change on the Spellings dialog box will replace the selected word with the word that the spelling checker has suggested.

Clicking Add on the Spellings dialog box adds the selected word to the custom dictionary. This will ensure that the next time the word is used it will not be flagged.

You can click the Spelling button on the Standard toolbar in any view other than Page view to perform a global spelling check. After the spelling checker has compiled the list of errors, you can double-click any page to begin correcting spellings anywhere you want.

Figure 7-4 Spelling dialog box

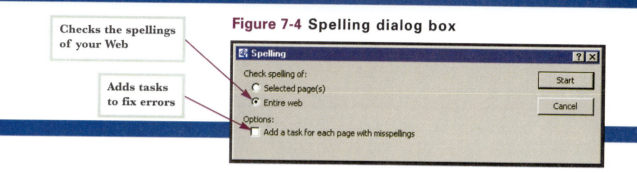

- Checks the spellings of your Web
- Adds tasks to fix errors

Figure 7-5 Search across Web is finished

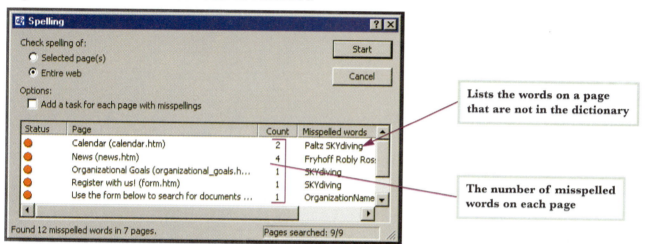

- Lists the words on a page that are not in the dictionary
- The number of misspelled words on each page

Figure 7-6 Fixing words not in dictionary

- Word that does not appear in dictionary
- The word in the dictionary that is the closest match to the misspelled word
- Suggests words to replace ones in the Web

Practice

Check the spellings in the Caddy Shop Web. Add any words that are not in the dictionary but you know are spelled correctly. Change any typos or misspelled words.

skill | Using Shared Borders

concept

The Shared Borders command enables you to add Navigation bars. You can even create other effects that are shared by all the pages in your Web. Any graphic, text, or HTML element can be placed in a shared border and appear on the top, bottom, or sides of every page in your Web. You can use shared borders to insert a company logo or slogan throughout your site.

do it!

Add text and page banners to the shared borders so that every page in the Skydiver Web will display them.

1. Click Format on the Menu bar and click the Shared Border command. The Shared Borders dialog box opens.

2. Select the Top check box. Then, click the Include navigation buttons check box under the Top check box. Clear the Include navigation buttons check box under the Left check box. Your dialog box should look like the one in Figure 7-7.

3. Click [OK]. A message box will warn you that changing the settings for the top or left shared borders will overwrite any content you have added. Click [Yes] to overwrite the shared borders. A navigation banner and hyperlinks are added to every page. Switch to another page to view the Navigation bar in the top shared border.

4. Return to the Home page. Right-click the text that says, Edit the properties for this Navigation bar to display hyperlinks here and click Link Bar Properties from the shortcut menu. The Link Bar Properties dialog box opens.

5. Click the Child pages under Home option button, as shown in Figure 7-8.

6. Click [OK]. Click anywhere outside the selection.

7. Delete the text, in the left shared border, that instructs you to replace the text with your own content.

8. Type Speed Demons: A National Skydiving Organization.

9. Your Home page should look like the one in Figure 7-9. The text you added will be visible on every page. When you use shared borders, you can only place navigation buttons on the left or top of the page, but you can manually add text hyperlinks to the bottom or right shared border.

10. Save the changes you made.

more

You can add graphics to the shared borders as easily as you added text in the above exercise. Place the insertion point inside the border to which you want to add the graphic. Insert the image just as you would anywhere else on the page. The image will be added to the shared border and will appear on every page in your Web.

Figure 7-7 Shared Borders dialog box

Figure 7-8 Link Bar Properties dialog box

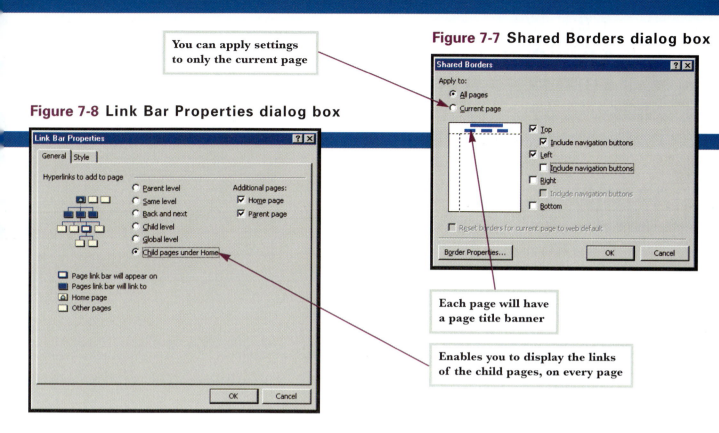

Figure 7-9 Banner and text in a shared border

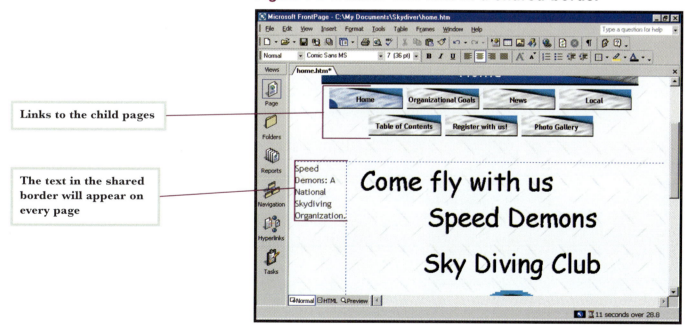

Practice

Add a banner to a shared border at the top of your Web pages in the Caddy Shop Web.

skill | Adding and Modifying Banners

concept

One commonly used component is a banner ad. Banner ads are slideshow style presentations usually used to advertise products. Companies can send images for a banner ad to a Web master who will post them on the site. You can also use the Banner Ad Manager to create a special effect that is attractive and fun. You can set the interval at which the images rotate and add transition effects to create a unique element for your site.

do it!

Use the Banner Ad Manager to make your Home page more exciting.

1. Place the insertion point in front of the banner that says Home and press [Enter]. Now, place the insertion point on the line above the banner.

2. Click Insert on the Menu bar and then click the Web Component command. The Insert Web Component dialog box appears.

3. Double-click the Banner Ad Manager option in the Choose an effect section. The Banner Ad Manager Properties dialog box appears.

4. In the Width text box, type 75, to make the banner 75 pixels wide. Double-click in the Height text box. Type 75, to select it as the height of the banner in pixels.

5. Leave the transition effect. Double-click in the Show each picture for (seconds) text box. Type 3.

6. In the Link to text box, type calendar.htm. If you were creating an advertisement, you would enter the URL of the company whose ad you were going to display.

7. Click [Add] next to the Pictures to display box. The Add Picture for Banner Ad dialog box opens.

8. Locate the folder where you have stored the student files. Click earth.jpg to select it, and click [Open]. The image is added to the Banner Ad Manager Properties dialog box.

9. Add Fish.jpg and Leopard.jpg, in the similar way, to the Banner Ad Manager Properties dialog box. When you are finished your dialog box should look like the one in Figure 7-10.

10. Click [OK].

11. Save your Home page.

12. To view your banner, open the Web page in a browser. The Web page will look like Figure 7-11.

You can set various properties to the banner ads that you create. Some of the banner ad properties are:

Height: This property enables you to set the height of the banner ad in pixels or percentage.

Width: This property enables you to set the width of the banner ad in pixels or percentage.

Transition effect: This property enables you to select the effect you want to use when the banner ad switches from one picture to another.

Show each picture for (seconds): This property enables you to specify (in seconds) how long to show each picture.

Link to: This property enables you to create a hyperlink from the banner ad. To change the size, transition effect, duration per picture, or hyperlink for a banner ad, right-click it and choose Banner Ad Manager Properties to open the Banner Ad Manager Properties dialog box.

Figure 7-10 Banner Ad Manager Properties dialog box

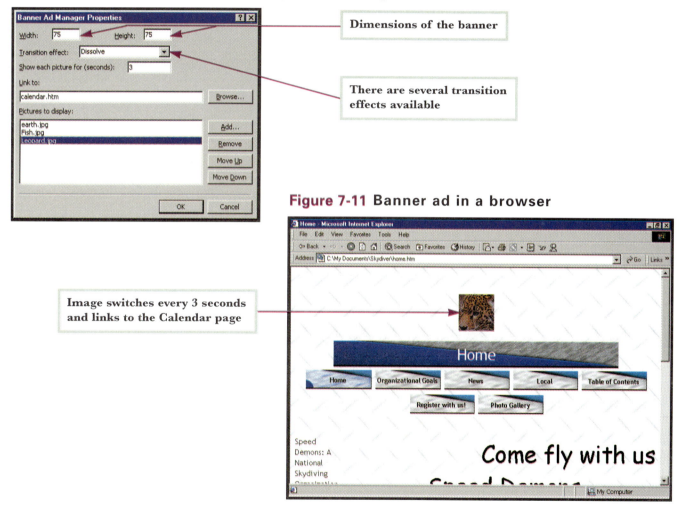

Figure 7-11 Banner ad in a browser

Practice

Put a banner at the bottom of the Home page in the Caddy Shop Web. Use the same images you used in the Do it steps. Change some settings so your banner is different than the one you created earlier.

skill Using Dynamic HTML Effects

concept

One of the newest advances in Internet technology is Dynamic HTML or DHTML. DHTML is used to add special motion effects to your Web pages. DHTML combines JavaScript, CSS, and internal browser technology to add spice to your Web pages. Using FrontPage, you can create vibrant animations for text or images with no knowledge of these programming codes.

do it!

Add DHTML effects to the Home page in the Skydiver Web to make it more lively.

1. Select the text that makes up the marquee, Come fly with us and the text Speed Demons on your Home page.

2. Click Format on the Menu bar.

3. Click Dynamic HTML Effects on the Format menu. You may have to access the extended menu to find the Dynamic HTML Effects command. The DHTML Effects toolbar appears.

4. Click the arrow next to the On list box. Click Page load from the list. The Apply list box becomes active.

5. Click the arrow next to the Apply list box. Click Fly in on the list.

6. Click the arrow next to the Effect list box. Microsoft has chosen not to label the Effect list box. However a ScreenTip identifies it as such. Click From top from the list (see Figure 7-12). Your Home page should now look like Figure 7-13.

7. Switch to Preview view to preview the page. The effect will look something like Figure 7-14. Notice that the text you animated is selected in Page view. To remove the selection, click the Highlight Dynamic HTML Effects button on the DHTML Effects toolbar.

8. Click View on the Menu bar, point to Toolbars, and click DHTML Effects. The DHTML Effects toolbar closes.

9. Save and close the Home page.

more

You can also use the DHTML Effects toolbar to remove an effect that you have added to a page. Simply click the text or graphic to which you applied the effect. Then, click Remove Effect on the DHTML Effects toolbar. Different effects are available when you select different text, objects, and elements on your Web page. To reopen the DHTML Effects toolbar, open the View menu and point to Toolbars, then click DHTML Effects on the submenu.

Figure 7-12 DHTML Effects toolbar

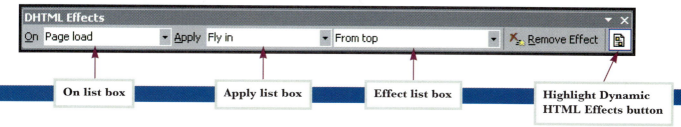

Figure 7-13 A DHTML effect applied to a Web page element

Figure 7-14 Previewing a DHTML effect

Practice

Create a DHTML effect on the caption of the table on the Home page in the Caddy Shop Web. Choose whatever settings you like. Save your changes and preview the page to make sure you like the effect.

skill: Inserting an ActiveX Control

concept

ActiveX controls are compact computer programs that you can embed in your Web pages. These controls cause something to happen in response to an action by the user. Some of the available interactive ActiveX controls are: a media player to run a video, a calculator, images that change when the visitor moves the pointer over them, a stock ticker, and an interactive calendar.

do it!

Insert an ActiveX interactive calendar in one of your Web pages.

1. Open the Calendar page in the Skydiver Web.
2. Scroll to the bottom of the page and place the insertion point at the bottom.
3. Press [Enter] twice.
4. Click Insert on the Menu bar and then click Web Component. The Insert Web Component dialog box opens.
5. Scroll down till the end of the Component type section and click the Advanced Controls option. Various controls appear in the Choose a control section.
6. Click ActiveX Control, as shown in Figure 7-15.
7. Click [Next >]. This changes the contents of the Insert Web Component dialog box. These contents are now specific to ActiveX controls.
8. Click Calendar Control 10.0 option in the Choose a control section, as shown in Figure 7-16. If your Office XP products are not yet activated with Microsoft, Calendar Control 9.0 instead of Calendar Control 10.0 may appear in the Choose a control section. This earlier version of Calendar Control will work, however, for completing this Skill.
9. Click [Finish]. To change the dimensions, colors, font, effects, or style of a control, right-click it and choose ActiveX Control Properties to open the ActiveX Control Properties dialog box.
10. Switch to the Preview view to preview the page. Your page should look like Figure 7-17.
11. Save the changes to the Calendar page and close it.

more

When you use ActiveX controls on a Web page, you can use many different programs along with it. Click [Customize...] in the Insert Web Component dialog box to open the Customize ActiveX Control List dialog box. This is a list of ActiveX programs you can use with the controls you insert on your pages. To be safe, do not customize your ActiveX controls unless you know the program you are selecting or have been instructed to do so.

To find more ActiveX controls to add to your Web pages, visit www.activex.com, or www.browserwatch.com/activex.html.

Figure 7-15 Insert Web Component

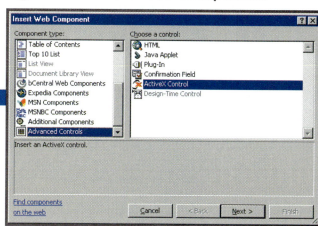

Figure 7-16 Choosing an ActiveX Control

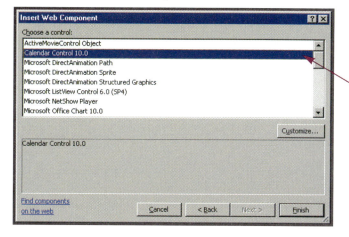

Inserts a calendar control in a Web page

Figure 7-17 Previewing an ActiveX Control

You can view any year from 1900 to 2100

You can view a different month using this list box

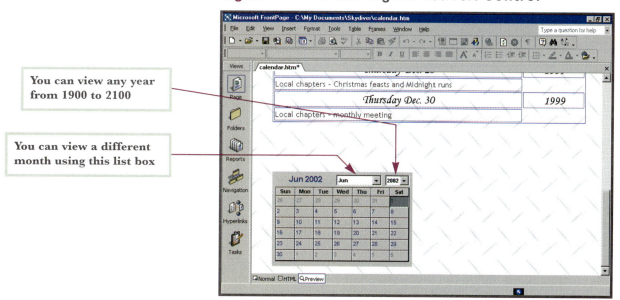

Practice

Insert an ActiveX calendar on the Home page in the Caddy Shop Web. If the download time of the document exceeds twenty seconds on a 28.8k modem, create a new calendar page and insert the control there instead.

Add a Photo Gallery

concept

Photo Gallery is a new feature in FrontPage 2002. Using the Photo Gallery feature you can create a Web page that contains a collection of photos arranged in a specific layout. FrontPage provides four different layouts in which you can arrange your photos, and if you are creating a photo album, each page can have a different layout. A photo album is a collection of two or more photo galleries linked together.

do it!

Add a photo gallery to a new Web page in the Skydiver Web.

1. Click the New button on the Standard toolbar to insert a new page.
2. Save the page as photo gallery.htm.
3. Switch to the Navigation view and drag the photo gallery.htm file from the Folder Options section under the Home page, in the Navigation structure.
4. Right-click the page you have just added, and click the Rename option from the shortcut menu.
5. Name the page as Photo Gallery. The Navigation structure should now look like Figure 7-18.
6. Switch back to the Page view.
7. Click Insert on the Menu bar and then click Web Components. The Insert Web Component dialog box opens.
8. Click Photo Gallery in the Component type section. Four kinds of photo gallery layout appear in the Choose a Photo Gallery Option section, as shown in Figure 7-19.
9. Double-click the third layout. The Photo Gallery Properties dialog box opens.
10. Click Add and then click Pictures from Files from the submenu. The File Open dialog box opens.
11. Navigate to the location where you have stored the student files and double-click the Photo Gallery folder to place it in the Look in list box.
12. Select all the images and click Open. The images appear in the list box on the Pictures tab of the Photo Gallery Properties dialog box.

(continued on FP 7.16)

Figure 7-18 New page added to the Navigation structure

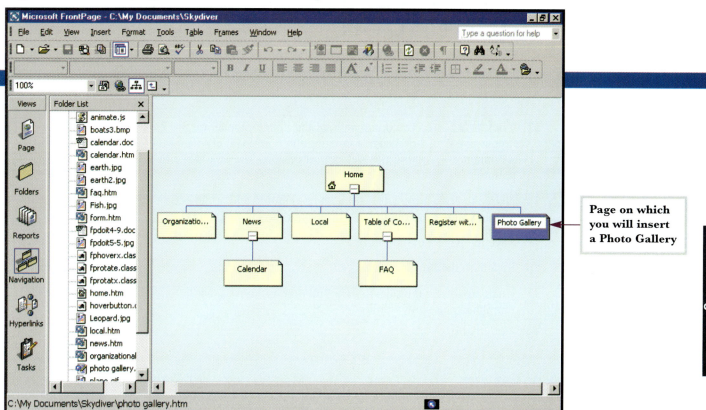

Figure 7-19 Different layouts of a Photo Gallery

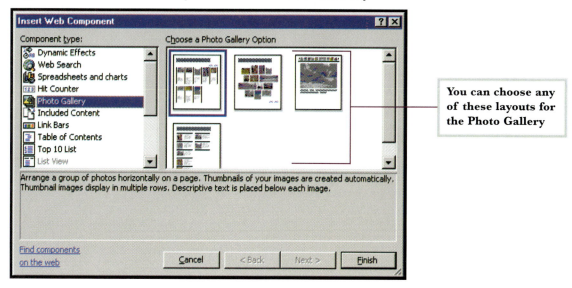

skill Add a Photo Gallery (continued)

13. Click [OK]. The thumbnails of the images appear on the Photo Gallery page, in the layout you had chosen while creating the Photo Gallery (see Figure 7-20). A thumbnail is a miniature version of the picture and contains the link to the full-size version of the picture.

14. Notice the two arrows present at the beginning and at the end of thumbnails. These arrows enable you to horizontally scroll through the Photo Gallery.

15. Save the page and the images.

16. Switch to the Preview view.

17. Click any of the thumbnails. The full-size version of that thumbnail appears below the thumbnails, as shown in Figure 7-21.

18. Close the Web page.

more

Once you have created a Photo Gallery in a Web page, you can change its layout. To change the layout of the Photo Gallery, double-click the Photo Gallery and access the Layout tab. Then choose the layout from the Choose a layout section. You can also specify the number of pictures in one row. However, if you have chosen the Slide Show layout or Mortgage Layout, then the option to choose the number of pictures per row will be disabled. You cannot specify number of pictures per row, in these layouts.

Figure 7-20 A Photo Gallery in a Web page

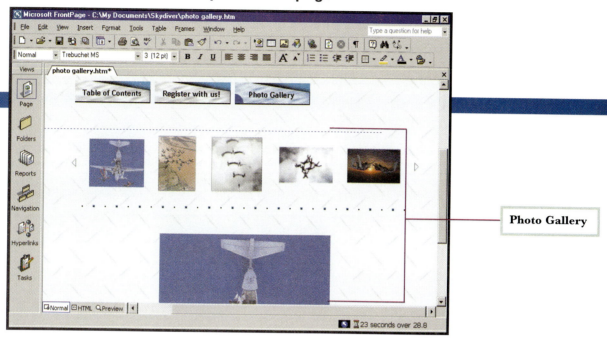

Figure 7-21 Previewing a full-size version of a thumbnail

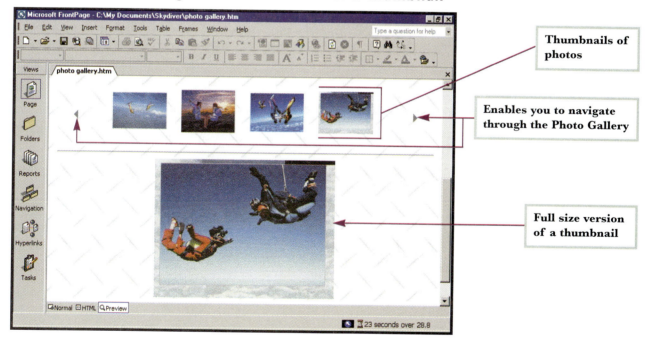

Practice

Add a Photo Gallery to a new page in the Caddy Shop Web. Use the student folder, Golf pics, to insert the pictures.

LESSON SEVEN Advanced Web Management and Design

skill: Reaching a Target Audience

concept

In order to maximize the number of people who will be able to view your Web site in its entirety, you can target your Web for compatibility with certain browsers and technologies. If you target your Web for older browser versions, commands for components not supported by those versions will no longer be available. You can choose settings for multiple browsers to ensure that your pages will display properly for all of your visitors.

do it!

Make your Web compatible with multiple browsers so it can be viewed by the maximum amount of people.

1. Open the Home page in the Skydiver Web.
2. Click Tools on the Menu bar.
3. Click Page Options on the Tools menu. The Page Options dialog box opens.
4. Click the Compatibility tab to select it and bring it to the front.
5. Click the arrow underneath the Browsers section. Click Both Internet Explorer and Navigator on the list. This will make your Web work with both Internet Explorer and Netscape Navigator. These are the two most popular browsers on the market today.
6. Click the Browser versions arrow. Click 4.0 browsers and later from the list. This will allow you to use some of the more advanced options available in FrontPage.
7. Leave the rest of the settings as they are. The dialog box should look like the one in Figure 7-22.
8. Click OK.
9. The dialog box closes and the options you selected are enabled. You will not be able to add any options that are not compatible with the settings you chose. When you select certain browsers, some technologies will be excluded. You can target specific technologies instead of browsers, but if you override the defaults for a specific browser or version, your page may not display properly for those visitors.
10. Save your changes.

more

As you select different browsers and different versions of those browsers, the available options will change. Many earlier browsers will not support Java, Frames, Dynamic HTML, and other more advanced options. If you are creating a simple page, it is not important that you select browsers that support these technologies. If you are creating a simple page with few special effects, you can target a wider audience. However, if you want to use many of the advanced components available in FrontPage, only Internet Explorer users will be able to fully view your site. For example, ActiveX controls are only supported by Internet Explorer 3.0 and above.

Figure 7-22 Page Options dialog box

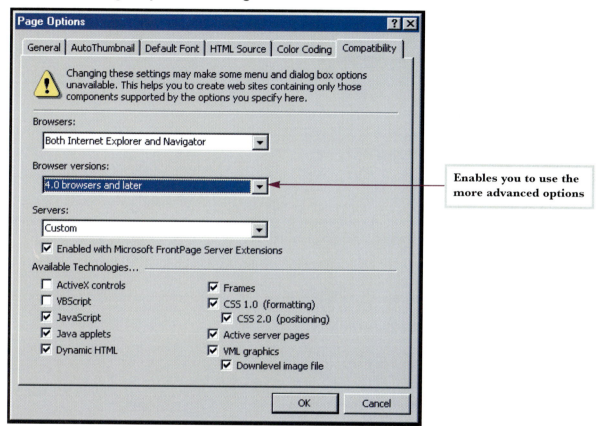

Practice

Create settings for browser compatibility for the Caddy Shop Web. Select Internet Explorer 4.0 and later as your compatible browser. Disable the Cascading Style Sheets and Frames options for your Web.

skill Creating Frames Pages

concept

A frames page is a Web page that divides the browser window into several different areas. Most frames pages use a layout with divisions on the top and left of the page. Generally, one or both of the smaller frames will contain navigation controls. When you click a hyperlink, the target page will open in the main, center frame. Frames can make your entire site accessible on a single screen.

do it!

Create a frames page in the Skydiver Web.

1. Click File on the Menu bar, point to New, and then click Page or Web. The New Page or Web Task Pane opens.

2. Click the Page Templates hyperlink. The Page Templates dialog box opens. Verify that the Frames Pages tab is available. If it isn't, close the dialog box, click Tools, click Page Options to open the Page Options dialog box, and click the Compatibility tab to bring it forward. In the Available Technologies section, add a check mark to the Frames check box, close the dialog box, and reopen the Page Templates dialog box.

3. Click the Frames Pages tab. Click the Banner and Contents icon, the first icon in the top left of the dialog box. Click [OK]. The frames page is created, as shown in Figure 7-23. There are many different arrangements for frames pages available in the Frames Pages tab. All frames pages will function the same way. They will simply use different layouts.

4. In the frame on the left, click [New Page]. A new page in the theme of the Web is created in the left frame.

5. In the center frame, click [Set Initial Page...]. In the Insert Hyperlink dialog box locate your Skydiver Web. Select the Home page. Click [OK].

6. Copy the text, Speed Demons, from the Home page.

7. In the top frame, click [New Page]. A new page in the theme of the Web is created in the top frame. Paste the text in the top frame.

8. Move the pointer over the border of the top frame until it turns into a vertical resizing arrow. Drag the border down until the words Speed Demons are visible. Center the text in the frame if necessary.

9. Place the insertion point in the left frame. Create hyperlinks to all eight pages in your Web so that your page looks like Figure 7-24.

more

The method outlined in the above exercise will guide you in creating frames pages. The purpose of a frames page is smooth navigation. Each hyperlink will open the corresponding page in the center frame while the frames on the left and top remain the same. The frame with the navigation controls will not change. You can also create a title, as in the exercise above, that will display no matter what page the visitor is viewing. Each frame can contain any HTML elements you can insert in a regular Web page. However, since frames are primarily used to construct a useful navigational scheme, if you overdo the design elements in the frame with the navigation controls it will detract from the function.

Although this exercise created a frames page using a page with shared borders applied, in general, if you use frames to design your page layout you should not use shared borders, particularly those with Navigation bars.

Figure 7-23 An empty frames page

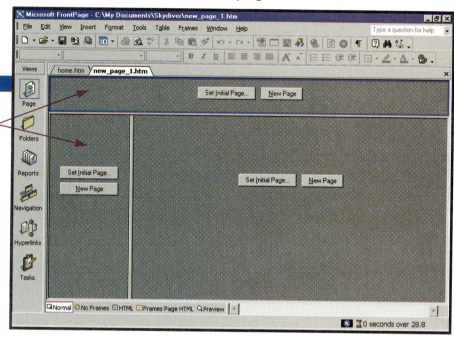

These frames will remain constant while the center frame changes

Figure 7-24 A complete frames page

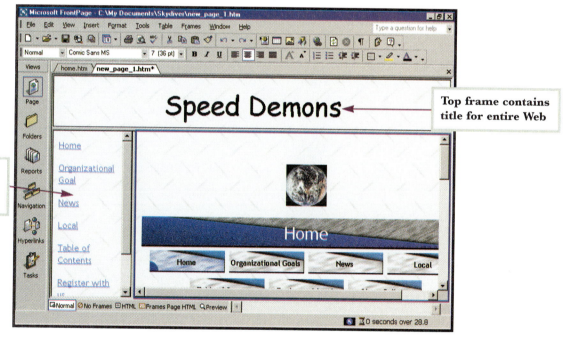

Top frame contains title for entire Web

Left frame contains navigation controls for the frames page

Practice

Create a frames page in the Caddy Shop Web. Set the center frame to the Home page. Create a new page on the top. Enter the words Caddy Shop in the top frame. Create a new page in the left frame. Create hyperlinks to the other pages in the Web.

skill | Saving Frames Pages

concept

When you save a frames page, you are actually saving the frames page, which contains the instructions for the layout and design of the page, and the rest of the frameset. The frameset includes all of the individual pages within the frames page. Any initial pages that have been saved previously will simply be saved with the whole, but any new pages will have to be saved individually.

do it!

Save the frameset, and the entire frames page in the Skydiver Web.

1. With the frames page still open, click File on the Menu bar.
2. Click Save on the File menu. The Save As dialog box opens with the top frame selected in a preview window, as shown in Figure 7-25.
3. Accept the default name for the top frame. Click [Save]. The top frame is saved.
4. The Save As dialog box opens again with the left frame selected. Change the file name to menu.htm and the page title to Menu. Click [Save].
5. The Save As dialog box opens one last time with the entire page selected in the preview window.
6. In the File name text box, type frame.htm, as the name for the page, as shown in Figure 7-26. Change the page title to Frames Page. Click [Save]. After you have saved your frames page for the first time, the Save As command will save the frames page as a whole. Any changes you have made to the individual frames will be saved in the corresponding frame file.
7. Switch to the Preview view. The Web page should look like Figure 7-27.
8. Click the hyperlink in the left frame that links to the Calendar page.
9. Include it in the Navigation structure.

more

Do not save the entire frames page as your Home page. Always save the frames page under a new and unique file name. If you save the frames page with the same name as another file in the Web, your page will not work. Rather than opening the original page, the hyperlink will target the entire frames page. Essentially you will have created a frames page within a frames page. For example, in the exercise above, if you had saved the frames page as home.htm replacing the original file, the entire frames page would open in the center frame.

Figure 7-25 Saving the top frame in Save As dialog box

Selected frame in preview is the frame currently being saved

Figure 7-26 Saving the entire page

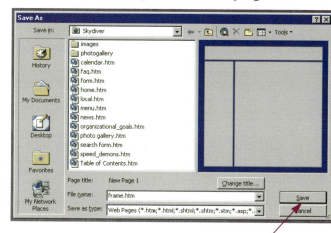

All the frames are selected and saved as one Web page

Figure 7-27 Previewing a frames page

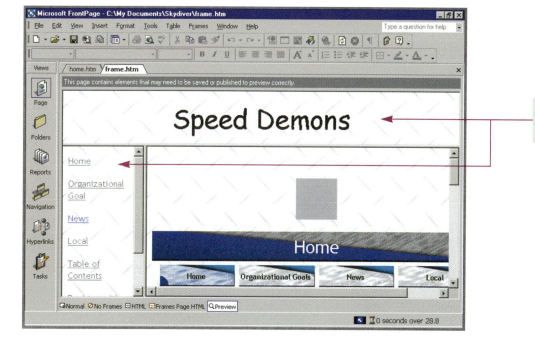

Frames stay the same as center frame changes

Practice

Save your new frames page in the Caddy Shop Web. Accept the default names for the left and top frame. Save the entire page as Frame.

Manipulating Frames Pages

concept

As they continue to build a site, Web authors often end up redesigning their pages. Using FrontPage, you can easily remodel any of the predefined frames templates. As you have seen, you can resize frames to modify your page layout. You can also delete frames and split frames. You split a frame either horizontally or vertically to add a new frame to your frames page.

do it!

Delete a frame from the Frame page in the Skydiver Web, and then add a frame to the same page.

1. Place the insertion point anywhere in the top frame.
2. Click Frames on the Menu bar.
3. Click Delete Frame on the Frames menu. The top frame is deleted as shown in Figure 7-28.
4. Click the Save button on the Standard toolbar to save the page.
5. Place the insertion point in the right frame so it is selected.
6. Click Frames on the Menu bar.
7. Click Split Frame on the Frames menu.
8. The Split Frame dialog box opens, as shown in Figure 7-29.
9. Click the Split into rows option button to split the page horizontally.
10. Click OK.
11. The frame is split into two, as shown in Figure 7-30. You can drag the frame border to change the size of the frame.
12. Close the Frame page and the Home page. Do not save changes.

more

When you deleted the top frame, you did not delete it from the Web. Remember that the frame was saved in the Web with its own file name. You can easily reuse the frame as you redesign your page. Simply click Set Initial Page... in the frame where you want to use it. Then select the file name in the Insert Hyperlinks dialog box. You can also use the resizing pointer to create a new frame. Press the [Ctrl] key while you drag a frame border. When you release the mouse button, a new frame with the Set Initial Page button Set Initial Page... and New Page button New Page will appear.

Figure 7-28 A frame deleted from the page

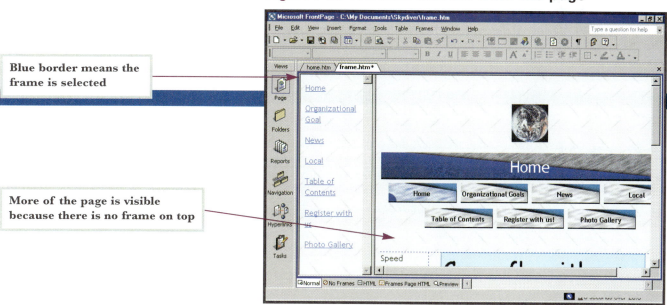

Blue border means the frame is selected

More of the page is visible because there is no frame on top

Figure 7-29 Split Frame dialog box

Preview of how the frame will split

Figure 7-30 A new frame added to a page

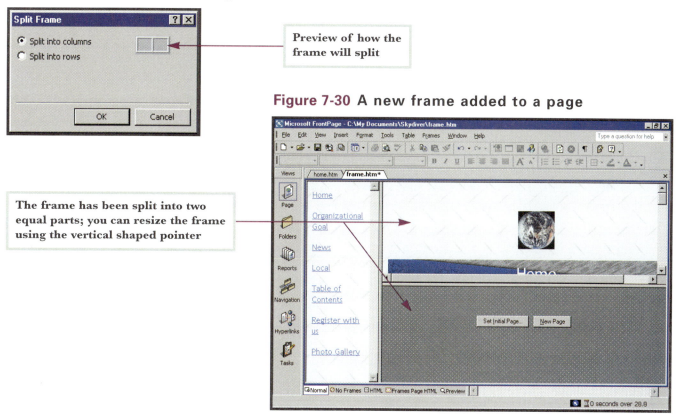

The frame has been split into two equal parts; you can resize the frame using the vertical shaped pointer

Practice

Delete the top frame in the frame page in the Caddy Shop Web. Then, save the page. Finally add another frame to the page, it can be a row or column. Close the frame page without saving the changes.

skill | Creating No-Frames Pages

concept

Many older browsers and browser versions do not support frames. Some visitors do not like frames pages and will set their browser preferences to avoid sites that use them. You do not have to lose potential customers or turn visitors away. You can create a no-frames page to ensure that everyone will be able to view your site, even those who do not have the browsers needed to view all of your elements. If you are creating a Web for a corporate intranet, the Americans with Disabilities Act (ADA) may require a no-frames alternative. Employees who do not use visual browsers cannot use frames pages.

do it!

Create a no-frames page for the Frames Page page in the Skydiver Web.

1. Open the Frames Page page in the Skydiver Web.
2. Click the No Frames tab at the bottom of the screen.
3. When you create a frames page, FrontPage creates a default no-frames page, as shown in Figure 7-31.
4. Place the insertion point at the end of the default no-frames text.
5. Press the [Enter] key. Type: Click here to view the no-frames version of this Web site.
6. Turn the word here into a hyperlink, which links to the home.htm file. Save your changes. Your no-frames page should look like Figure 7-32.
7. You will not be able to view the no-frames page. You can test it by previewing it in a browser that either does not support or is set to not view frames pages.

Figure 7-31 Default no-frames page

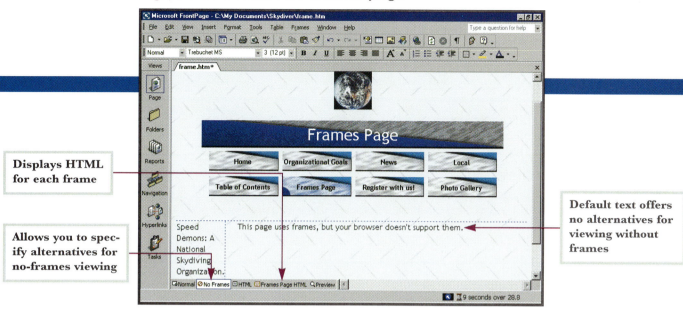

Figure 7-32 Link to no-frames version of Web site

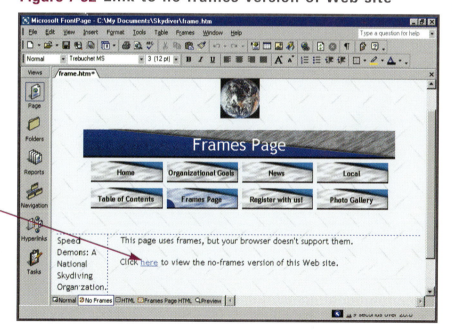

Practice

Create a no-frames page for the Frame page in the Caddy Shop Web. Make sure the user has the ability to link to your Home page in a no-frames setting.

shortcuts

Function	Button/Mouse	Menu	Keyboard
Insert a new page		Click File, then New, then Page or Web	[Ctrl]+[N]
Check Spellings		Click Tools, then click Spelling	[F7]
Save a Web page		Click File, then click Save	[Ctrl]+[S]

INTERACTIVE COMPUTING | FrontPage 2002 | FP 7.29

A. Identify Key Features

Name the items indicated by callouts in Figure 7-33.

1. _____
2. _____
3. _____
4. _____
5. _____
6. _____

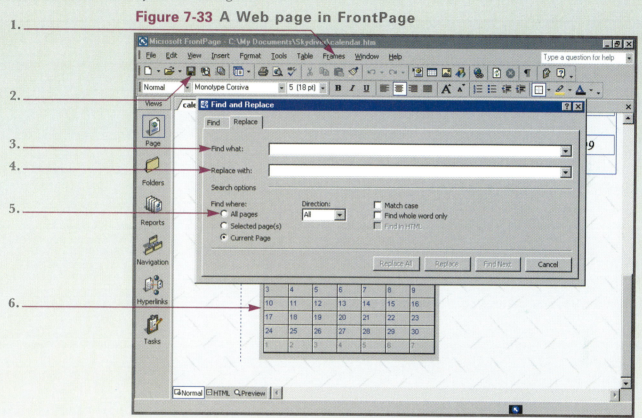

Figure 7-33 A Web page in FrontPage

B. Select the Best Answer

7. Allows you to search a Web for a specific character or piece of text
8. This tab in the Page Options dialog box allows you to target a browser audience
9. When you add elements to these, any changes will appear on all the changes in your Web
10. Click this in the Spelling dialog box to check your Web
11. Inserts a slideshow presentation of images to advertise products or Web pages
12. One of the newest advances in Internet technology
13. You could use this to insert a video player on your Web pages
14. A way of letting visitors move smoothly throughout your Web

a. ActiveX Control
b. Banner Ad Manager
c. Compatibility
d. Dynamic HTML
e. Entire Webs
f. Frames pages
g. Global Find and Replace
h. Shared Borders

quiz (continued)

C. Complete the Statement

15. Click this option button in the Replace dialog box to search your Entire Web:
    a. Entire Web
    b. All Pages
    c. Whole Web
    d. Current Web

16. You can select certain advanced options in this section of the Compatibility tab of the Page Options dialog box:
    a. Servers
    b. HTML Source
    c. Technologies
    d. Browser Versions

17. If a word has been selected by the Spelling checker, it means:
    a. Nothing
    b. The word must be changed to the suggestion in the Spelling dialog box
    c. You should ignore it
    d. It does not appear in the Spelling dictionary

18. You can create Dynamic HTML effects by using the:
    a. Formatting toolbar
    b. DHTML Effects toolbar
    c. Special Effects toolbar
    d. Advanced Effects toolbar

19. The following item is not an ActiveX control:
    a. Stockticker
    b. Banner Ad
    c. Video Player
    d. Calendar

20. In order to completely save all the elements of a frames page you must:
    a. Save only the whole page
    b. Save only the center frame
    c. Save all the frames separately as well as the whole page
    d. Save all the frames separately but not the whole page

21. For viewers who cannot or choose not to view pages with frames you should:
    a. Provide a no-frames page
    b. Create a whole new Web from scratch
    c. Provide alternate Web sites with similar topics
    d. Do nothing

22. You can add a frame to a page using this command:
    a. Add Frame
    b. Multiply Frame
    c. More Frames
    d. Split Frame

23. The Spelling dialog box contains all of the following boxes except:
    a. Not in Dictionary
    b. Change from
    c. Change to
    d. Suggestions

24. The Shared Borders command enables you to add:
    a. Table and chart borders
    b. Navigation bars
    c. Hyperlink borders
    d. Banner and button borders

Build Your Skills

1. Use the global Find and Replace function to search the entire Water Taxi Web:

   a. Open the Index page in the Water Taxi Web.

   b. Open the Find and Replace dialog box.

   c. Replace all occurrences of the word leaving with the word departing.

   d. Save your changes.

2. Change settings in your Web so that you are targeting a specific audience:

   a. Open the Page Options dialog box.

   b. Activate the Compatibility tab in the Page Options dialog box.

   c. Set the browsers so that the Web is compatible with both Internet Explorer and Netscape Navigator.

   d. Set the versions so the Web is compatible with browsers that are 4.0 and later.

   e. Select the ActiveX controls check box in the Technologies section, so you can add an interactive calendar.

   f. Save your changes.

3. Use Shared Borders in the Water Taxi Web:

   a. Open the Shared Borders dialog box.

   b. Add a top shared border, and create a header at the top of the page. Delete the left shared border. In the top shared border, type Water Taxi. Format the header any way you want to complement the site.

   c. Add two rows to the table. Add hyperlinks to the table for every page in the Web. Format the text to match the rest of the table. Leave one cell blank for a page you will add later.

   d. Add a Home hyperlink to all the other pages. Add an Up hyperlink for all the pages beneath a parent page other than Home (e.g., FAQ is below Information). Do not add these links in the shared border; they are for the no-frames site.

4. Check the spellings in the entire Water Taxi Web:

   a. Switch to Navigation view.

   b. Open the Spelling dialog box, and check the spelling in the entire Web.

   c. Make any spelling corrections. You can ignore proper nouns or add them to the custom dictionary if you prefer.

   d. Save any changes you make.

interactivity (continued)

Build Your Skills (continued)

5. Add a Banner Ad to the top shared border in the Water Taxi Web:

   a. Open the Index page in the Water Taxi Web. Place the insertion point in front of the header.

   b. Use the boats 1, boats 2, and boats 3 images from the location where you have stored your Student Files. Set the duration for 3 seconds, and leave the effect set to dissolve. Link the Banner Ad to the Information page, and set the size to 100x100.

   c. Save your changes.

6. Create a Dynamic HTML effect on your Index page in the Water Taxi Web:

   a. Open the Index page in the Water Taxi Web.

   b. Open the DHTML Effects toolbar.

   c. Create an effect on the header above the table. Select any effect you would like to see on this page.

   d. Save your changes.

7. Insert an ActiveX control on the Reservations page in your Water Taxi Web:

   a. Open the Reservations page in the Water Taxi Web. Press [Enter] twice.

   b. Open the Insert ActiveX Control dialog box.

   c. Insert the Windows Media Player program on the Reservations page. Center the calendar on the page.

   d. Save your changes.

8. Create a frames page, save it, modify it, and supply no-frames page in your Water Taxi Web.

   a. Create a new frames page in the Water Taxi Web. Make it so there is only one frame on the left.

   b. In the left frame, create hyperlinks to the other pages in the Web. In the center frame, set the initial page to the Index page in your Water Taxi Web.

   c. Save the frame with filename menu.htm. Change the page title to Menu. Save the frames page as frame.htm and change the page title to Home.

   d. Add a frame to the top of the page.

   e. Delete the frame at the top of the page.

   f. Click the No Frames tab at the bottom of the screen. Create a hyperlink on the page that links to the Index page. The text should read, To view this Web site without frames click here. The word here should be the connecting hyperlink.

interactivity

Problem Solving Exercises

1. Create a new Web called Frames. Add three Web pages with some text and graphics to it. Name them as Home, Calender, and Gallery. First, use the Find and Replace command to find a word and replace it with its alternative. Next, use the Spelling feature to check the spellings in the entire Web. Remember, there may be a lot of proper names and titles that you will have to add to the dictionary. Make sure all the necessary spelling changes are made. Set the target audience for your browser. Make sure your Web is compatible with both Internet Explorer and Netscape Navigator. The settings should be at 4.0 browsers and later. Make sure the ActiveX Control check box is selected in the Technologies section of the Page Options dialog box.

2. Create a banner ad on the Home page of the Frames Web. Use three clip art images that are related to books and the publishing industry. These images should each appear for a duration of 5 seconds. Add a Dynamic HTML effect to one of the images in your Web. Your friends would like to see the different ways you can make an image move and choose the one they like best. Insert the ActiveX device, Calendar Control 10.0 on the Home page. Finally, create a frames page for the Frames Web. Create a frame on the left with hyperlinks to all the other pages in the Web. In the main frame, set the initial page to the Home page. Make sure you create a no-frames alternative. Save the frame and the frames page under the default file names.

3. Now open your personal Web. Apply any of the layout options, or insert any of the HTML elements you learned about in this lesson. Use the Compatibility tab in the Page Options dialog box to set the browser compatibility for your Web. If you know that most of your visitors will have 3.0 versions, make your pages compatible with those browsers. If you do not have headings for your pages, add a shared border at the top of your page. If you have advertisers lined up or graphics that will promote a friend's site, use the Banner Ad Manager to support these sites. You can use images from or associated with the site you want to advertise or a corporate logo. Finally, decide whether or not to apply DHTML effects or insert ActiveX Controls. If you set your target audience for browsers other than Internet Explorer, the ActiveX command will be inactive. You will have to change the compatibility settings to add the control. Some of your audience will not be able to see these special effects. You can insert an ActiveX video player and use DHTML effects for your high-tech visitors.

4. Finally, create a frames page in your personal Web. Create a single frame on the left side of the page. Create hyperlinks in this frame to all the pages in your Web. Set the other frame to your Home page. Preview the frames page and make sure it works. Provide a no-frames alternative for visitors who cannot or choose not to view frames. You can either provide a link to your Home page or create a portal page where visitors can choose which version of your Web site to visit. When you are finished, check the spellings of your entire Web to ensure that it is professional in appearance. Add words to the custom dictionary as appropriate. If there is any text you want to change, use the Find and Replace command to change all occurrences of the word or words in the Web.

Creating and Managing Tasks

Creating a large Web site, even with all the FrontPage shortcuts, is a big job that can sometimes seem overwhelming. Fortunately, FrontPage includes a task manager called Tasks view. In Tasks view, you can organize the work that must be completed on your Web, assign tasks to co-workers, and track what jobs have been completed, when and by whom for a multi-authored site.

Tasks are simply reminders about actions that you need to perform in your Web. You can build a Tasks list to provide a clear and accurate account of what work has been finished and what remains to be done before your Web can be published. The Tasks list is a to-do list that will also provide valuable documentation, especially for team projects.

Some FrontPage wizards automatically create tasks for you. You can also create tasks right from the beginning.

skills

- Creating New Tasks
- Adding a Task Linked to a Page
- Starting and Completing Tasks
- Sorting Tasks
- Viewing Task History

Lesson Goal:

In this lesson, you will learn how to create your own tasks, assign tasks to others and add tasks that are linked to a particular page. You will learn how to edit and delete tasks and how to start and complete them. You will also learn how to mark tasks as completed. Next, you will learn how to sort your tasks by who is assigned to complete the task, date modified, status, priority and other criteria. Finally, you will learn how to use the Show History command to limit the Tasks list to jobs that have not been started or are still in progress or to view the complete task history.

skill Creating New Tasks

concept

Although some wizards add tasks automatically, most do not. In general, you will have to manually add tasks. You will need to add to the Tasks list created by a wizard or create a Tasks list for a Web you are constructing from the beginning or with a template. When you create a task, you can specify to whom it is assigned and any other pertinent information. This documentation is especially important for large corporate Web sites with many contributors.

do it!

Create a new task in the Skydiver Web.

1. Open the Home page of the Skydiver Web, in FrontPage.
2. Click File on the Menu bar.
3. Move the pointer over New.
4. Click Task on the submenu that appears, as shown in Figure 8-1. You may have to access the extended menu to find the Task command. The New Task dialog box opens.
5. In the Task name text box, type Recalculate Hyperlinks.
6. In the Description text box, type Check all hyperlinks in Web. Recalculate if necessary.
7. Click the Low option button in the Priority section of the New Task dialog box. The New Task dialog box should resemble Figure 8-2.
8. Click [OK]. The task is added to your Tasks list. To edit a task, right-click it and choose the Edit Task command from the shortcut menu. You can view or make modifications to the task details in the Task Details dialog box.

more

If you are managing a project, you can assign tasks to other people. Employees can then open a Web to see if any work has been assigned to them and complete the tasks. You can also create tasks for yourself to serve as reminders of what you need to do before your Web is ready to be published.

There are two kinds of tasks, linked and unlinked or general tasks. In the above exercise, you created a general task. A linked task is associated with a particular file or page. For example, replacing text on one page would be linked to only the page on which it occurred. You can also create a linked task to remind yourself to add a paragraph, table, or graphic to a particular page.

Figure 8-1 Accessing the Task command from the File menu

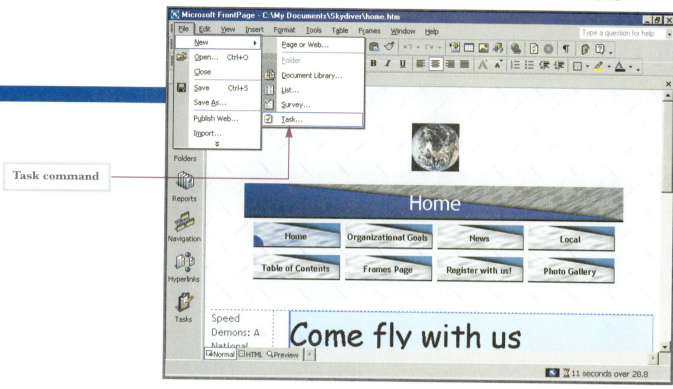

Figure 8-2 New Task dialog box

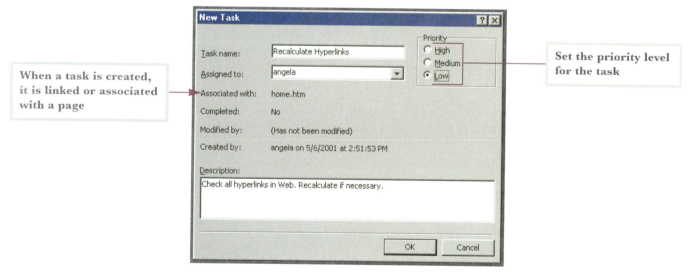

Practice

Create a new task in the Caddy Shop Web. The task is a high priority. Name the task, Check Spellings. For a description, type Check Web for spelling errors.

FP 8.4 LESSON EIGHT Creating and Managing Tasks

 Adding a Task Linked to a Page

concept

Some FrontPage features allow you to add a task to your Tasks list while you are performing another function. When you are starting a new page, you can create a task in the Page Templates dialog box, as shown in Figure 8-3. Rather than actually creating the page, you can create a task to remind you to finish the page later. The task will be linked to the new blank page.

do it!

Add a task to remind yourself to complete a new page in the Skydiver Web.

1. Click File on the Menu bar. Point to New and click Page or Web in the submenu. The New Page or Web Task Pane opens.

2. Click the Page Templates hyperlink. The Page Templates dialog box opens.

3. Leave the Normal Page template selected and make sure that the Just add Web task check box is selected. Click [OK]. The Save As dialog box opens.

4. Type Task.htm in the File name text box.

5. Click [Save].

6. Click the Tasks button on the Views bar. The new page appears as a high priority task on the Tasks list, as shown in Figure 8-4.

7. Right-click the new task. Click Edit Task on the shortcut menu to open the Task Details dialog box. You can reassign the task, change or add to the description or change the priority level.

8. Click [OK] when you are finished. Add two more tasks and name these tasks as Creation of Web page and Spelling Check. Associate these tasks with FAQ and Organizational pages, respectively.

more

The priority level automatically assigned to a task by FrontPage depends on the type of task. Finishing a new page, as in the exercise above, is treated as a high priority task. Each Spelling or Replace task you add while using the Replace and Spelling checking tools is linked to the page on which it occurs and is considered a medium priority task.

To add a task that is linked to an existing page, first select the page in any view. Then, follow the steps mentioned in the exercise section of this skill. For example, select a page in Navigation view. Then, open and complete the New Task dialog box. The task will be added to the Tasks list associated with that page. You can also add a task to an existing file by right-clicking the file in the Folder list. Click Add Task on the shortcut menu to open the New Task dialog box. The task will be associated with the file you selected.

Figure 8-3 Adding a task in the New dialog box

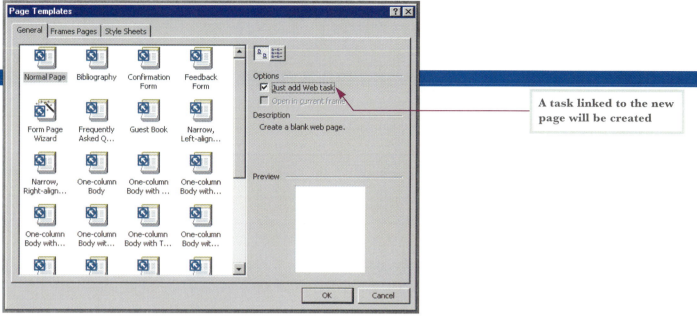

Figure 8-4 New task in Tasks list

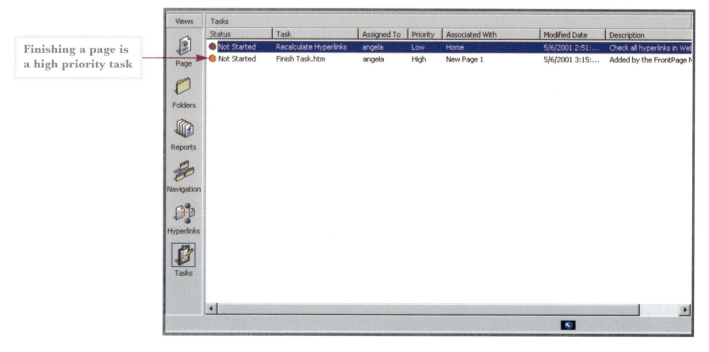

Practice

Create a new page in the **Caddy Shop** Web, but create it as a high priority task. Save the page as **caddytask.htm**. Create two more tasks of your choice and assign them a medium priority.

FP 8.6 | LESSON EIGHT — Creating and Managing Tasks

skill: Starting and Completing Tasks

concept

When you are ready to start working on a task, you must first select the task so the appropriate page will open. When everything is done, mark the task as completed to keep your Task list up to date. Tasks can be started and completed in any order by the person to whom they have been assigned.

do it!

Execute your highest priority task in the Skydiver Web and then mark the task as completed.

1. Right-click the Finish Task.htm task.
2. Click Start Task on the shortcut menu that opens. The new page, Task.htm opens.
3. Type Skydiving is fun and adventurous.
4. Press the [Enter] key.
5. Click Insert on the Menu bar, point to Picture and click From File from the submenu. The Picture dialog box opens.
6. Locate the photo gallery folder in your student files and double-click the file fpdoit8-3.gif. The image is inserted in the Web page, as shown in Figure 8-5.
7. Save this page. The Microsoft FrontPage dialog box appears, prompting you to mark the page as completed. Click [Yes]. Save the embedded image.
8. Place this page under Photo Gallery page in the Navigation structure.
9. Rename the page as Finished Task.
10. Click the Tasks button 📋 on the Views bar.
11. The Task list opens. Notice that now there are only three tasks left to be completed. The Finish task.htm no longer exists in the Task list (see Figure 8-6).
12. Switch back to Page view and close the Task.htm file.

more

If you create a general task, you will have to start and complete the task yourself. When you are done, save any changes, return to Tasks view and mark the task completed.

When you mark a task completed, it cannot be reversed. For a multi-authored site, this may mean that even when a task is complete it should not be marked as such until it has been reviewed and approved by a department head or supervisor. If you prematurely mark a task completed, you will have to delete it and create a new task to replace it. 🌈 To determine who completed a task and when it was finished, right-click the completed task and click Edit Task to open the Task Details dialog box. The updated information will include the completion date and time.

Figure 8-5 Completing a task

Task.htm page created in New dialog box with an associated task

An image inserted in the Web page

Figure 8-6 Task list

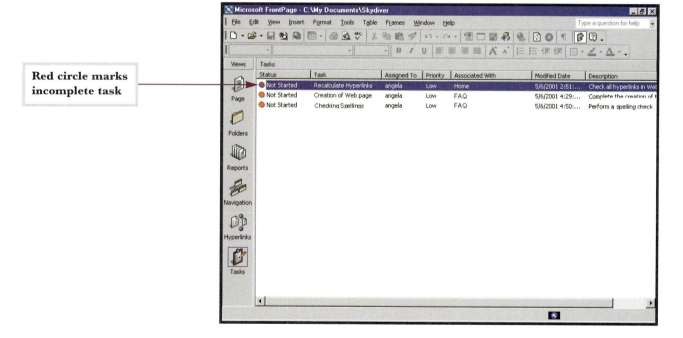

Red circle marks incomplete task

Practice

Start and complete the highest priority task in your Caddy Shop Web.

FP 8.8 — LESSON EIGHT — Creating and Managing Tasks

 ## Sorting Tasks

concept

By default, tasks appear in the Tasks list in the order in which they were created. You can sort your tasks to view them in a different order by clicking the column heading you want to use as the sort criterion. This can be useful in large Web sites with many tasks assigned to different individuals. You can sort your Tasks list by status, the people assigned to complete the tasks, priority, or any other column heading to organize your tasks.

do it!

Sort the tasks in your Tasks list to view them in different ways.

1. Click the Tasks button on the Views bar to access the Task list, if required.
2. Click the Priority button at the top of the Tasks list.
3. Your tasks will be sorted by priority, as shown in Figure 8-7.
4. Click the Associated With button at the top of the Tasks list.
5. The tasks are now sorted by the pages in the Web they are associated with. This is shown in Figure 8-8.
6. Close the Task list.

more

You can sort tasks in either ascending or descending order. If the category you are sorting contains letters, for example, names in the Assigned To category, the first time you click the column heading the names will be listed in ascending order alphabetically from A to Z. Clicking the Assigned To column heading a second time will reverse the order. If you click the Associated With column heading, your tasks will be listed alphabetically by page title in ascending order. To restore the default order, click the Modified Date column heading. If you click the Modified Date column heading again, the tasks will be listed in descending order with the most recently created or modified tasks listed first.

To resize a column, move the pointer over the vertical bar on the right edge of the column heading until it becomes a resizing pointer. Drag to the right to widen a column and to the left to shrink a column. To make a column in the Tasks list exactly as wide as the information in the column, double-click the vertical bar. To delete a task, right-click it and click the Delete command on the shortcut menu. The Undo command will not reverse the deletion.

Figure 8-7 Sorting tasks by Priority

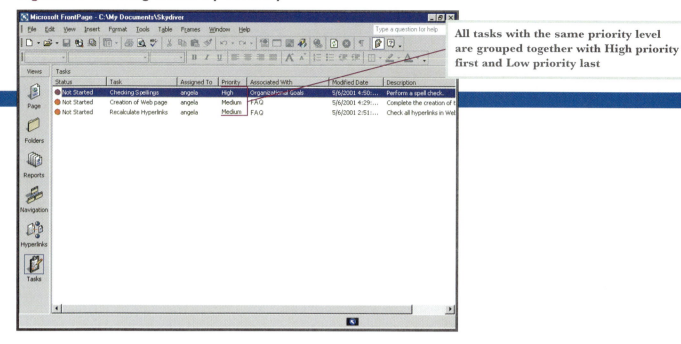

Figure 8-8 Tasks sorted according to the Web pages associated

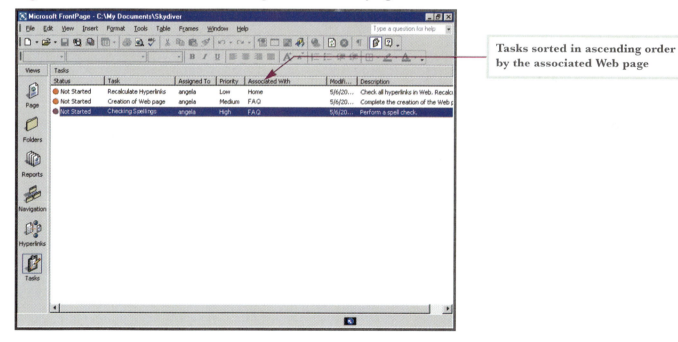

Practice

Open the Tasks list for your Caddy Shop Web. Sort the tasks in all the different ways you can. Take note of the differences, and why each sorting criteria would be useful.

skill | Viewing Task History

concept

When the Show History command is enabled, all tasks, even those completed, will be listed in the Tasks list. If the Show History command is inactive, the completed tasks will not be listed. In large Tasks lists, you may want to turn off the Show History function to limit the list to those tasks that must still be completed.

do it!

Use the Show History command to view the tasks you have completed.

1. Open the Home page in the Skydiver Web.
2. Click the Tasks button on the Views bar.
3. Complete the Creation of Web Page task that is associated with the FAQ page.
4. Return to Task view.
5. Click Edit on the Menu bar, move the pointer over Task and click Show History from the submenu. The information about the completed and the uncompleted tasks will be displayed in the Task list, as shown in Figure 8-9. If you right-click the background in Tasks view, a shortcut menu including the Show History command will open. You can check to see if the function is activated and turn it on or off.
6. Close FrontPage.

more

When the Show History command is checked, the command is active and all completed tasks will appear in the Tasks list. When the Show History command is not activated, any action that refreshes the page such as the Refresh command or closing the Web or FrontPage will remove the completed tasks. When managing the construction of a large site and coordinating many tasks, you may want to deactivate the Show History command to keep the size of the Tasks list manageable and avoid any possible confusion.

The Refresh command is a useful tool for team projects with multiple authors. For example, if you have already created a Site Summary you will have to refresh Reports view to display changes another author has made to the site.

Figure 8-9 Task history with Show History command active

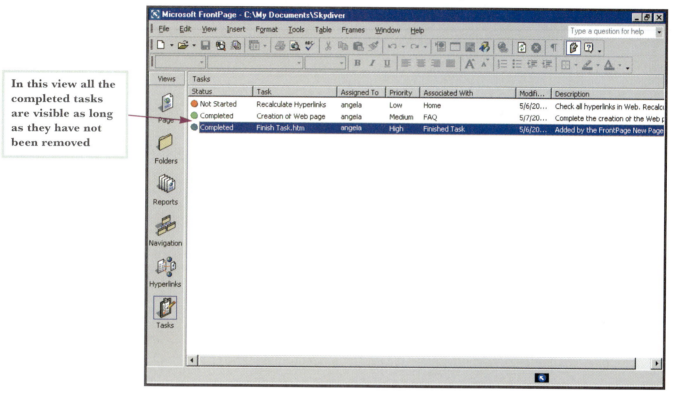

In this view all the completed tasks are visible as long as they have not been removed

Practice

Mark two tasks as being completed in your Task list. Then deactivate the Show History command. Refresh the page. Then, activate the Show History command again.

shortcuts

Function	Button/Mouse	Menu	Keyboard
Activate Tasks view		Click View, then click Tasks	[Alt]+[V], [A]
Refresh Page		Click View, then click Refresh	[F5]

A. Identify Key Features

Name the items indicated by callouts in Figure 8-10.

Figure 8-10 Task list

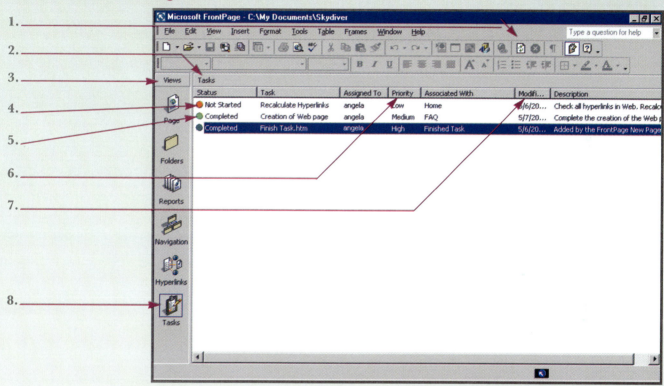

1. ____
2. ____
3. ____
4. ____
5. ____
6. ____
7. ____
8. ____

B. Select the Best Answer

9. Tells you how important a task is
10. Use this to edit tasks
11. This opens the function used to create a task or the page with which it is associated
12. Sorts tasks from A to Z
13. Sorts tasks from Z to A
14. Displays all tasks, including those that have been completed
15. A job associated with a particular file or page
16. A job not associated with one particular file or page

a. Ascending order
b. Descending order
c. Priority
d. Start Tasks
e. Show History
f. Task Details dialog box
g. General task
h. Linked task

quiz (continued)

C. Complete the Statement

17. The purpose of assigning tasks is to:
    a. Delegate the tasks
    b. Spread tasks to different co-workers
    c. Keep track of who has completed what tasks
    d. All of the above

18. You can view a task using:
    a. Task Details
    b. Edit Task
    c. New Task
    d. Add Task

19. You can sort tasks using all the following categories except:
    a. Task History
    b. Priority
    c. Assigned To
    d. Modified Date

20. You can mark a task as complete:
    a. Only after you have used FrontPage to complete the task
    b. Only in the Task Details dialog box
    c. At any time by clicking Mark as Completed
    d. At any time by clicking Task Finished

21. If you sort tasks by who they are assigned to in descending order, this name would appear first:
    a. Sydney
    b. Ronald
    c. Raymond
    d. Matthew

22. You can delete a task by right-clicking it to open a shortcut menu and clicking:
    a. Edit Task
    b. Delete Task
    c. Cut Task
    d. End Task

23. When the Show History command is checked it means:
    a. None of the completed tasks will be visible
    b. Only the completed tasks will be visible
    c. All the completed and unfinished tasks will be visible
    d. None of the unfinished tasks will be visible

24. You can create a linked task to remind yourself to add a:
    a. Paragraph
    b. Table
    c. Graphic
    d. All of the above

25. To start working on a previously created task, you first must:
    a. Select the task so the proper page will open
    b. Go to the home page of the Web site
    c. Assign a priority to the task
    d. Assign a description to the task

Build Your Skills

1. Create new tasks in the Water Taxi Web:

    a. Open the Home page in the Water Taxi Web.

    b. View the Tasks list.

    c. Open the New Task dialog box.

    d. The task name is Test Hyperlinks.

    e. The description is Test all the hyperlinks in the Web. If there are faulty hyperlinks, recalculate them.

    f. The priority of this task is Medium.

    g. Make sure this task has been added properly to your Tasks list.

2. Add a task to the Water Taxi Web while performing another function:

    a. View the Tasks list.

    b. Open the New dialog box to create a new page.

    c. Select the Just add Web task check box.

    d. Save the file under the name newtask. Return to Tasks view.

    e. Right-click the new task.

    f. Click Edit Task on the shortcut menu. View the details of the new task in the Task Details dialog box. Change the description to Create a new page listing popular fishing locations.

    g. Close the Home page.

3. Start and complete tasks in the Water Taxi Web:

    a. Open the Index page in the Water Taxi Web.

    b. View the Tasks list.

    c. Right-click on the task Finish newtask.htm.

    d. Click Start Task on the submenu menu that opens.

    e. Complete the new page and save it as fishing.htm. Change the page title to Fishing Locations.

    f. When the message box opens reminding you that the page was opened from Tasks view and asking if you would like to mark the task as completed, click Yes.

    g. Add the page to the navigation structure below the the Locations page.

    h. Close the Index page.

interactivity (continued)

Build Your Skills (continued)

4. Sort the tasks in the Tasks list.

   a. Open the Home page in the Water Taxi Web.

   b. View the Tasks list.

   c. Click the Associated With button at the top of the Tasks list to sort the tasks in ascending order of the pages they are associated with.

   d. Click the Modified Date button at the top of the Tasks list to view the tasks in ascending order of the date they were last modified.

   e. Click the Modified Date button at the top of the Tasks list again to view the tasks in descending order of the date they were last modified.

5. View the history of your tasks:

   a. Create a new task by the name of Test Hyperlink.

   b. View the Tasks list. Mark the Test Hyperlinks task complete.

   c. If the Show History command is active, deactivate it.

   d. Refresh the page.

   e. Activate the Show History command to view your task history.

   f. Close the Web site, then close FrontPage.

Problem Solving Exercises

1. Use the Skydiver Web and assign work to the three employees who will be taking over the maintenance of the Web, John, Martha, and Alan. If you have any Spelling check or Replace text tasks left, divide them up as evenly as possible. Create three new linked tasks to remind each employee to finish a new page. Create three new general tasks. Ask John to perform a final spelling check on the Web, Martha to test all hyperlinks and Alan to check all interactive and advanced components. Assign priorities to these tasks as you see fit.

2. Sort the Tasks list in different ways. First, sort them according to the person assigned to complete the task. Make sure each employee has approximately an equal amount of work. Tasks that were previously assigned to you must be reassigned. Next, sort the tasks by priority. Make sure you have equally divided the number of high, medium and low priority tasks. Finally, return to the default view so that each task is listed by the date it was created or last modified. Turn off the Show History command if necessary, so that only uncompleted tasks will display.

3. You are now ready to finish your personal Web. Perform a final spelling check. Add a task for each page with misspellings to perform this task more efficiently. Open the Tasks list and complete all tasks including those you have created while performing other functions. If you still have pages to create or other maintenance to perform, create tasks for each job. Be sure to complete all tasks.

4. Sort the list in various ways to decide how to proceed. You may want to perform all tasks associated with a certain page or high priority tasks first. To avoid confusion, do not enable the Show History command until you have marked all tasks as completed. Then, use the Show History command to ensure you have not accidentally marked a task completed.

glossary

a

ActiveX Control
A control added to your Web pages, often interactive, created by a program written especially for that control.

Align left, right
Command buttons on the Formatting toolbar that change the alignment of the text on a Web page by aligning the text to the left or the right side of the page.

Answer Wizard
A part of the FrontPage Help feature, it allows you to type a question, and will search for the help topics that might be useful in answering that question.

Applet
A set of instructions written in Java that tells your browser how to interpret a certain object and effect; it works only with Java-enabled browsers.

b

Background
A command on the Format menu that allows you to make formatting changes to different aspects of Web pages.

Banner
An image that usually appears at the top of a Web page, containing text and/or graphics, often but not necessarily for advertising purposes.

Banner Ad Manager
Creates a slideshow-like presentation of images which can be linked to other Web pages. Often used for advertisements that appear on Web pages.

Bevel
Formatting around an image that makes the image appear to have a picture frame around it.

Bold
A command button on the Formatting toolbar that makes the selected text appear in bold lettering.

Broken hyperlink
A hyperlink that has a target page that does not exist, has been moved, or changed, or for some other reason the hyperlink does not work, or link to an appropriate file.

Browser
See Web Browser.

Bulleted list
A type of list in which the information is organized by graphical marks, called bullets, representing a new section of information on the list.

c

Caption
A feature that creates a message to appear with a table, usually used to explain information in a table.

Cascading Style Sheets
A FrontPage feature that uses a text file to affect the way elements on your Web are positioned.

Cell
The empty spaces that are created by the rows and columns of a table. Contains the information in a table.

Center
A command button on the Formatting toolbar that changes the alignment of the text on a Web page by aligning it in the center of the page.

Check box
A check box is another way of answering a yes or no question, the user has an option of checking the box to select it, a yes answer, or not checking it, a no answer.

Child page
A page, in a Web hierarchy, that appears below another page in the hierarchy, and therefore can only be linked to from that page; see "Parent page."

Click
To press and release a mouse button in one motion; usually refers to the left mouse button.

Clickable image
Another name for a hotspot or an image map, an image that is formatted so that a hyperlink is added to a particular place on the image. When clicked this spot acts as a hyperlink.

Clip Art Gallery, Microsoft
A gallery of images that Microsoft provides that you can search and use to add graphics to your Web pages.

Close button
A sizing button that appears on the Title bar, when clicked it closes the application.

Column
The vertical border of a table, that intersects with the rows to make up the empty spaces of the table called cells.

Contents
A part of the FrontPage Help feature, this allows you to search for help based on a table of contents with help topics that you can choose to look at.

Control
An object that makes data entry easier and more efficient; most controls appear on form pages, such as check boxes, and radio buttons.

Control Menu icon
An icon that appears in the Title bar that opens a menu; when clicked, it enables you to manipulate the FrontPage window.

Convert
A function on the Table menu that allows you to change plain text into a table and a table into plain text.

Copy
A command found on the Edit menu that copies the selected text and places the copy in the Office Clipboard.

Cut
A command found on the Edit menu that cuts the selected text and moves it to the Office Clipboard.

Decrease indents
A command button on the Formatting toolbar enabling you to decrease indentation between text and margins.

Desktop
The standard Microsoft Windows screen, it is designed to have the appearance of an actual desktop.

Dialog Box
A box that groups functions together, it performs actions depending on the commands you use and options you select.

Drag
To hold the mouse button down while moving the mouse.

Draw Table
A function on the Tables toolbar that allows you to draw a table to your own specifications, and insert columns and rows.

Drop-Down arrow
An arrow that appears in a text box, clicking it opens up a menu of options to choose from.

Drop-Down Menu
A menu of options that opens by clicking the drop-down arrow. You can also use FrontPage to create a drop-down menu on a form page.

Dynamic HTML (DHTML)
A code used to create motion effects on a Web page, such as banner ads and other special effects.

Edit
A menu on the Menu bar that provides you with commands enabling you to make changes and edit your Web and Web pages.

File
A menu on the menu bar, it provides commands that have to do with saving, opening, printing, storing, and performing other filing options on your Web and Web pages.

Find
A command found on the Edit menu, it searches for text that you specify and takes you to where the text is located on a page, or in a Web.

Folder List
A list of files and folders appearing to the left of the FrontPage screen; you also can access it by opening the View menu.

Folders view
Allows you to view and organize the folders and files that are associated with a Web.

Font
The style in which text appears. Bold, italic, script, serif, and sans serif are all styles associated with different fonts.

Form page
A type of Web page that asks the user for information; once the information has been entered the page, it may be sent to the Web manager, and saved, or sent to an e-mail address so the data can be recorded.

Format
A menu on the Menu bar that allows you to make formatting changes to your Web and Web pages.

Format Painter
A FrontPage feature that enables you to copy and paste the format from a body of text and apply it to text in a different location.

Formatting
The process of adding elements to your Web page, including objects, text, colors, and other important Web components to give your Web a certain look or style, and make it attractive.

Formatting toolbar
A bar full of buttons and icons that allows you to perform certain formatting actions on your Web pages.

Frames
A menu on the Menu bar that allows you to add frames to a page, create a frames page, and make changes to frame pages.

Frames page
Pages that contain an extra frame, which is another Web page, that allows visitors to move smoothly through your Web site.

Graphic Interchange Format (GIF)
A format in which images are saved, where the image is compressed so that it does not take up much space, and doesn't take long to download.

Global Find and Replace
The same function as the Find command and the Replace command. The difference is that global means these commands are applied to an entire Web.

Help
A Microsoft feature that provides several different ways of searching for help and information while you are using a Microsoft program. You can access this feature with the Help menu on the Menu bar.

Hit Counter
An interactive feature on a Web page. When inserted, it displays the number of visitors that have opened a Web page.

Home page
The first page that visitors see when they enter your Web site. It is where they begin to navigate through your Web.

Hotspot
Another name for an image map or a clickable image, when an image is formatted so that a particular spot on the image is linked to a target page. When clicked, the hotspot acts as a hyperlink.

Hover button
A button added to a Web page which creates an effect when the pointer hovers over it, the button is actually a Java applet.

HTML Editor
Any program like FrontPage that takes the work you have created in a Normal view and converts it into HTML format.

HTML tab
Found in Page view, this mode of viewing pages enables you to view and edit the HTML code that makes up the Web page.

Hyperlink
A hyperlink is a piece of text that links to another page inside the Web, or externally to another Web altogether.

Hyperlinks View
Displays every hyperlink to and from each page in a Web.

Hypertext Markup Language (HTML)
A code used for designing Web pages. FrontPage writes HTML code for you, but a knowledgeable user may also write HTML code for a page in FrontPage.

i

I-beam
When you move the mouse pointer over text or an area of a page where text may be inserted, it turns into an I-beam; so named because it looks like an I-beam.

Icon
A small graphic that identifies an object or a button.

Image map
Another name for a hotspot or clickable image, when an image is formatted so a particular spot on the image is linked to a target page. When clicked the spot acts as a hyperlink.

Image toolbar
A bar containing buttons that perform specific actions when clicked, this particular toolbar contains command buttons that act on images alone.

Import
A command that enables you to take files from another location, such as another folder, drive, or even from the Web, and place them in your current Web.

Increase indents
A command button on the Formatting toolbar that allows you to increase the indent between the text and the margins.

Index
A part of the FrontPage Help feature, this function allows you to get help by typing a keyword and searching for the help topics related to that keyword.

Insert
A menu on the Menu bar that allows you to insert certain objects and files into your Webs and Web pages.

Insertion point
A flashing point on a page, it marks the point where text will be entered on the page, or where an object will be placed.

Internet
A global network of computers exchanging information over the network, it includes the Web servers, the individual user, and organizations that manage the networks.

Internet Explorer
Microsoft's Web browser application that enables you to search for, view, and navigate through Web sites.

Italic
A command button on the Formatting toolbar that makes the selected text appear italicized.

j

Java
A Web designing language. Similar to HTML, Java is read by browsers and then used to display Web pages, but Java allows certain effects to be created which are not possible in HTML.

Java applet
A set of instructions written in the Java language that tells the browser which effects to perform when the page is displayed. These applets are visible only with Java-enabled browsers.

Joint Photographic Experts Group (JPEG)
A format in which images are saved, where the image is compressed so that it does not take up much space, and doesn't take long to download.

k

Keyword
A part of the Index help feature, type in a keyword and the help feature will find a help topic related to that keyword.

l

Layout buttons
The Align Left, Align Right, and Center buttons on the Formatting toolbar that align text in relation to the left and right margins of a page; also called alignment buttons.

List
A list is a way of organizing information on a Web page by displaying it in list format.

Lotus 1-2-3
A spreadsheet program, using FrontPage you can open documents from this program and put them on a Web page.

m

Marquee
An object that takes text and moves it across the screen in order to grab the viewer's attention.

Maximize button
A sizing button found on the Title bar that maximizes the size of the FrontPage window.

Menu
A list of related commands.

Menu bar
Found below the Title bar, it contains the names of menus that present lists of commands to choose from.

Merge Cells
A function performed on a table that turns two separate cells into one.

Microsoft Paint (MS Paint)
A program installed in the Accessories category of Microsoft Windows that you can use to draw lines and shapes, put text in pictures, work with color, and otherwise format and edit drawn objects.

Microsoft Personal Web Server
A program that publishes Webs to a local hard drive or any other local area on your computer.

Minimize button
A sizing button the Title bar that minimizes the size of the FrontPage window so that it no longer appears on the screen.

Mouse pointer
The arrow shaped cursor on the screen that you control by guiding the mouse on your desk. You use the mouse to select and drag items, choose commands, and start or exit programs. The shape of the mouse pointer can change depending on the task being executed.

n

Navigation bar
A group of hyperlinks appearing as buttons or simply as text that guide a user through the navigation of your Web, by providing hyperlinks, internally, to pages in the Web.

Navigation button
A button that links to other pages to help navigate a user through a Web.

Navigation view
Displays the navigation structure of a Web. It also enables you to add Navigation buttons and a Navigation bar to your pages.

Netscape Navigator
The main Web browser competition to Microsoft Internet Explorer; Navigator 5.0 and later versions are enabled for using JavaScript, Java applets, DHTML, frames, and some other features used in Internet Explorer.

New Page
A command found on the File menu that allows you to create a new page with a template, a wizard, or just a blank page.

New Web
A command found on the File menu that allows you to create a Web using a template, a Wizard or a simple one-page Web.

No-Frames page
An alternative page created simultaneously with a frames page for users who cannot or choose not to view frames.

Normal Tab
Found in Page view, this mode of viewing a page allows you to add objects and elements, and perform some of the formatting options available to you in FrontPage.

Numbered list
A type of list in which the information is organized by numbers representing a new section of information on the list.

o

Office Clipboard
Enables you to send up to 24 pieces of data from programs to the Clipboard, by cutting or copying, then enables you to take data off the clipboard and use it in other programs.

Open File
A command found on the File menu that allows you to open any previously saved file.

Open Web
A command found on the Menu bar that allows you to open any previously saved Web.

Option buttons
A group of buttons enabling you to select one of several options; you will be limited to only one selection, out of several option buttons.

p

Page banner
A rectangular area in FrontPage that enables you to quickly add titles to Web pages; page banners are visible on a page only if the page is part of the navigation structure.

Page view
This view allows you to work on an individual Web page. Most of the formatting of additional elements and graphics to a Web page is done in this mode.

Page transition
A formatting feature that creates an effect as different pages are viewed in a Web.

Parent page
The page that appears above another page in the Web hierarchy, so that it links to the child page.

Paste
A command found on the Edit menu that allows you to take data from the clipboard and paste it in a document.

Paste Special
A command on the Edit menu that enables users to paste data onto the clipboard in different formats—as a paragraph, several paragraphs, formatted paragraphs, or as HTML.

Photo gallery
A new feature in FrontPage 2002, it is a Web page containing a collection of graphics arranged in one of four layouts offered in FrontPage; if creating an album, you can have different pages with different layouts.

Plain Text (TXT or ASCII)
A format in which data appears. It is significant because you can use FrontPage to open data in this format and place it on a Web page.

Preview in Browser
A command found on the File menu, it enables you to open your Web in a browser; you may use any browser that is used by your computer.

Preview Tab
Found in Page view, this mode of viewing a page allows you to see what the page would look like if it were published on the Internet and viewed with a browser.

Print
A command found on the File menu that allows you to print a copy of the FrontPage screen, so that you can have a hard copy of the pages that will be published.

Print Preview
A view that shows how an object will appear when printed on paper. Useful for evaluating the layout or structure of a Web, before publishing it.

Publish Web
A command found on the File menu that publishes your Web to a Web server or to another location that you specify.

Push button
A button that is added to a form page that enables a user to submit a form or to reset a form; these options may be set when the button is created.

r

Recalculate Hyperlinks
A command found on the Tools menu that fixes broken hyperlinks, by locating the intended target pages.

Recent File
A command found on the File menu that enables you to instantly open one of the most recent files you have been working on.

Recent Web
A command found on the File menu that enables you to instantly open one of the most recent Webs you have been working on.

Rename
A command found on many shortcut menus that enables you to rename an object using the Rename dialog box.

Replace
A command found on the Edit menu that is related to the Find command. It allows you to find information on a page or in a Web and replace it with the text you specify.

Reports view
Provides reports and updates on the status of the files and hyperlinks of a Web, so you can keep it up to date.

Resizing arrow
When the mouse pointer is moved over an object and you have the option of resizing it, the pointer will turn into a double-headed arrow; clicking and dragging the arrow will resize the object.

Restore button
A sizing button found on the Title bar that enables you to revert the FrontPage window to its previous size.

Rich Text Format (RTF)
A format in which data sometimes appears, FrontPage can open a document in this format and place it on a Web page in HTML format.

Right-click
To click the right mouse button; often used to access specialized menus and shortcuts.

Row
The horizontal border of a table, it intersects with columns to create the empty spaces called cells.

S

Save
A command found on the File menu that saves a file simply by overwriting the existing saved document.

Save As
A command found on the File menu that enables you to save a file with a new name and a new location.

Scroll arrow
Arrows that appear on the right and bottom of the FrontPage screen, they allow you to scroll through a document one line at a time, by clicking the arrow in the direction you want the view to move.

Scroll bar
A graphical device for moving vertically or horizontally through the FrontPage screen with the mouse. Scroll bars are located along the right and bottom edges of the FrontPage window.

Scroll bar box
A small gray box located inside a scroll bar indicating your current position relative to the rest of the window. You can advance a scroll bar box by dragging it or by clicking the scroll arrows.

Search form
A form control that allows users to search for specific information in a Web.

Shared borders
A command found on the Format menu that enables you to add a Navigation bar to a Web; this is most useful when you add the shared borders in Navigation view; text, images, or other elements added to the shared borders will be applied on all the pages in a Web.

Shortcut key
A keyboard equivalent of a menu command such as [Ctrl]+[S] for Save.

Shortcut menu
A pop-up menu accessed by right-clicking the mouse. The contents of the menu depend on your current activity.

Site Summary
A type of report provided in Reports view that evaluates files, folders, and hyperlinks to make sure that every element of your Web is kept up to date.

Sizing buttons
Three buttons found on the Title bar that allow you to manipulate the size of the FrontPage window.

Sizing handles
The small black squares that appear on the border of an object when it is selected. Dragging these handles will allow you to resize the object.

Smart Tag
Enables you to perform external actions on types of data that FrontPage recognizes; FrontPage uses a smart tag called the Paste Options button to keep the formatting of the source item or keep only the data that you have pasted.

Spelling Checker
A command found on the Tools menu, it checks the spelling of words on a page or in a Web with the words in its internal dictionary.

Split Cells
A function performed on tables that creates two cells from a single cell.

Standard toolbar
Found below the Menu bar, it contains graphical buttons that execute specific commands.

Status bar
Appears at the bottom of the screen and displays the activity being performed, as well as displaying currently active features, including the loading time for a Web page.

Style box
A box on the Formatting toolbar that allows you to set and change the style of text that appears in a Web page.

Style sheets
See Cascading style sheets.

Table
An object that you can insert into a Web page to help organize information. The table is made up of rows and columns which create cells, the cells contain the information. The Table menu on the Menu bar is used to insert and format tables.

Tables toolbar
A toolbar that contains different graphical buttons used to work with a table.

Target
The page, Web, or location that a hyperlink links to. When creating a hyperlink the target page or URL must be specified. The target page must also be in working order for the hyperlink to work.

Task
A task provides a reminder as well as documentation as to what work is to be done in your Web, who is doing the work, and when that work is taking place.

Task pane
A new feature to FrontPage 2002 and other Office XP programs that organizes common program tasks in one pane that is convenient to access. In FrontPage 2002, the common task panes are New Page or Web, Clipboard, and Search.

Tasks view
Displays the tasks that are and must be completed in a Web.

Template
A basic structure or outline that FrontPage provides you with to help you start your Web. The pages may include placeholder text which you simply overwrite to create your page.

Text box
A box that appears on a form page that allows users to enter text into it, a one-line box allows a short entries, while scrolling text boxes allow longer entries.

Theme
An overall style or look that is applied to a Web page or an entire Web; it is customizable so you can create your own.

Time stamp
A FrontPage component that displays the most recent date and/or time that a Web page was edited or updated.

Title bar
Contains the application Control menu icon, name of the application, and sizing buttons, it appears at the very top of the FrontPage screen.

Toolbar
A graphical bar containing buttons that act as shortcuts for common commands.

Tools
A menu on the Menu bar that enables you to select options that are useful for setting the technical properties of the FrontPage screen, Webs, and Web pages.

Tree diagram
Another name for a Web hierarchy, it is the basic structure of a Web displaying all parent and child pages and their relationships to one another.

Underline
A command button on the Formatting toolbar that makes the selected text underlined.

Uniform Resource Location (URL)
The address of a Web page. Every page has its own URL, no two URLs are exactly the same.

View

A menu on the Menu bar that allows you to choose certain ways of viewing your Web and Web pages, and allows you to manipulate what tools and toolbars are visible.

View buttons

Found on the Views bar, these buttons enable you to control the way you view a Web, and allow you to perform different functions in a Web.

Views bar

The bar of buttons found on the left side of the FrontPage screen. This is where you find the View buttons that allow you to perform different functions in a Web.

Warning

A dialog box that opens to ensure that you are performing the action that you want, permits you to continue the action, or to cancel it; the box is used to prevent you from losing data or making irreversible changes that you don't want to make.

Web

An assortment of Web pages that make up a Web site.

Web authoring application

Any computer program like FrontPage that is useful for easily and quickly creating, editing, and enhancing Web pages without having to use HTML.

Web browser

A program that has the ability to display Web pages, and can access them off of the Internet, it displays pages by reading the code they are written in.

Web hierarchy

Another name for a tree diagram, it is the basic structure of a Web displaying all parent and child pages and their relationships to one another.

Web page

A document that appears on the Internet with its own URL. It may contain graphics, text, or any number of elements that may be viewed once it is published.

Web server

A computer running software that stores Web pages and objects, so that when a browser requests a page or object, the server furnishes the request, the browser interprets the objects as pages, text, graphics, etc.

Web site

One or more Web pages that are linked and may be navigated by a visitor. Web sites are managed and owned by a person, company, or an organization.

What's This

A help feature that enables you to point to an object on the screen, a small box will open describing what that object is.

Window

A menu on the Menu bar that enables you to manipulate the FrontPage window. Also a rectangular area on the screen where you view and work on files.

Windows Taskbar

Usually located at the bottom of your screen, it contains buttons that allow you to open programs and perform certain functions.

Wizard

A series of dialog boxes that enables you to enter data and choose options and uses those choices to create a page or a Web for you, based on your specifications.

Word

A Microsoft program used for word processing, you can use FrontPage to open a document from Word on a Web page.

WordPerfect

A word processing program, FrontPage can open this document and place it on a Web page.

index

a

ActiveX controls, inserting, FP 7.12-7.13
Adding:
   and formatting lists, FP 2.16-2.17
   and modifying banners, FP 7.8-7.9
   check boxes and option buttons, FP 3.28-3.29
   images, FP 3.16-3.17
   navigation bars, FP 4.4-4.5
   photo galleries, FP 7.14-7.17
   tasks linked to a page, FP 8.4-8.5
   text to a Web page, FP 2.12-2.13

b

Banners, adding and modifying, FP 7.8-7.9
Beveled borders, FP 5.8-5.9
Browser, defined, FP 1.8, 2.22

c

Captions, inserting, FP 6.12-6.13
Check boxes, adding, FP 3.28-3.29
Creating:
   and printing reports, FP 4.20-4.21
   drop-down list boxes, FP 3.30-3.31
   frames pages, FP 7.20-7.21
   hover buttons, FP 3.22-3.23
   marquees, FP 3.24-3.25
   new tasks, FP 8.2-8.3
   new Web pages using a template, FP 2.2-2.3
   new Webs using a template, FP 2.4-2.5
   no-frames pages, FP 7.26-7.27
   push buttons, FP 3.32-3.33
   search forms, FP 5.22-5.23
   tables, FP 3.2-3.3
   text hyperlinks, FP 3.12-3.13
   Web hierarchies, FP 4.2-4.3

d

Deleting tables and rows, FP 6.2-6.3

Dialog boxes:
   Add Editor Association, FP 5.10-5.11
   Add File to Import, FP 5.6-5.7
   Banner Ad Manager Properties, FP 7.8-7.9
   Caption Properties, FP 6.12-6.13
   Cell Properties, FP 6.6-6.7
   Convert Text to Table, FP 6.10-6.11
   Date and Time, FP 5.20-5.21
   Find and Replace, FP 7.2-7.3
   Hit Counter Properties, FP 5.18-5.19
   Import, FP 5.2-5.5
   Insert Web Component, FP 7.12-7.15
   Link Bar Properties, FP 7.6-7.7
   New Task, FP 8.2-8.3
   Options, FP 5.10-5.11
   Page Options, FP 7.18-7.19
   Page Templates, FP 5.22-5.23, 8.4-8.5
   Page Transitions, FP 5.24-5.25
   Position, FP 5.26-5.27
   Save As, FP 7.22-7.23
   Shared Borders, FP 7.6-7.7
   Spelling, FP 7.4-7.5
   Split Cells, FP 6.8-6.9
   Split Frame, FP 7.24-7.25
Drop-down list boxes, creating, FP 3.30-3.31
Dynamic HTML (DHTML) effects, using, FP 7.10-7.11

e

Editing
   graphics on one or more pages, FP 5.10-5.13
   Web pages, FP 2.18-2.19

f

Files, organizing in Folders View, FP 4.8-4.9
Find command, using, FP 2.20-2.21
Find and Replace, using, global, FP 7.2-7.3
Folders button, FP 1.6
Folders View, organizing files in, FP 4.8-4.9

Format Painter, using, FP 5.16-5.17
Formatting:
   images, FP 3.18-3.19, 5.8-5.9
   tables, FP 3.4-3.5
   Web page transitions, FP 5.24-5.25
Formatting toolbar, FP 1.6
Frames pages:
   creating, FP 7.20-7.21
   manipulating, FP 7.24-7.25
   saving, FP 7.22-7.23
FrontPage:
   exiting, FP 1.16-1.17
   exploring the screen, FP 1.6-1.7
   introducing, FP 1.2-1.3
   starting, FP 1.4-1.5

g

Graphics, editing on Web pages, FP 5.10-5.13

h

Help, getting FrontPage, FP 1.14-1.15
Hit counters, inserting, FP 5.18-5.19
Hover buttons, creating, FP 3.22-3.23
HTML (Hypertext Markup Language), FP 1.2, 1.12
Hyperlinks:
   creating text, FP 3.12-3.13
   editing, FP 3.14-3.15
   verifying, FP 4.10-4.11
Hyperlinks button, FP 1.6

i

Images:
   adding, FP 3.16-3.17
   formatting, FP 3.18-3.19, 5.8-5.9
   importing, FP 5.6-5.7
   mapping, FP 3.20-3.21
Import Web Wizard, using, FP 2.10-2.11
Importing:
   images, FP 5.6-5.7
   text, FP 5.2-5.3
   Web pages, FP 5.4-5.5

Inserting:
   ActiveX controls, FP 7.12-7.13
   captions, FP 6.12-6.13
   hit counters, FP 5.18-5.19
   text boxes, FP 3.26-3.27
   time stamps, FP 5.20-5.21

l

Lists, adding and formatting, FP 2.16-2.17

m

Marquees, creating, FP 3.24-3.25
Menu bar, FP 1.6
Microsoft (MS) Paint, FP 5.10-5.13
Microsoft Personal Web Server, FP 5.18

n

Navigation bars, adding, FP 4.4-4.5
Navigation button, FP 1.6
New tasks, creating, FP 8.2-8.3
No-frames pages, creating, FP 7.26-7.27

o

Office documents, opening in a Web, FP 4.16-4.17
Office Clipboard, using, FP 4.18-4.19
Opening:
   Office documents in Webs, FP 4.16-4.17
   Web pages, FP 1.8-1.9
Option buttons, adding, FP 3.28-3.29

p

Page button, FP 1.6
Page titles, changing in page banners, FP 4.14-4.15
Page View, using, FP 1.12-1.13
Pages, renaming, FP 4.12-4.13
Photo galleries, adding, FP 7.14-7.17
Pixels, FP 6.6
Push buttons, creating, FP 3.32-3.33

r

Replace command, FP 2.20
Reports, creating and printing, FP 4.20-4.21
Reports button, FP 1.6

s

Saving Web pages, FP 1.10-1.11
Search forms, creating, FP 5.22-5.23
Shared borders, using, FP 7.6-7.7
Spelling of a Web, checking, FP 7.4-7.5
Standard toolbar, FP 1.6
Status bar, FP 1.6
Style sheet positioning, relative and absolute, FP 5.26
Style sheets, using, FP 5.26-5.27

t

Table rows and columns, deleting, FP 6.2-6.3
Table cells:
   merging, FP 6.8-6.9
   resizing, FP 6.6-6.7
Tables:
   and columns, drawing, FP 6.4-6.5
   creating, FP 3.2-3.3
   formatting, FP 3.4-3.5
   toolbar, FP 6.4-6.5
Target audiences, reaching, FP 7.18-7.19
Task histories, viewing, FP 8.10-8.11
Tasks:
   adding linked to a page, FP 8.4-8.5
   button, FP 1.6
   sorting, FP 8.8-8.9
   starting and completing, FP 8.6-8.7
Templates:
   defined, FP 2.2
   examples of, FP 2.4
   using to create new Web pages, FP 2.2-2.3
   using to create new Webs, FP 2.4-2.5
Text:
   converting to a table, FP 6.10-6.11
   importing, FP 5.2-5.3
   placing over an image, FP 5.14-5.15
Text boxes, inserting, FP 3.26-3.27

Themes:
   applying custom, FP 3.8-3.9
   applying to individual pages, FP 3.10-3.11
   applying to Webs, FP 3.6-3.7
Time stamps, inserting, FP 5.20-5.21
Title bar, FP 1.6
Toolbars:
   DHTML Effects, FP 7.10-7.11
   Formatting, FP 1.6
   Tables, FP 6.4-6.5

u

URLs, changing, FP 4.12-4.13

v

Views bar, FP 1.6

w

Web hierarchies, creating, FP 4.2-4.3
Web pages:
   adding text to, FP 2.12-2.13
   creating new using templates, FP 2.2-2.3
   formatting text on, FP 2.14-2.15
   formatting transitions of, FP 5.24-5.25
   importing, FP 5.4-5.5
   opening, FP 1.8-1.9
   previewing in a browser, FP 2.22-2.23
   saving, FP 1.10-1.11
   spell checking and editing, FP 2.18-2.19
Web structures, viewing and printing, FP 4.6-4.7
Web Wizard, using the, FP 2.6-2.9
Webs, publishing, FP 4.22-4.23
What's This? command, FP 1.14
Windows control buttons, FP 1.6, 1.16

FILE DIRECTORY

The table below summarizes the data files that have been provided for the student. Many of the exercises in this book cannot be completed without these files. The files are distributed as part of the Instructor's Resource Kit and are also available for download at http://www.mhhe.com/it/cit/index.mhtml. Please note that the table below lists both the raw files provided to students before they start working on them and the three major Webs created by students as they work through the Lessons and end-of-chapter exercises. Students should use the version of a Web that is located in the folder for the particular Lesson on which they are working.

Lesson	Skill Name/Page #	File Name	Introduced In
Lesson 1	Opening a Web Page/FP 1.8	fpdoit1-4.htm	do it! step 4
	Opening a Web Page/FP 1.9	fpprac1-4.htm	Practice
	Saving a Web Page/FP 1.11	fpprac1-5.htm	Practice
	Interactivity/FP 1.21	fpskill1.htm	Build Your Skills #2
Lesson 2	Using the Import Web Wizard/FP 2.10	fpdoit2.4.htm	do it! step 7
	Using the Import Web Wizard/FP 2.11	fpprac2.4.htm	Practice
	Spell Checking and Editing a Web Page/FP 2.18	fpdoit2-8.htm	do it! step 1
	Spell Checking and Editing a Web Page/FP 2.19	fpprac2-8.htm	Practice
	Using the Find Command/FP 2.21	order_form.htm	Practice
	Interactivity/FP 2.27	fpskill2.htm	Build Your Skills #4
Lesson 3	Creating Tables/FP 3.2	Skydiver Web	do it! step 1
	Creating Tables/FP 3.3	Caddy Shop Web	Practice
	Interactivity/FP 3.37	Water Taxi Web	Build Your Skills #1
Lesson 4	Creating a Web Hierarchy/FP 4.3	Caddy Shop Web	Practice
	Adding a Navigation Bar/FP 4.4	Skydiver Web	do it! step 1
	Organizing Files in Folders View/FP 4.8	jo336982[1].gif	do it! step 3
	Organizing Files in Folders View/FP 4.8	fphoverx.class	do it! step 4
	Opening an Office Document in a Web/FP 4.16	fpdoit4-8.doc	do it! step 4
	Opening an Office Document in a Web/FP 4.17	fpprac4-8.doc	Practice
	Using the Office Clipboard/FP 4.18	fpdoit4-9.doc	do it! step 1
	Using the Office Clipboard/FP 4.19	fpprac4-9.doc	Practice
	Creating and Printing Reports/FP 4.20	form.htm	do it! step 2
	Publishing a Web/FP 4.22	fpdoit4-11.htm	do it! step 1
	Interactivity/FP 4.27	Water Taxi Web	Build Your Skills #1
	Interactivity/FP 4.27	fpskill4.doc	Build Your Skills #5
Lesson 5	Importing Text/FP 5.2	Skydiver Web	do it! step 1
	Importing Text/FP 5.2	calendar.doc	do it! step 4
	Importing Text/FP 5.3	Caddy Shop Web	Practice
	Importing Text/FP 5.3	fpprac5-1.doc	Practice
	Importing Web Pages/FP 5.4	fpdoit5-2 folder	do it! step 4
	Importing Web Pages/FP 5.4	faq.htm	do it! step 4
	Importing Images/FP 5.6	fpdoit5-3 folder	do it! step 4
	Importing Images/FP 5.6	plane.wmf	do it! step 4
	Importing Images/FP 5.7	money.gif	Practice
	Advanced Image Formatting/FP 5.9	fpprac5-4.gif	Practice
	Editing Graphics on Web Pages/FP 5.10	airplane.bmp	do it! step 4
	Editing Graphics on Web Pages/FP 5.13	fpprac5-5.gif	Practice
	Placing Text over an Image/FP 5.15	leopard.jpg	Practice
	Interactivity/FP 5.31	Water Taxi Web	Build Your Skills #1
	Interactivity/FP 5.31	Water Taxi Calendar.doc	Build Your Skills #1
	Interactivity/FP 5.31	fpskill5.htm	Build Your Skills #2
	Interactivity/FP 5.31	boats1.bmp	Build Your Skills #3

Lesson	Skill Name/Page #	File Name	Introduced In
Lesson 6	Deleting Table Rows and Columns/FP 6.2	Skydiver Web	do it! step 1
	Deleting Table Rows and Columns/FP 6.3	Caddy Shop Web	Practice
	Interactivity/FP 6.17	Water Taxi Web	Build Your Skills #1
Lesson 7	Using Global Find and Replace/FP 7.2	Skydiver Web	do it! step 1
	Using Global Find and Replace/FP 7.3	Caddy Shop Web	Practice
	Adding and Modifying Banners/FP 7.8	earth.jpg	do it! step 8
	Adding and Modifying Banners/FP 7.8	fish.jpg	do it! step 9
	Adding a Photo Gallery/FP 7.14	Photo Gallery folder	do it! step 11
	Adding a Photo Gallery/FP 7.17	Golf pics folder	Practice
	Interactivity/FP 7.32	Water Taxi Web	Build Your Skills #1
	Interactivity/FP 7.32	boats 2.bmp	Build Your Skills #5
	Interactivity/FP 7.32	boats 3.bmp	Build Your Skills #5
Lesson 8	Creating New Tasks/FP 8.2	Skydiver Web	do it! step 1
	Creating New Tasks/FP 8.3	Caddy Shop Web	Practice
	Starting and Completing Tasks/FP 8.6	fpdoit8-3.gif	do it! step 6
	Interactivity/FP 8.15	Water Taxi Web	Build Your Skills #1

MOUS OBJECTIVES MAP

The Introductory Editions of the Interactive Computing Series prepare students for Microsoft Office User Specialist (MOUS) Core certification. The table below outlines where in the book the certification exam objectives are covered. If you are using an Interactive Computing Series Brief Edition (equal to the first four lessons of an Introductory Edition), you can still see which MOUS skills you have learned. However, completion of the Brief Edition does not fully prepare you for the MOUS Core certification exam.

Reference Numbers	Skill Sets and Skills	Pages
FP2002-1	**Creating and Modifying Web Sites**	
FP2002-1-1	Create and manage a FrontPage Web	FP 2.2-2.5
FP2002-1-2	Create and preview Web pages	FP 2.16-2.17
FP2002-1-3	Open, view, and rename Web pages	FP 1.8-1.9, 1.12-1.13, 4.6-4.7, 4.10-4.13
FP2002-1-4	Change the title for a Web page on banners and buttons	FP 3.22-3.23, 4.14-4.15
FP2002-2	**Importing Web Content**	
FP2002-2-1	Insert text and images	FP 4.18-4.19
FP2002-2-2	Insert Office drawings, AutoShapes, and WordArt	FP 3.16-3.17
FP2002-3	**Formatting Web Pages**	
FP2002-3-1	Apply text and paragraph formats	FP 2.14-2.15
FP2002-3-2	Insert hyperlinks	FP 3.12-3.13
FP2002-3-3	Insert a date using shared borders	FP 5.20-5.21
FP2002-3-4	Create and edit tables	FP 3.2-3.3, 6.2-6.3, 6.8-6.9
FP2002-3-5	Apply Web themes	FP 3.6-3.13
FP2002-4	**Working with Graphic and Dynamic Elements**	
FP2002-4-1	Edit graphic elements	FP 3.18-3.19
FP2002-4-2	Create image maps	FP 3.20-3.21
FP2002-4-3	Add a FrontPage Web component to a Web page	FP 3.22-3.25, 3.28-3.33
FP2002-4-4	Add a Photo Gallery	FP 7.14-7.17
FP2002-5	**Organizing and Viewing FrontPage Web Sites**	
FP2002-5-1	Use FrontPage views	FP 1.8-1.9, 1.12-1.13, 4.6-4.7, 4.10-4.11
FP2002-5-2	Manage Web structures	FP 4.2-4.5
FP2002-5-3	Organize Web files	FP 4.8-4.9
FP2002-5-4	Manage tasks	FP 8.2-8.11
FP2002-6	**Managing Web Sites**	
FP2002-6-1	Publish a Web page	FP 4.22-4.23
FP2002-6-2	Create custom reports	FP 4.20-4.21

NOTES

NOTES

NOTES